JOHN A. DeMAY

DISCOVERY &
SETTLEMENT

HOW TO WIN
YOUR CASE
WITHOUT TRIAL

PRENTICE HALL

This publication is designed to provide accurate and authoritative information in regard to the subject matter covered. It is sold with the understanding that the publisher is not engaged in rendering legal, accounting, or other professional service. If legal advice or other expert assistance is required, the services of a competent professional person should be sought.

—From the Declaration of Principles jointly adopted by a Committee of the American Bar Association and a Committee of Publishers and Associations.

ISBN 0-13-224882-4

Library of Congress Cataloging-in-Publication Data
DeMay, John A. [date]
    Discovery and settlement : how to win your case without trial /
John A. DeMay.
        p. cm.
        Rev. ed. of: Discovery, how to win your case without trial. © 1982.
        Includes bibliographical references and index.
        ISBN 0-13-224882-4
        1. Discovery (Law)—United States. 2. Compromise (Law)—United
States. I. DeMay, John A., [date] Discovery, how to win your case
without trial. II. Title.
KF8900.D45 1992
347.73'72—dc20
[347.30772]   92-16404
                                                                          CIP

PRENTICE HALL
Business Information & Publishing Division
Englewood Cliffs, NJ 07632
Simon & Schuster, A Paramount Communications Company

Printed in the United States of America

ABOUT THE AUTHOR

John A. DeMay is a trial lawyer and the founder of the firm of DeMay, DeMay, Donelly & Todd, P.C., in Pittsburgh, Pennsylvania. Since 1957, he has devoted himself principally to representing the Plaintiff's case, particularly in personal injury actions. A graduate of the University of Pittsburgh Law School, Order of the Coif, he was admitted to the Bar in 1953. He is a former Assistant United States Attorney for the Western District of Pennsylvania and is admitted to practice before the U.S. Supreme Court, the U.S. Court of Appeals, 2nd and 3rd Circuits, the U.S. District Court, Western Pennsylvania, the U.S. District Court for the Western District of New York, the U.S. District Court for the Northern District of Ohio, and all state courts in Pennsylvania. He is a member of the Academy of Trial Lawyers of Allegheny County, the American Trial Lawyers Association, and many other legal organizations.

DEDICATION

This book is dedicated to my wife, **Helen Louise,** who inspired me with the courage to attempt it, the tenacity to complete it, and whose threats to impose sanctions were a constant spur to good work. Her love of the Law and the understanding of the problems of trial lawyers are reflected in this book.

It is also dedicated to my sons—**John,** whose experience as a Claims Supervisor lends balance to my attitudes; **Patrick,** who, as an experienced Trial Lawyer, now casts long shadows of his own; and **David,** a law student, who revels in the glory of the Law.

Preface to the Second Edition

The first edition of this book, published in 1982, was well received by attorneys in this country.

While the information set forth in the original book is as sound and applicable today as it was when it was originally published, I couldn't help but wonder whether it would be helpful to expand on that basic knowledge. For example, too little attention was paid to the subject of settlement, which is, after all, a goal much to be desired. Accordingly three chapters are now included dealing with settlements in general (Chapter 12), with the preparation of a Settlement Brochure (Chapter 13), and with structured settlements (Chapter 14). In addition, of course, the title was changed to add the important word "Settlement."

Then it was thought to be appropriate to devote an entire chapter to the subject of the use of discovery in medical malpractice and products liability cases. These types of cases are very lucrative—every attorney should handle them—but they are difficult. At the same time they are very "winnable" through the aggressive and effective use of the discovery tools. Chapter 9 helps you learn how to accomplish this.

Thoughts about difficult cases naturally led to thoughts about the "hopeless" case. Now there are hopeless cases; but there are also cases that just look that way. If you have a client with very serious injuries and very doubtful liability, you better read Chapter 11 before you either reject the case or file it. This chapter "Winning The Hopeless Case with Discovery," by itself, could be worth the price of this book. None of us are looking for trouble, but neither do we want to reject a million-dollar case.

Also, in this era of the camcorder, instant replay, and videotapes, Chapter 8 tells you in detail how to use videotapes to their utmost advantage in depositions, taking statements from witnesses, and Day in the Life films.

Finally, since we live in a world of uniformity and exactitude, which we try to achieve through rules and regulations, Chapter 10 has been included to discuss this subject as it relates to discovery. There are, out there somewhere, industry standards, professional society guidelines, and government regulations. If you can find them, you can use them, with devastating effect in Interrogatories and Depositions. This chapter gives you a hand in that regard.

So we have here a new book for you. With apologies for a certain degree of immodesty, I must say that there are some powerful, workable ideas in this book that can make you a better lawyer and increase your success in the handling of lawsuits.

John A. DeMay

Foreword

No phase of litigation process has received more critical comment in recent years than discovery. Opinions of the United States Supreme Court, as well as other courts, proposals by the Civil Procedure Rules Advisory Committee, and articles in legal journals all reflect growing disenchantment. What was originally expected to end trial by ambush and promote speedier, just resolution of law suits has instead led to complaints of harassment, delay, and unnecessary expense. Reports that discovery has been used as a weapon of attrition rather than a means of developing truth are widespread.

Although abuse of discovery may be intentional in some instances, a lack of skill in the art in many cases is at least as likely a cause. The practitioner who would increase his competence in this very important part of the litigation, however, has had surprisingly little in the way of text material to guide him. It is particularly fortunate, therefore that John DeMay has chosen to devote his latest book to the very timely topic of discovery.

Mr. DeMay is a highly regarded trial lawyer who has drawn on his years of active practice in the courtroom to explain how discovery can be used effectively, not only in winning a verdict but also, and more often, to bring about a favorable settlement. He analyzes the relative advantages of interrogatories, depositions, and requests for admission, and suggests when each should be used. He writes candidly of the need to establish goals for discovery in each case so that the client's money, the lawyer's energy, and the court's time are not wasted.

Recognizing the growing belief that trial judges should become more active in a supervisory role, Mr. DeMay even suggests proper steps to pave the way to secure sanctions against recalcitrant adversaries. He writes in a readable and interesting style, frequently illustrating his points with instructive anecdotes from his extensive career at the trial bar, and making generous use of illustrative forms.

Many lawyers do not realize the value of discovery in bringing about an early and satisfactory disposition of a lawsuit. In an era of overcrowded dockets and inevitable delay in bringing a case to trial, effective discovery as a means to resolving factual issues is an alternative that Mr. DeMay argues persuasively.

I am confident that if the principles in this book were put into practice by the majority of the bar, much pretrial skirmishing would disappear and the aims of the original proponents of discovery would be met. Consequently, I have no hesitancy in saying that active trial lawyers will find the book to be valuable indeed. Those who enter the courts only occasionally should consider it as essential reading.

Judge Joseph F. Weis, Jr.
United States Court of
Appeals for the Third Circuit

How You Can Benefit from This Book

There is one good question that might well be asked of any Trial Lawyer, whether a Plaintiff's attorney or Defense counsel: when you take on a new case, do you give any thought to how you're going to win it? Probably not. If you are like most attorneys, you will have some vague concept of "trying the case"—someday; or some equally ill-defined notion that it "may settle"—eventually. How often have you heard your fellow-practitioners say that they are "waiting for the case to come to trial" or "hoping for a settlement," as though "waiting" and "hoping" were the roads to success. They're not.

This book is about winning cases—your cases, whether they involve Trespass, Assumpsit, Eminent Domain or a Will Contest. And it's about winning your case in one-half the time it will take for the case to come to trial. This book is about discovery and settlement.

You probably think you know enough about discovery—depositions, interrogatories, and the like. You do know the words and you have used these legal tools from time to time, but the question is whether you have invoked discovery, wisely and well, *to win a case* rather than as a routine procedure. There is a vast difference between the two approaches, and unfortunately most attorneys invoke discovery with little zeal and no faith in its effectiveness. Let's face it: most lawyers—possibly even including yourself—look upon discovery as a drudge, a chore, more akin to digging a ditch than to practicing law. That's too bad. As many old-time Forty-Niners could attest, there is a lot of incentive to digging if there is a good possibility of uncovering gold. And that is what lies before you when you really work at discovery and know what you are doing.

This applies no matter which side of the case you are handling. If it is correct that many Plaintiff's attorneys are somewhat hesitant about admitting that they can win a case via Discovery, then it must be said that an equal number of Defense attorneys are absolute nonbelievers. And that's not right. In this book, we cite a concrete example of a good Defense attorney winning a case by preparing an excellent set of Requests for Admissions followed by a Motion for Summary Judgment. The same thing has happened *often* (and illustrations are provided here) when a Plaintiff's or Defense attorney takes a good deposition of the opposing party, secures damning admissions, and follows up with a Summary Judgement Motion. It can be done! Defense attorneys can do a great job of either winning a case outright by the skillful use of Discovery or of devastating the Plaintiff's case so badly that a low settlement results.

Plaintiff's attorneys can do the same thing. If you are a Plaintiff's lawyer, just pause for a moment to think about your new case and you will soon realize that you don't know much about it. Your client has given you a biased, fragmentary and disjointed account of an event, or series of events, that occurred some time ago. Based on this information (hopefully supported by some investigation), you will prepare and file a Complaint. This Complaint isn't going to scare anyone. It is, in essence, a notice of suit accompanied by a statement of some facts (which you hope to be correct) and a theory of liability (which you may have conjured up out of the facts with crossed fingers and a muttered prayer).

Now what? Is any defendant going to come running to you to discuss settlement just because you filed a Complaint? Not at all. So what happens? You could do your usual thing and half-heartedly serve a Notice of Deposition on the principal defendant, prepare a few Interrogatories to get the names of witnesses, and let it go at that. Then you could set the file aside for a questionable result at some distant trial date. Or, after reading this book, you can buckle down for some hearty discovery that is going to win your case, and in much less time than it will take to get it to trial.

Look at a lawsuit from the defendant's point of view. The Complaint is nothing more than you intended it to be. The defendant knows that he is being sued, he disputes many of your facts, and he may be amused, intrigued or annoyed at your theory of liability. But he isn't going to panic and rush to pay you any money.

Now, suppose you follow up that Complaint with a well-constructed, detailed set of Interrogatories; then take several Depositions—not merely of the principal defendant but also of vital, peripheral witnesses; then serve a Motion to Produce very specific documents; and finally, nail down key facts with a Request for Admissions. Then watch the attitude of your opponent change. When you develop a case in this manner, the defendant begins to see that what began as a questionable case is evolving into a sure thing—for you. Thereafter, the correspondence between the Defense attorney and his client changes from "Is there any liability?" to "What are the damages and how much will we have to pay?"

That is exactly the position in which you want to place your opponent. When he begins to think like that, he is ready for the final step—serious settlement negotiations.

That's the way to win a case.

You will be on your way to the bank with a substantial settlement check while your buddy across the hall twiddles his thumbs, his file still in a drawer gathering dust as he waits for that elusive and protracted "trial date."

Discovery is the key to success in every case. If yours is a good case, discovery will force opposing counsel to recognize that fact; if you have a poor case, discovery will help you to realize that you're not going anywhere with it and will enable you to avoid the expenditure of great quantities of time and money in a fruitless cause.

Finally, the proper use of discovery is an art—a talent that has to be developed. The first thing we want to discuss is your attitude toward it and the "atmosphere," if you will, in which you work. Those important matters are discussed in Chapter 1, followed promptly by a review of the principal discovery tools, the sequence in which to use them, and the ways of combining them with each other and with Motions. Subsequent chapters will explore in detail the intricacies of taking Depositions, preparing Interrogatories and Requests for Admissions, and Motions to Produce Documents.

Special attention will be given to the use of discovery in those difficult, but so lucrative, medical malpractice and products liability cases. Chapter 9 will provide guidance and some helpful hints when you get involved in those cases—as you should.

Certain matters are peripheral to discovery but vital to it. Thus, in Chapter 8 we go into detail regarding the use of videotape not only in depositions, but also in taking statements from witnesses and in the preparation of Day in the Life films. Chapter 10, aptly titled "Paper Chase," helps you to learn about industry standards, government regulations and professional society guidelines. These are things you can use in Interrogatories and Depositions with devastating effect.

Then there are the "Hopeless cases," some of which you ought to reject (and often don't!), and some of which can be worth many times their weight in gold. Chapter 11 will give you helpful pointers and provide direction so that you can handle these cases effectively and make them winners.

Then we come to settlement, that "pot of gold." Good settlements don't just happen; you have to make them happen. This is more hard work. In Chapter 12 we discuss settlements generally, with some sound ideas about how to arrive at the proper figure. Chapter 13 tells you how to prepare that essential Settlement Brochure when you are handling a big case, and Chapter 14 teaches you the "in's and out's" of structured settlements.

The goal of every attorney is to conclude a case to the satisfaction of his or client and himself or herself. For too long have you contemplated achieving the goal solely through a trial or a settlement at some indefinite date far in the future. You have the opportunity to force things to happen—to bring about prompt action on your case—without sitting and waiting. Above all, you have the means available to you to win your case in an expeditious manner. That means is called *Discovery*, and that is what this book is all about—winning through discovery—and doing so quickly. It takes time, effort, and some guidance. If you will take the time and exert the effort, this book will provide you with the guidance.

John A. DeMay

Contents

1

Strategy and Technique for Successful Discovery

DISCOVERY TODAY—A WHOLE NEW BALL GAME

A friend of mine—a prominent defense attorney—recently addressed a group of young lawyers on the subject of cross-examination. At one point he made the startling assertion: "Cross-examination is dead. Discovery killed it." I admit to choking a little on hearing that comment, having just lost a case based in good part on the devastating cross-examination of my client by opposing counsel. Of course my friend was emphasizing by exaggeration, but the thust of his argument is sound. Prior to the post-world-War-II era there was very little discovery, and lawyers prepared their cases in deliberate isolation with a great emphasis placed on "hiding" facts, documents and even witnesses from the other side. As a result the first contact an attorney had to the facts known by his opponent was in the courtroom during the direct examination of a witness. In just a few moments he had to analyze that testimony and then attack it through cross-examination. Is it any wonder that the art of cross-examination was developed to a high degree and its successful practitioners greatly esteemed? They were functioning in a "now or never" situation. Lawyers of that era still talk of trying a lawsuit "by the seat of the pants"—much like the way the pilots of the time flew their fabric-covered biplanes. It must have been an exciting and dramatic way to handle a lawsuit and, of course, *the trial* was everything. Apparently, though, many thinking persons began to wonder whether the cause of justice was well served by this procedure and decided that the answer was "no." Cross-examination, as the sine qua non of trial, was seen as so subjective and personal an art, and skillful cross-examination so beyond the capability of many trial lawyers, that it was felt some other way had to be found to advance the cause of justice between disputing parties. Certainly the major change wrought by this reasoning was in the Discovery Rules incorporated in the new Federal Rules of Civil Procedure which came into being in 1946. They may have been technical rules, but they dramatically changed the whole attitude and approach of lawyers in the handling of lawsuits.

DISCOVERY EXISTS TO INFORM LAWYERS, SHORTEN TRIALS AND ENCOURAGE SETTLEMENTS

It might jokingly be said that the old-time lawsuit was made up of equal parts of stealth, subterfuge, and surprise. If this was so, the new discovery rules were expressly designed to completely reverse those attributes and to expose the entire preparatory process to fresh air and sunshine. Open disclosure became the name of the game. The older lawyers may have been shocked, but under the prodding of a determined judiciary, they were required to identify witnesses, produce documents, and answer pointed questions abut the conduct of their client; and the client was subjected to intensive interrogation by the process of deposition.

The thought behind the changes was that through a policy of open disclosure each party to a dispute could learn in detail all the facts concerning it, and then could analyze these facts at leisure. In this way, it was hoped, lawyer and client could view their position more intelligently, and settlement would necessarily result. (Of course, this presumed a certain degree of good faith and a willingness to face the facts developed by discovery—two qualities that are often lacking in litigants, be they irate individuals or bureaucratic corporations.) In addition, it was thought, if the parties could not settle their dispute, thorough discovery would certainly reduce the time of trial itself. Since each side would know the details of the other's case there could be stipulations, a waiver of proof as to documents, fewer witnesses and shorter cross-examination.

To the credit of the originators of these ideas, things have pretty much worked out the way they had hoped. In the jurisdiction in which I practice, fully 80 percent of the cases are settled prior to trial and the trial of a routine negligence or assumpsit case rarely takes more than three to five days.

GETTING ALL THE FACTS

It is rare to find a case in which the issues are exclusively legal ones. Can you remember the last time you sat down with your opponent, stipulated every fact involved in a case, and then presented it to the Court for determination as a pure question of law? We call that a Case Stated. I have a vague memory of having done that once a long time ago, but it is such a rarity that I have long since dismissed it from my mind. Almost by definition lawsuits involve factual disputes. To be sure, legal issues arise in interpreting the facts, but disputed facts are the first matter that requires resolution in a trial. The problem of who said what is usually the issue in a contract dispute, and the problem of who did what is at the heart of every negligence case. The answers to these questions lie in the facts known, or believed, by each party and the surrounding witnesses. Discovery enables the attorney to learn these facts. With them he can sensibly decide what kind of case he has; without them he is blind and has no idea where he is going. That important difference is more than enough to justify the discovery rules and the devotion of serious effort to utilizing them.

In addition, there is another virtue in Discovery, and it arises because of the honest ignorance of one's client.

YOUR CLIENT KNOWS ONLY SOME OF THE FACTS—YOUR OPPONENT KNOWS THE REST

Too often, attorneys proceed on these two false assumptions:

1. Their client knows the facts and can tell them all they need to know; and,
2. Their client tells the truth, the whole truth and nothing but the truth.

In the vernacular—and bluntly put—"It just ain't so!"

Every experienced attorney knows this; the inexperienced ones should learn it promptly. The tale is often told—and constantly bears repeating—about the psychology teacher who stages a disruption in his classroom with two boys rushing in, shouting and fighting, and then running out of the room. Then he asks the class to write a report describing the event and the participants. Amazingly, if he has 25 students, he will get 25 variations of who, what, where and when. Our powers of observation and recollection are simply not acute enough, or properly developed enough, to enable us to report exactly what happened. How much more difficult it is when we are personally involved—in an accident, for example, where things happen very quickly, or in a Will Contest among family members where emotionalism runs rampant.

Let's face it—your client doesn't know all the facts and even the ones he or she claims to know are often distorted by self-interest, anger, vindictiveness, or an honest desire to explain that it simply "must have been that way."

Your opponent knows many facts that your client doesn't know. Even in such an elemental matter as the names of witnesses, he knows things that your client doesn't know. In addition, he may have been in a better position to observe facts, he may have more ready access to documents, and he may simply have a better memory than your client. To illustrate: who knows most about what happened during an operation—the patient or the surgeon?

Happily one need not rely solely on one's client. Because of the discovery rules you can expand your knowledge to include everything the other side knows or believes. These rules enable you to fill in the gaps in your own knowledge of what happened, and also enable you to get the attitude, opinions and views of your opposing litigant regarding those facts. That later can be just as important as the facts.

THE WEAPONS IN YOUR DISCOVERY ARMORY

There are four major tools available to you for the purpose of gathering information from your adversary. They are described here:

1. Interrogatories: A series of questions that must be answered under oath. Those questions need not relate directly to the subject matter of the lawsuit, although as a matter of generality and common sense they will. One is permitted to ask questions which can lead to information that relates to the subject matter of the case.

2. Requests for Admission: A series of statements of fact which the other side must admit or deny under oath. This procedure has value in clearing the air of facts that are necessary to prove and that the other side has no interest in contesting. They are easily evaded because so much depends on the precision of the wording.

3. Motion to Produce Documents: A procedure designed to permit one to secure, inspect and copy written material in the possession or control of your opponent. This is an invaluable tool.

4. Depositions: A procedure in which one compels a party or witness to appear and, under oath, submit to a verbal examination concerning any matter relevant to the lawsuit. Probably this is the most widely used discovery tool, and it is highly effective if the attorney is properly prepared and knows what he's after. While this technique is nearly always utilized by attorneys, it is not often utilized wisely and well.

There are some miscellaneous techniques that are available for specific purposes. Thus, for example, a defendant in a personal injury action can compel an injured plaintiff to submit to a physical examination. There is a procedure whereby one can take a deposition by written interrogatories. These are not used often and need only be touched upon in this book.

DEFINE THE ISSUES! A LEGAL IMPERATIVE

The call has been repeated over and over again from the first day of law school: "Define the issues!" That is just as important in discovery as it is in any other aspect of a lawsuit. Without a clear understanding of the issues your discovery will proceed in a willy-nilly fashion, without rhyme or reason, and will result in your collecting information that is not pertinent to the issues and your spending a lot of time gathering useless facts. If, in an Assumpsit action, the issue is when and where a party mailed his acceptance of an offer, why spend a lot of time on discovery about the consideration supporting the contract? In a slander action the central issue may well be the identity of the precise words used; why go to great lengths inquiring about the time, place and circumstances of the usage? This is what I mean about identifying the issues. Know what you want and need—then spend your time achieving this goal.

RESEARCH THE APPLICABLE LAW

With the facts your client can give you, you have a fair idea of what happened and a reasonable appreciation of the issues. But, before you start running off to dictate interrogatories or schedule a deposition, take time to do some research on the applicable law. It could well be that your general knowledge has some important gaps in it, that the statutory law has changed since the last time you handled a case such as this, or that there have been recent court opinions emphasizing the need for additional proof of some element of liability or damages that exists in your case. Such research can't take much time, and that time will be well spent. First of all it insures that you aren't overlooking a significant aspect of your case and, second, it enables you to frame your discovery so as to pinpoint a matter that you have to prove. As we all know, the law is a vibrant and lively subject, and a few minutes in a library will help you to be certain that you have a clear idea concerning matters that you have to prove.

HAVE A SPECIFIC GOAL IN MIND

There's more to this than merely saving time, although we are certainly all concerned with that subject. It's also a matter of purpose or intent. Why are you serving Interrogatories? What documents do you want from the defendant? What admissions do you want him to make? Whether you call it a purpose or a goal, you must have some clear-cut idea of what you are after when you proceed with discovery. Defining the issues is a great help; thereafter you should plan just what facts you need to win your case and then decide on the appropriate discovery tool to gather this information. The whole idea is to concentrate your efforts on gathering the precise data you need rather than proceeding with discovery indiscriminately.

MIX AND MATCH—USE ALL THE AVAILABLE TOOLS

There is no rule that restricts you to any one type of discovery; they are all available to you. Use them. In addition, there is no law that says you can use them only once and then not again. Use them often—and mix them up. Suppose you start with Interrogatories and then learn that certain documents you need are in the possession of your opponent. Go ahead and serve a Request for Production of Documents. But after you have received and reviewed the documents you may very well find they have raised additional questions in your mind. That's fine; get the answers by serving additional Interrogatories. With background material securely in hand, go ahead with a deposition of a party or witness. You may learn that someone else has documents that sound interesting. You can get them by preparing another Request for Production. Finally, to establish the validity of some of the documents and to avoid proof in Court of some essential but non-disputed facts, serve a Request for Admissions. In other words, use all your discovery tools and mix them up as needed.

DON'T ABUSE DISCOVERY

The abuse of discovery continues to be a serious problem. The Federal Discovery Rules were revised in 1980 in an effort to put teeth into sanctions that the courts could impose and it did some good. But the problem is an ongoing one.

A deposition that should take one afternoon is stretched out to a full week; instead of serving 30 specific interrogatories an attorney will serve 150, 90 percent of which are really irrelevant but just enough within the rules to make it necessary to answer them. A corporation will be asked to produce enormous quantities of documents that may span a decade, well knowing that the requesting party will use a mere handful of them and may not even look at the majority of them.

This is unfortunate, and it is my observation that it is principally a fault of the major law firms in each city. They are the only ones with clients who are willing to pay for endless hours spent on this foolishness. The sole practitioner who has a case on a contingent fee basis and the small law firm whose insurance-company client watches the bills like a hawk simply cannot afford the time for what is essentially unnecessary and unjustifiable discovery. It is in their interest to get to the heart of the matter quickly at the least cost to their client and with as little expenditure of time as possible.

By way of example let me refer to that deposition that lasted a week. The lawsuit was against a major corporation which was represented by a large law firm. I deposed four corporate officers in one afternoon. I knew exactly what I wanted and got it, promptly and concisely. The deposition of my client lasted a week. Why? In essence the deposition covered his entire life—the jobs he held, why he left them, arguments with his superiors, who said what and when, his military career—nothing was left out. The transcript is so voluminous that it is painful to look at. From those hundreds of pages of transcripts there aren't more than 150-200 that have any utility. The rest is biography and sociology. Interesting, but with no genuine relevance to the issues involved in the lawsuit. About the only way it could be justified is on the theory that *every* event in a person's life could *possibly* become relevant in a trial.

That's true, but it's not a good enough reason to go to such lengths in discovery. It does do one thing, though—it earns a substantial income for the law firm.

In my opinion this is an abuse of discovery. Because of many instances like this we may get substantial restrictions on discovery in the future.

A rather hilarious and concrete illustration of the abuse of discovery can be found in the case of *Jankins* v. *TDC Management Corp., Inc.*, 131 FRD 629 (D.D.C. 1989), which ought to be required reading for all attorneys. There the court states at P. 632:

> The misconduct of defendants' counsel has violated not only the letter and spirit of Rules 11 and 26 of the Federal Rules of Civil Procedure and the Local Rules of this Court, but also at least 11 express orders of the trial court and the Magistrate. The misconduct of defendants' counsel has also occasioned two extensions of the discovery cut-off and one continuance of the trial, thereby unnecessarily taxing judicial resources and delaying the resolution of the action on the merits.

Now, that represents real abuse of Discovery! The Court did impose some powerful sanctions, which were appropriate—but it was all so unnecessary.

In any event, don't do it. Use discovery as a rapier, not as a broadsword. Pick and choose what you need, then go get it. Know the issues, decide the facts you need to resolve them, then choose the discovery procedure that will help you to gather those precise facts. Nothing more is needed. There is such a thing as overkill in discovery just as there is in nuclear weaponry.

DISCOVERY AND INVESTIGATION ARE PARTNERS— NOT COMPETITORS

Discovery will never take the place of investigation. It will supplement investigation and help you to limit the extent and scope of your investigation, thereby saving you some money, but it will never replace investigation. There are certain times, however, and they occur frequently, when an investigator cannot gather the information you need. A manufacturing company, or a hospital, will not open its files to an investigator, but it will do so in response to an Order of Court. A person may refuse to talk to an investigator but can be compelled to come to your office and answer questions at a deposition. The two procedures—discovery and investigation—should work together, hand in hand, each accomplishing what the other cannot. In some cases an investigator may not even be able to start his work until you have secured the identity of witnesses by serving Interrogatories on your opposing counsel, and your architect-expert may need drawings that you will have to secure by a Motion to Produce. Discovery can never preempt the field of investigation· it can only supplement it.

BUILD A SOLID CASE—FOR SETTLEMENT, A SUMMARY JUDGMENT OR A QUICK AND EASY TRIAL

The whole purpose of discovery is to elicit facts from your opponent which, together with the ones that you already have, will enable you to win your case.

If you are very diligent and skillful, you may be able to gather enough admitted facts to enable you to get a Summary Judgment and avoid a trial entirely. Admittedly that is rare, but it does happen. More frequently you will gather sufficient evidence to convince your opponent that there is no hope of his winning the lawsuit and he will be very receptive to settlement negotiations.

Let me illustrate these statements by two examples:

In my jurisdiction we have the Doctrine of Informed Consent in medical malpractice actions. In a case involving surgery I deposed the defendant doctor and led him through the specific requirements of Informed Consent. We covered the "part of the body involved," "nature of the operation," and "alternatives to the operation," and he did just fine. Then we reached the part about "possible ill effects" of the operation. At this point he faltered and fell. I moved for a Summary Judgment and got it.

In a recent case against an insurance company which issued a disability insurance policy—and then refused to pay on the ground of a relation back to a "preexistent" condition—I deposed the underwriter, the claims man and the president. The more information I secured, the more I felt that a claim for punitive damages was in order. In a highly technical medical matter all the decisions were being made by persons who were completely untrained in medicine, and not one of them had even tried to get a medical opinion. When it became obvious that things were getting very bad, the insurance company suggested that a settlement was in order. I agreed.

These things just didn't happen—like lightning out of a clear blue sky. The end result was the product of hard work, deliberate planning, and discovery techniques that were carefully thought out and executed according to a definite outline—a written, prepared outline that was part of the file while the entire proceeding was going on.

Finally, if the case must be tried, your efforts in discovery can shorten your trial time—and isolate the remaining issues so that you can concentrate your talents on a few vital issues rather than worrying and proving a veritable host of important but miscellaneous matters.

Discovery can accomplish great things for you. Use if freely, but wisely.

2

The Effective Use of Legal Assistants

No lawyer works on a case alone. Each of us solicits and receives some kind of help in the development and preparation of a lawsuit. Certainly the first line of support is our secretary, in whom we place a great deal of trust and confidence and, depending on his or her experience, to whom we can assign significant tasks in the discovery phase of a case. Frequently we have an associate attorney in our office who is assigned to work with us on a case, or a referring attorney who wants to participate. Finally, in today's world, the paralegal has become a standard fixture in many law offices. All of these persons can be of great help to you in the discovery process, but it does take some special effort on your part to utilize them effectively.

When assistants work with you there has to be organization of the work to be done and an understanding—a ''modus operandi'' if you will—as to how it is to be done. If either is ignored, the partnership breaks down very quickly and becomes quite ineffective.

This chapter explores the problems of how to work with others in discovery proceedings, and gives you some practical ideas on how to make the team perform efficiently and successfully.

In thinking about your discovery you must give some consideration to these factors:

1. Deciding what facts you need;
2. Determining which discovery technique best secures those facts;

3. Preparing the appropriate pleading;
4. Analyzing the answers or response; and
5. Deciding the additional data you need and how to get it.

In answering these questions you have to work closely with your assistant—explaining, supervising, criticizing and directing. These duties have problems of their own and they deserve a close look.

THE ROLE OF THE LEGAL ASSISTANT IN DISCOVERY PROCEDURES

It is good to remember that any aid and assistance you receive from others is designed to help you, not replace you. That is a distinction that lawyers ought to think about. Too many of them look upon their assistant as *the* person to take over all the hard work of preparation in a lawsuit. When these attorneys assign work they seem to proceed on the assumption that the secretary, paralegal, or associate attorney ought to know everything *they* know about the law and the case, and ought to be able to do everything *they* can do. (Naturally this presumption is never permitted to extend to such mundane matters as equal pay and equal rights around the office.) This attitude is unfortunate because it inevitably leads to a breakdown in a system that is supposed to work smoothly and to result in an increase in the effective productivity of an office. Note the key word "effective."

Most of the blame rests with the lawyer. He is in charge and gives the orders. Unless there is an out-and-out personality conflict, any reasonably trained person should be of great help to the lawyer, provided the attorney *takes the time to*

Explain the facts,

Outline the issues,

Discuss the law, and

Assign specific tasks.

I am certain that some reader will feel obliged to make the flippant comment: "If I do all of that, I might as well do the discovery work myself." That's not so, and the comment reveals hasty, ill-considered reasoning. It may require one hour of an attorney's time to carefully explain the things that have to be done—the kind of interrogatories you want, for example—but it may well take eight hours for the paralegal (or the attorney) to do the work. These same proportions, in time spent by the attorney and time saved for him, exist to one degree or another in all phases of discovery. The saving in time and effort on the part of the lawyer is very substantial, provided the assistant has a clear idea of just what he or she is supposed to do.

Essentially the choice must be made by you, the attorney! You can either explain carefully the work you want done and its purpose so that your assistant goes about the detailed work with understanding, or you can give abrupt and general instructions and permit your assistant to work in ignorance. One method results in a lot of good work; the other leads to ill feelings and a waste of time.

ASKING AND GETTING—MAKING YOUR NEEDS UNDERSTANDABLE TO PRODUCE GOOD RESULTS

I pointed out earlier that a common problem of attorneys vis-à-vis their paralegal assistant is that they act as though the assistant knows as much as they do. Unfortunately, one's assistant is not one's clone or alter ego. You simply cannot give the instruction, "Draw up interrogatories," and let it go at that. Your helper does not know the questions that might be specific for your factual situation as opposed to those that provide general background information; he or she cannot be expected to realize those facts that are legally necessary—an essential element of proof—in your case; and finally, the assistant cannot, in the abstract, appreciate what the central issues are so as to emphasize questions relating to these issues in the interrogatories. It is simply asking too much to expect your assistant to know these things and to do a creditable job for you, without detailed knowledge of the case and explicit instructions as to how to proceed.

Some attorneys even compound the error by telling their assistant: "In addition, you decide what documents we need and see if you can get the other side to admit some of the facts we know are so. I'll take the depositions—after you decide who is to be deposed—but you get everything else ready."

The assistant will leave the room with head whirling and in a state of bewilderment. He or she will seek help from the first person he or she meets who will explain just what has to be done. Both of them may hope that in their ignorance of what you have in mind they are doing the right thing.

This sounds like an extravagant example, but is it? Haven't you done this from time to time—and don't you have an acquaintance who does it all the time? It could be called the Big Shot Syndrome. To test yourself, just ask your secretary if you have ever done anything like this to him or her. You may be surprised to observe how quickly he or she answers "yes."

This is no way to work with your associate. You must limit your demands to one subject—i.e., interrogatories, or a motion to produce—and then you must narrow your instructions even more by limiting the scope of the immediate task to one aspect of the subject matter. If you are dealing with the production of documents, tell your assistant to get those documents you need from one opponent before you turn your attention to another one, or within one time period, or one class of documents, leaving to a later date your instructions pertaining to another class. I'm talking here about your instructions to your assistant, not about filing pleadings in court. The actual work-product can be as lengthy, complicated and all-inclusive as you desire, but in the preparatory stage—for goodness' sake and your assistant's sake—break it into manageable and understandable portions.

TAKE TIME TO COMMUNICATE

As you can appreciate, all these things require communication. You have to talk to make yourself heard. You have to meet so that you can talk. At these meetings you have to explain what you want, answer questions, give directions regarding the best way to get the information you want, analyze the work that has been done to date, and criticize.

Certainly this takes time. No one ever said that your having an assistant means that you don't have to work on a file at all! It only means that now you don't have to spend a great deal of time on the detail work on one case, but instead can supervise the work on several cases at once. But, to supervise, you have to communicate. Accordingly, plan on a regular schedule of meetings. You could arrange to get together after your assistant has completed a particular assignment, or you could meet daily or biweekly at a specified time. However you care to do it is a matter of personal choice—just do it! Your assistant cannot read your mind, and you will never know whether the work is proceeding well or poorly unless the two of you get together and talk about it. That is your opportunity to make corrections in whatever work is being done, to give additional facts to your assistant, and to give new directions, if necessary, to the course of the work.

However you care to do it, good communication between you and your paralegal is essential.

REVIEW THE CASE IN DETAIL

The first important step in working with your paralegal is to go over the case in detail. If your assistant doesn't understand what the case is all about, he or she cannot do any assigned task really well. With regard to your explanation of the facts of the case, a word of warning is appropriate right now: do not give your assistant the file with instructions to read it, and with the expectation that once having done so he or she will know all about the case. That is not true and you know it is not true. If you are the one who took in the case, met with the client and, possibly, a member of the family or a friendly witness, you know very well that fully one-quarter to one-third of the information about the case is in your head and not in the file. This is where the need for communication is vital. I remember very clearly several incidents of this kind when, as a young attorney, I was working with a senior partner of the law firm. When we were discussing my handling of a case of his I might mention an essential fact that was missing in our case, to which he would respond: "Oh, we have that," or, "Didn't I mention that?" The answer was, "No, you didn't mention that," and it was frustrating in the extreme. (In retrospect I hope I barked out that answer, or said it caustically; but as I recall, the words were spoken definitely but with a degree of discretion and deference. Perhaps you know what I mean.) In either event the facts that I didn't know completely fouled up the work I had done. It was as simple as that. So, certainly, let your assistant begin with a reading of the file since it contains all the basic information, but follow that up with a meeting at which you can explain the several matters that are not in the file but in your head.

At the conclusion of that meeting your assistant should have all the information that is known, at that time, about the case. You should also have expressed some cautions about those aspects of it on which you have doubts, and should discuss the extent of your client's knowledge and its likely accuracy and completeness. Talking about the client in this way gives your assistant a "feel" or a "sense" for the person and enables him or her to develop an intuition about the case. I do believe in intuition but not as a novel, somewhat weird kind of extra-sensory perception. I perceive it as a judgmental reaction based on one's knowledge and experience. Intuition, so defined, is a valuable aid in making decisions, and its formation begins at this time, when you and your assistant go over every fact, evaluate the client, and engage in conversation about what might have occurred and how you are going to find out what, in fact, did occur.

HAVE YOUR ASSISTANT PREPARE A LIST OF KNOWN AND PROVABLE FACTS

If you are lost in the woods someday, a good way to get back to civilization is to take the time to try to figure out where you are. You can study a map, take compass readings, look for prominent terrain features, watch the movement of the sun, or whatever. But first figure out where you are rather than aimlessly wandering about just hoping that, by luck, you will find your way.

So with the start of a new case. Before you invoke discovery have your paralegal prepare a list of all known—and provable—facts. At this stage it doesn't do any good to list a fact that you are pretty sure is true, but can't prove. The Request for Admissions exists as a discovery tool for just such a purpose. For now, just stay with the facts you can prove. Preparing such a list is an excellent way for your helper to organize his or her thoughts and, seeing them in black and white, to begin to think about all the facts he or she cannot prove and how to go about securing those facts. It's a good way to begin to plan your work.

Let us take a simple automobile intersection accident for illustration. Your assistant might prepare a list like this:

Known and Provable Facts

1. Accident occurred on September 6, 198___, at 2:00 P.M.
2. Intersection of Elm and First Avenue.
3. Plaintiff proceeding East on Elm Street.
4. Defendant proceeding North on First Avenue.
5. A stop sign exists on Elm Street at the intersection.
6. Plaintiff driving a 1980 Buick Sedan.
7. Defendant driving a dark Cadillac.
8. Weather conditions: sunny, clear, dry.
9. James Jones saw the accident and assisted Plaintiff.
10. Plaintiff's car badly damaged at right front—fender, hood and wheel.
11. No passengers in Plaintiff's car.
12. Plaintiff was into the intersection when the collision occurred.
13. Plaintiff was badly injured; could not get out of car; ambulance arrived and crew removed him from car.

Suppose for a moment that these are all the facts that you can prove at this time. It takes only a moment to realize that there are a host of things you don't know. Where in the intersection did the accident occur? Was there a traffic control signal for cars traveling on First Avenue? What did the witness, James Jones, observe? Were there any other witnesses? How fast were the respective vehicles going? Where were the Plaintiff and Defendant coming from and going to? Was either of them in a hurry? What was the point of impact on Defendant's car?

One would go on with a dozen more similar questions. They all need to be answered. The important point is that by making out a list such as the one above, your assistant can recognize how many facts are not known.

Let us take one moment for an aside about a comparison of the state of the attorney's general knowledge with that of his paralegal assistant. Just by glancing at the facts of this elemental, basic—one might almost say "grade school"—legal problem the mind of the attorney recognizes the issues, the facts he needs, and the discovery techniques he will use to get the facts. Almost without thinking he knows that he must prepare interrogatories to get the identity of witnesses and other data known to defendant, or a police report, file a Motion to Produce to get the itemized repair bill for defendant's car, take a deposition of defendant and send an investigator out to interview Mr. Jones and the crew of the ambulance.

Unfortunately, the average paralegal, who does not have a considerable amount of experience, doesn't think along these lines with the rapidity and understanding of the lawyer. This is why consultation with the lawyer and instructions from him are so important.

Returning to the illustrative problem, you can see that by listing the known, provable facts the paralegal can begin to understand how many additional details will be needed.

As one examines the complexity of a case one realizes how much more difficult things become for the paralegal and how necessary it is to divide the proposed work into understandable portions that can be effectively handled, and to give direction as to how one wants the information collected—i.e., the discovery process to be utilized.

EXPLAIN THE APPLICABLE LAW

When your assistant has a clear understanding of the facts of the case, it is necessary to explain the general principles of law applicable to those facts. Without such an explanation your paralegal will fail to understand the context in which the facts are going to be used and why some are more important than others. Thus, in our hypothetical intersection case, you could explain the duties of each driver as he came to the intersection and why it is important to learn which of them was committed to the intersection first; you might point out the requirements of statutes regulating speeds as they apply if this intersection is in a school zone, a residential area, or along a major highway. It might be helpful to discuss the use of a police report as evidence, and, if a Business Records Act or local rule prescribes certain formalities for using it, how one can comply with those requirements. In addition, if either party made an admission at the scene of the accident, you could point out how important that could be as evidence of liability.

With a little knowledge of this kind the whole process of discovery becomes more sensible to your assistant. Now he or she is not merely trying to ascertain a fact, but is collecting a fact that has a certain meaning to the overall case. In other words, the work begins to make sense.

A discussion of this kind can also help your assistant to know that certain information is positively essential (did plaintiff stop at the "stop" sign?); other matters are interesting and informative but not really vital (had plaintiff received medical treatment in the past to any parts of his anatomy injured in this accident?); and some data is for general background only (date of birth, place of employment, Social Security number).

It is good for all of us to bear in mind that facts in and of themselves do not have much significance. After a little understanding of the applicable law, however, the facts become important and it becomes clear that they have differing degrees of importance.

DISCUSS YOUR THEORY OF LIABILITY OR DEFENSE

At the beginning of every case, I'm sure that you can think of several different theories by which the case might be won. Naturally the key to success is in developing sufficient evidence to justify your proceeding to trial on one theory rather than another. While your paralegal is helping you to gather the evidence, he or she ought to know what approach you are taking. This is another area in which misapprehension can lead to wasted time and energy. Therefore, it behooves you to explain just how you intend to win this case and the facts that you need to accomplish that purpose. Referring once again to our hypothetical example, a Plaintiff's attorney might say:

> Look, we'll work on the idea that defendant was traveling at a high rate of speed; that he saw Plaintiff stop and then proceed into the intersection; that he thought Plaintiff would clear the intersection in time and when he didn't our defendant could not stop and the accident occurred.

That is a good theory. Your assistant, after additional instructions, can now begin to utilize the appropriate discovery methods to support this hypothesis. Now suppose you also order some investigation and the investigator learns from witness Jones that the defendant was proceeding at a very sensible speed, that it appeared to Jones that defendant tried to apply his brakes to slow down for the intersection, that the brakes didn't work and thus the collision. Jones even tried to operate the brakes of defendant's car after the accident, while moving it to the curb, and the brakes were inoperable.

At this point your original theory is no longer valid, and you're going to have to switch to a new one involving the brakes on defendant's car. You might even start wondering whether defendant's brakes were improperly repaired recently, and consider the possibility of your bringing a mechanic or repair garage into the case.

Immediately you will have to call in your paralegal, explain the newly received information, stop the work on the earlier theory, and start all over again with a new hypothesis of liability and a whole new approach to the discovery necessary to support this concept.

The point is that you have to keep your assistant apprised of changes in the case, of new and different ideas you have, and of what you want him or her to do now. Don't keep the poor soul in the dark and then get upset when you are presented with a nice set of discovery documents that have nothing whatsoever to do with your current ideas.

The same sort of thing can happen to you as a defense attorney. You start off with the idea that Plaintiff failed to stop before entering the intersection and put your paralegal to work on that theory. Then you discover that he did stop, but started again like the proverbial jack-rabbit and shot in front of your defendant. You had better call in your assistant and explain the change in circumstances and in approach.

Whatever the case may be, and irrespective of your position as representing either a plaintiff or a defendant, you have to have a theory of liability or defense and your assistant has to be thoroughly conversant with it. When it changes due to changing circumstances, don't keep that a secret. Let your paralegal know about the change so that there isn't a waste of time and effort.

OUTLINE THE FACTS NEEDED TO SUPPORT
YOUR THEORY

Once you have decided where you are going, the next step is to figure out how to get there; having determined upon a theory of liability or defense you are now faced with the task of accumulating the facts you need to support it. This involves a little more than determining the facts you need, comparing this list with the facts you have, and then itemizing the ones you still need. The question is: how do you get them?

The easiest way to handle this is to prepare an outline that will sketch out what you need and how you propose to get it. This accomplishes two purposes— it clarifies your thinking and represents a work schedule for your assistant, and, equally important, it almost automatically breaks down the work into definable, easily understood objectives for your assistant.

The outline need not be lengthy, but it should be complete. For example, turning again to our automobile case, you could work up something like this:

Facts Needed

 1. Speed of defendant as he approached intersection.
 2. Speed of defendant immediately prior to accident.
 3. Condition of brakes after accident.
 4. If they are defective:
     a. Did the accident damage them?
     b. Was the defect a preexistent condition?
     c. Should the defendant have known of their condition?
     d. Was it a sudden emergency situation?
 5. Words or conduct of defendant at the scene.
 6. Repairs to brakes—who, when, why and nature of repairs.
 7. Witnesses.
 8. Areas of damage to defendant's car and cost of repair.
 9. Background information regarding defendant.
10. Any evidence of drinking or drunkedness.
11. Where defendant was coming from and going to.
12. General data regarding car—age, condition, mileage.
13. Data regarding the scene of the accident.

You should prepare a list like this with your assistant so that there is a clear understanding between you concerning what you are looking for.

EXPLORE TOGETHER THE BEST WAYS TO GET THE INFORMATION YOU NEED

After you have your outline prepared, the next topic for discussion is how you are going to get the information. This is the time when the attorney has to begin giving instructions. It will be easy for him to select the most appropriate discovery tool for each type of fact. Look over that list of facts needed. It would appear that No. 3, "Condition of brakes after accident," No. 4, "If they are defective..," No. 5, "Words or conduct of defendant at the scene," and No. 13, "Data regarding the scene of the accident" can best be secured by investigation and supplemented by the deposition of the defendant. A deposition should also be used to secure Nos. 1 and 2, "Speed of defendant as he approached the intersection and immediately prior to the accident," No. 6, "Repairs to brakes..," and No. 11, "Where defendant was coming from and going to." Interrogatories can be used for No., 7, "Witnesses," No. 9, "Background information regarding defendant," and No. 12, "General data regarding car..." You will probably file a Motion to Produce a repair bill or estimate to secure the answer to No. 8, "Areas of damage to defendant's car..." and possibly No. 6, "Repairs to brakes...."

You can then give your assistant a simple outline that will determine not only the facts that he or she must collect but also the way to do it. The work is laid out for the paralegal. Something like this will do fine:

Interrogatories—Nos. 7, 9 and 12

Investigation—Nos. 3, 4, 5 and 13

Deposition—Nos. 1, 2, 3, 4, 5, 6 and 11

Motion to produce—Nos. 6 and 8

Your assistant can now leave you alone and begin to work with a clear idea of what he or she is doing. In due course of time the discovery will be underway with a reasonable likelihood that it will be effective and productive.

Don't forget that there is a certain element of priority to these discovery techniques. Thus investigation and interrogatories are generally used first, followed by the deposition. A motion to produce can only be filed after you learn what data is available and who has it. This is probably going to be after you have taken the deposition or received the answers to interrogatories. Last of all will be your Requests for Admissions; these will be filed to establish a fact already known or strongly suspected and thus avoid proof at trial, rather than to seek after facts.

STUDY THE RESULTS, ANALYZE THEM, REGROUP AND MOVE AHEAD

When opposing counsel begins to answer the interrogatories, when the investigation report comes in, and when documents are produced for inspection, it is time again to meet with your assistant to analyze this information. What have you learned and where do you stand now? It is to be expected that you will be disappointed with some of the information you received, while other data will be very helpful. It is time to talk over different ideas. Perhaps your theory of liability or defense will change again; possibly you will have discovered another party who ought to be brought into the case; and inevitably you will come up with new questions you want answered, another deposition to be taken, or documents secured from some other person or organization. It is from such a meeting that you outline the additional data you want and determine how your paralegal will secure it.

It is also a time to criticize—objectively, dispassionately and in a friendly manner. You may well observe that the interrogatories were too vague and imprecise; that the motion to produce was so broad that it evoked a motion for a protective order that you will now have to argue; or, just as bad, that you now have a stack of documents on your desk which you have to go through, well knowing that most of them are not of help.

This is your opportunity to sharpen the skills of your assistant by pointing out the errors and correcting them. It does no good to keep still if mistakes have been made, but at the same time incentive is destroyed by harsh criticism.

At any rate, after you have made a thorough review of the new information and adjusted your plans, it's time to get back to the next step in the discovery process.

USE YOUR PARALEGAL TO DO OUT-OF-OFFICE RESEARCH AND DOCUMENT COLLECTION

Later chapters relate to the preparation of a Settlement Brochure, to medical research and to locating various industry and professional society standards and governmental rules and regulations.

This area of work is uniquely appropriate to the skills of your good paralegal. As you will see, the information is *absolutely essential*, but gathering it is:

Time-consuming,

Nerve-wracking,

Detailed, and

Frustrating.

Let's face it—you're no good at that sort of thing, and neither am I. It requires a special talent and a unique ability. Your paralegal has it; you don't. For that reason work closely with your associate but let him or her do it.

It takes weeks to gather the dozens of documents that must go into a Settlement Brochure: wage records, school records, photographs from a family album, letters from school teachers or supervisors at work, weather reports and detailed bills for past and future medical care, medicines and equipment. You need it all but give the assignment to your paralegal to collect it, get it authenticated if you think that is necessary and then begin to get it into some sort of usable order.

The Effective Use of Legal Assistants   **23**

Much the same is true of the hard work and extensive time needed to track down medical books and articles, university research, governmental regulations and industry standards. Somebody has to spend hours browsing in a medical school library looking for pertinent writings, and someone has to travel to a municipal building or state office complex and wander around with the distinct likelihood of being shunted from office to office while trying to track down a specific local ordinance, state building regulation, or industry code. That someone ought to be your paralegal. He or she is the person who has the training, the time and the energy to do this work.

Just remember that you are going to have to take the time to explain in detail what it is you are after before you send him or her out on this scouting expedition. And it is an expedition! Too often attorneys contemplate the matter for awhile then decide that it is too time-consuming for him or her to do. Then they turn the job over to the paralegal and later complain. About what? That it is taking so much time! Let's cut that out. You know the job is going to be time-consuming; so don't be surprised or annoyed when your paralegal is gone for hours or days working on this project. It simply has to be done.

DISCOVERY IS A CONTINUING PROCESS UNTIL YOU HAVE ALL THE DATA YOU NEED—OR CAN GET

Fortunately there are no rules that allow you only a single chance at any given discovery technique. The answers to interrogatories will lead to your additional questions and to a motion to produce. The documents produced will compel you to take a deposition, and this in turn may lead you to order more investigation. It's an ongoing process and it ends only when you have all the information you need. Thus, it's important that you keep in close contact with your assistant—prodding, advising, correcting, supervising. Your paralegal will do the work if, between the two of you, there is a clear understanding of what's to be done and how it fits into the overall case. While the role of the assistant is to do the work, the job of the attorney is to guide and direct. Together you can have the pleasure of a case successfully concluded and a satisfied client. In addition, if you have worked well as a team you will have furthered a relationship that will continue to lead to happy results in the future.

3

Building a Solid Foundation—the Imaginative Use of Interrogatories

The Trial Lawyer should always keep in mind the following facts:

Interrogatories are the foundation blocks of successful cases.

★ ★ ★ ★ ★

They are a potent and effective tool.

★ ★ ★ ★ ★

They are free of charge.

★ ★ ★ ★ ★

If there were ever three good reasons for putting time and effort into a project that can only benefit you, these three should be persuasive. Yet, for some reason, many attorneys refuse to work at preparing a good set of Interrogatories.

Let me emphasize that Interrogatories are to Discovery as foundation blocks are to a house—unglamorous but necessary; they provide the support for the whole structure. In addition, like foundation stones in construction they come first. There is a good reason for this: one has to have some general background information and some basic data before one can engage in probing, carefully thought out, and case-winning depositions. Interrogatories are the foot soldiers of discovery, setting up the opponent for the sudden, decisive cavalry charge; in football parlance they are the running backs who continually pound away for a few yards until the linebackers and defensive backs begin to move up, thus setting the scene for the long touchdown pass.

Interrogatories are important, detailed, and somewhat laborious to prepare. As in all such office work they are often glossed over, done hurriedly, and viewed with some distaste—one might almost say active dislike—by many lawyers. What a mistake!

FORCE YOUR OPPONENT TO WORK FOR YOU—FOR FREE!

It is often said that nothing is free in this world. That's not true. The Answers to Interrogatories are free. Think of this for a moment: where else in the law (or in the world for that matter) can you force your opponent to work for you—with no payment expected or required! It happens every time you serve a set of Interrogatories. It is perfectly proper for you to prepare a set of Interrogatories that could have your opposition pulling his hair and shouting imprecations, but at the same time tearing apart records, interviewing people, holding meetings, and, in short, working for you to secure those mandatory answers to your questions. You can have fun with this discovery tool if you want to. But seriously, you are literally forcing the defendant (or plaintiff) to gather information that you need to win your lawsuit. He may not like it, but he has to do it.

HOW INTERROGATORIES CAN HELP YOU TO WIN YOUR CASE

Certainly the primary function of Interrogatories is to gather information—the necessary facts that your opponent knows and you do not. At the same time, however, you should always ask some very probing questions that touch on the most sensitive aspects of your liability problem and thus, hopefully, secure an answer that will win your case right then and there! Many attorneys are shy about this for some reason that has never been clear to me. Unless you ask a searching question there will never be an opportunity for the other side to come forward with the answer. This is clearly one instance in which the Biblical admonition still applies: *Ask and you shall receive.* You can rely on the fact that in most instances your opponent will respond to your question truthfully and accurately, so if you do ask a question that goes to the heart of the matter you may well get an admission that will end the case. Settlements result when your opponent is forced to admit that he is liable, or, if you represent a defendant, that your client is not liable in the cause of action that is the subject matter of the lawsuit. When you receive an answer that is obviously damaging to the cause of your adversary, the subject matter of negotiation quickly switches from ''Are we liable?'' to

"How much (or little) shall we pay?" Let us consider some actual instances in which specific Interrogatories resulted in cases being won very quickly.

Illustration No. 1—A Student Rider Thrown from a Horse

The plaintiff went to a prestigious riding academy to take horseback riding lessons. She stated that she was taking a lesson at the indoor ring under the supervision of the instructor when the horse suddenly veered or jerked to the right, throwing the rider to the ground and resulting in her injuring a cervical disc. She stated that there was no apparent reason for the horse to have made the sudden movement. She also mentioned that hers was the first lesson of the day at the academy.

The plaintiff's attorney discussed the incident with an experienced instructor, who advised him to make inquiry in four areas:

1. Was the horse kept in a box stall or a standup stall? The significance here is that the horse can lie down and rest in a box stall, which can contribute to its being a more tranquil and contented animal.
2. Was the horse exercised prior to the beginning of the lessons? This is important because a horse tends to be nervous and skittish in the morning; horses suffer from the "early morning blahs" just as people do.
3. Did the instructor use a lunge line? A lunge line is a rope, 30 feet or so in length, whereby the instructor maintains some control over the horse.
4. Did the horse have a bad reputation for throwing students or other riders?

Please note two things about these questions: first, an expert was consulted, who suggested the areas into which inquiry should be directed; and second, the questions would have to be tailored to the specific facts of the case. There are no "Form Interrogatories" that can be designed to apply to an accident of this kind. Certainly the average attorney is not going to have enough cases of this kind to justify the preparation of Form Interrogatories. The Interrogatories that were submitted included the following:

1. Identify the horse here involved, including the following:
   a. The name of the horse;
   b. Date of birth of the horse;
   c. Identity of the farm or stable at which it was reared;
   d. The date of purchase of this horse by the Defendant (if it was purchased);
   e. The uses to which the horse has been put by the Defendant during the time it has owned the horse.

Answer:

    a. Snoopy.

    b. November 10, 1976.

    c. Sunny Slopes Farm.

    d. December 1, 1980.

    e. Used for riding by students and other members of the public.

2. State whether the horse here involved was, on the night before this accident, kept in a box stall or a standup stall.

Answer:

    This horse was kept in a box stall.

3. State whether the riding lesson scheduled for Mrs. Jones was the first riding lesson given at the Defendant's academy on the day of the accident.

Answer:

    Yes.

4. Set forth the time at which Plaintiff's riding lesson began.

Answer:

    8:00 A.M.

5. State whether prior to the time the riding lesson began the horse here involved was exercised, and if the answer is "yes," set forth:

    a. The identity of the person who exercised the horse.

    b. The time at which the horse was exercised.

    c. The length of time during which the horse was exercised.

Answer:

    a. John Riley, stable hand.

    b. Approximately between 6:30 A.M. and 8:00 A.M. Exact time unknown.

    c. Approximately 30 minutes.

6. Identify the name and home address of the person who was instructing the Plaintiff at the time of this accident.

Answer:

    Mary Brown
    123 White Street
    Pittsburgh, Pennsylvania

7. State whether the instructor utilized a lunge line during the period of instruction.

Answer:

No.

8. State whether the Defendant has any knowledge of any student or rider being thrown from or falling from the horse here involved prior to the date of this accident, and if the answer is "yes," set forth:

   a. The name and home address of persons who have been thrown from or who have fallen from this horse.

   b. The date of each such incident.

   c. Whether the rider was injured.

   d. Whether any claim has been made against the Defendant by such rider.

Answer:

Yes.

   a. John Smith
      456 Jones Street
      Aspinwall, Pennsylvania.

      Susan Black
      789 Oriole Drive
      Pittsburgh, Pennsylvania.

      John Calgani
      10 Somerset Blvd.
      Pleasant Hills, Pennsylvania.

   b. John Smith-April 14, 1981.
      Susan Black-January 23, 1981.
      Joan Calgani-December 20, 1980.

   c. John Smith-Injured.
      Susan Black-Injured.
      John Calgani-Injured.

   d. John Smith and Susan black have filed claims against this Defendant.

   You will note from the answers that Plaintiff's counsel struck out regarding the questions about the box stall and the exercising of the horse, but the answers to the questions about the lunge line and prior accidents were pure gold. Since the instructor did not use a lunge line she had no control whatsoever over the movements of the horse, and we now know that the horse had thrown three other riders. Clearly the academy had prior notice that this horse was trouble.

   The answers to those two questions provided all the ammunition Plaintiff's counsel needed on liability. As a result, this case was settled promptly and for a substantial sum.

It is important to note that in this case proper specific questions were asked. The defendant could have avoided, evaded or even lied in its answers—but it did not. You will find that in 99 percent of the cases the defendant will not do so. The answers were straightforward and liability attached.

Illustration No. 2—An Electrical Arc Case

In this case the plaintiff was a painter whose duty it was to paint a tower carrying high voltage electrical lines, at a substation owned by a major public utility. Aside from the usual warning sign attached to the fence surrounding the tower, there were no other particular instructions given him. He related that about twenty feet up the tower there was a crossarm, on the outer edges of which electric wires were strung. The wires were attached by a ceramic device that looked like an inverted cup. The painter clung to a vertical beam and painted one side of it and then he began to move out on the horizontal beam, planning to paint it from its outer edge back toward the vertical beam. He took a few steps and was about four or five feet from the outer edge of the horizontal beam when he was struck by a bolt of electricity, thrown to the ground, and sustained injuries. He swore that he never touched the wires or the ceramic object. The facts seemed unusual—even weird. Can electricity jump and literally chase a man along a tower?

Inquiry to electrical engineers revealed that the device at the end of the horizontal beam is known as a "pothead," and that electricity can indeed arc over a distance of several feet and strike a person. They suggested that questions be asked of the defendant concerning why the electricity was not shut off at the tower; why the painters were not warned of the danger of arcing; and why barricades of some kind were not erected to keep the painters away from the "potheads" while they worked.

As a result of these conversations, some specific questions were prepared:

1. State whether the electrical power was shut off on the tower here involved while it was being painted.

Answer:

No.

2. State whether the device which holds the electric wires to the tower is known as a "pothead."

Answer:

Yes.

3   Set forth the amount of the voltage in the electric lines passing over the tower here involved at the time of this accident.

Answer:

25,000 volts.

4. State whether defendant knows that an electrical arc can be formed between the "pothead" and a person five feet away.

Answer:

Yes.

5. Set forth whether any person to the defendant's knowledge gave instructions to the plaintiff with regard to the risks, hazards or dangers of working near or around "potheads."

Answer:

Not to the knowledge of this Defendant.

6. Set forth whether there were any signs on or around the tower here involved warning persons concerning the danger of getting near the "potheads."

Answer:

A sign posted on the fence surrounding the tower reads:
    "High Voltage—Keep Away."

7. State whether there were any barricades or restraining devices of any kind to keep the painters from getting close to the "potheads."

Answer:

None.

8. If there were signs or other written notice of hazards placed on or around the tower here involved, please set forth:

    a. the exact wording on the signs;

    b. The precise loction of each and every sign.

Answer:

See answer to Number 6 above.

9. On the tower here involved and at the point where this accident happened, state whether there were any physical barriers, either wooden, rope or otherwise, to prevent plaintiff from stepping beyond the vertical beams of the tower.

Answer:

None.

As you can see, when the Defendant admitted that it knew that an arc could jump between the pothead and the place at which the Plaintiff was standing and that it neither warned Plaintiff of this nor shut down the electricity nor roped off the area near the potheads, the game was over. Realistically, where was the defense? Here again, because of a good set of Interrogatories the case was settled.

Consider for a moment that if the Interrogatories had not been asked, each of the cases set forth above could have dragged on for many months, possibly to the time of trial, before the facts became known and settlement became a practical reality. As it was, very early in the case this discovery tool was used and promptly after the answers were received a settlement was achieved.

Illustration No. 3—A Defective Intravenous Catheter

A catheter is nothing more than a tube designed to carry fluids. Its insertion into the human body is sometimes difficult, and manufacturers have developed various products to accomplish this purpose as easily as possible. In this case an injured women had a catheter inserted into a vein in the area of the right collar bone—a subclavian jugular catheter. Unfortunately the catheter broke and moved, and the doctors had a very difficult time removing it at surgery. Since the attending physician insisted that he had inserted the catheter properly, the question arose whether the product was defective. Among the Interrogatories asked were these:

1. Has this Defendant received any complaints concerning its catheter, Model No. 1234?

Answer:

Yes.

2. If the answer to the foregoing question is "yes," set forth:
   a. The date of each and every complaint received by Defendant concerning this catheter;
   b. The name and address of the complaining party;
   c. The nature of the complaint.

Answer:

[The answer to this question consisted of a long list of persons who had made complaints to the company, most of which were substantially similar in nature to the complaint of the doctor in the instant case.]

3. Has this catheter ever been recalled by the Defendant either voluntarily or at the request of any governmental agency?

Answer:

Yes, voluntarily.

4. If the answer to the question above is "yes," set forth:

   a. The date of recall;

   b. The reason for the recall.

Answer:

   a. June 26, 1980

   b. Sometime in 1980, Jones Manufacturing Co. began to receive complaints through a product complaint reporting service initiated by the Food & Drug Administration and the U.S. Pharmacopeia and also complaints directly from hospitals of problems relating to the adapter end of the catheter. An analysis of these complaints indicated that they were generally caused by errors of the physicians who were using the catheter. These errors consisted either of the insertion of the wrong end of the catheter through the needle and into the patient or of insufficient tightening of the adapter end of the catheter to the adapter. As a result of this, a "product recall" was initiated by Jones Manufacturing Co., which amounted to a change in the directions for use of the catheter to explicitly point out that the metal end of the catheter must be attached to the screw-on adapter and that the catheter must be snugly applied, even if this required the use of a hemostat.

As you can imagine, the doctor was exonerated in this case and a quick settlement was effected with the manufacturer. The complaints of the other doctors and the problems they had were nearly the same as the difficulties experienced in the instant case so that there was plenty of notice to the manufacturer. Then, to top it off, the recall date was just a few weeks before this unfortunate plaintiff had the catheter inserted into her upper chest.

These three illustrations—just a few among many that could be selected—illustrate that your cases can be won through the use of interrogatories and at a very early stage in its life as a lawsuit.

The important point to be made is that you don't have to hold onto a case clear up to the time of trial, which in some states is many months—or even years—after the date of filing. In most instances you can have a good set of interrogatories prepared within 30 days after the Complaint is filed. Then if we allow another 30 days for your opponent to answer and a month or so for settlement negotiations, it is very possible to conclude a case in 90 days, give or take a few.

There is absolutely no good reason for many cases to linger for years. The lawyer is earning no money, or very little, while the case sits; the client is unhappy with the delay; and the court has one more case overloading its dockets. All that it takes to clear away this unfortunate and unnecessary state of affairs is for the lawyer—you—to prepare a detailed, specific set of questions, which your opponent must answer at no cost to you—and many of these cases can be brought to a prompt conclusion. If you are a defense attorney you can move for a Summary Judgment on the Pleadings based on the answers to interrogatories. The principal value of the questions—and the answers—is that they force both parties to look at the strengths and weaknesses of their respective cases, and this encourages settlement. Many times your opposing counsel will not have really thought out his case or considered its problems until he or she has to make serious inquiries, ask tough questions, or search for documents to answer the questions. Just consider the position of the defense attorney in the case involving the lady who was thrown from the horse, when he had to ask his client about prior, similar incidents and learned that there were three such incidents, two of which involved claims against the riding academy. You know that very promptly he did three things: he opened settlement discussions with plaintiff's counsel, he notified his insurance carrier about the problem, and he told the client to get rid of the horse! Had the interrogatories not been served, it is very likely that none of those things would have been done and the case would have dragged on and on.

So interrogatories can accomplish a great deal for you. Frequently the answers will lead to settlement, but even if they do not they will certainly give you valuable information that you need in the preparation of your case for trial.

THERE ARE SEVERAL ADVANTAGES TO USING INTERROGATORIES INSTEAD OF INVESTIGATION

Interrogatories can never replace investigation but they can reduce the amount of investigation that you require. Let's face it—private investigators are expensive and their cost is going up, not down. To the extent that you can use Interrogatories to do your investigation, your costs will be reduced. Obviously that is an important consideration. There is one other aspect of this question of Interrogatory vs. Investigation that you might think about: when you send out an investigator he asks the questions his way; when you prepare Interrogatories you are asking the questions the way you want them asked. The difference can be very significant in terms of the answer you are looking for.

Finally, we must always keep in mind that your opposing party will be answering the Interrogatories and he, she, or it is going to be bound by those answers. The question and answer can be read into evidence during the trial. That is not true of an investigation report. Usually your investigator does not take sworn statements from the people he talks with; such persons can change their minds or claim to have been misquoted, and you're not going to read the investigation report into evidence.

These represent a few more good reasons for the careful preparation of interrogatories.

USE INTERROGATORIES TO UNCOVER STATIC FACTS

Interrogatories have a limited capacity; they are useful to uncover fixed, un-changeable, what may be referred to as "static," facts. In the very nature of things you can't use them to engage in dialogue with your opponent; save that for depositions. If you try it sometime you will soon learn that you can go crazy trying to come up with alternative questions in anticipation of your opponent's answers. And you lay yourself open to sarcastic or comic answers, to wit:

Q: When you came to the intersection of First Avenue and Green Street, which way did you go?

A: Through the intersection.

Q: Why did you proceed in that direction?

A: To get to the other side!

That's not very helpful—but it's an honest answer. Or this:

Q: Of the four recognized methods to perform this operation, which did you use?

A: Method No. 2.

Q: Why did you choose this technique?

A: To save the man's life.

What does one do with that answer?

It's no good. Your opponent can always answer a "why" question in a way that can evade, hurt or embarrass you. Don't give him or her the chance. Besides, such questions are a complete waste of time. They lead nowhere and provide no useful information.

Interrogatories are best used to answer the questions "who," "what," "when," and "where." Leave the "hows" and "whys" for depositions.

With these limitations, however, you are free to explore every facet of your lawsuit—to uncover information you don't have and to prove facts that you know are essential to your case.

YOU ARE NOT LIMITED TO INFORMATION THAT IS DIRECTLY RELATED TO THE ISSUES IN THE CASE

Don't be timid about asking questions and seeking information. You are not limited to questions that directly relate to the issues involved in the lawsuit. Remember that this is *discovery*—the purpose of which is to uncover all information you need. The rule is clear; you can discover information which, while not directly relevant, can lead to facts that are relevant to the lawsuit. This is very important; without this right your ability to gather information would be quite restricted and you might not learn some helpful information. Suppose you have a case in which the condition of the plaintiff's heart is very much at issue. It stands to reason that you can ask all sorts of questions about prior medical treatment of the plaintiff—examinations, diagnostic techniques, hospitalizations, drug and medications and restrictions on activities. But can you ask such questions about the parents of plaintiff? His brothers and sisters? Absolutely. There is a respected body of medical opinion that believes that certain heart conditions are hereditary in nature and that therefore your questions inquiring into familial difficulties with cardiac conditions are perfectly proper.

The same thing applies to prior difficulties with an instrumentality. Suppose your client was injured in a large department store when an elevator malfunctioned. Certainly you want to know all about the elevator on the day of the accident—but it is equally proper to inquire about prior accidents or malfunctions both as to this elevator and as to other similar ones in the store. Suppose the store has four Otis elevators. Let us additionally assume that the Plaintiff was hurt on Otis No. 2 due to some supposed defect in the operating mechanism. You are certainly justified in asking all the questions you deem pertinent as to Otis No. 2. If you suspect that the same defect existed in the other Otis elevators and that the store had prior notice of the condition, you can interrogate as to the other Otis elevators—inspections, maintenance, repairs, accidents, complaints to Otis, and anything else you think can help you. All of these questions may *lead you* to information that will be relevant to your case—questions of Notice and the like—and these questions constitute permissible discovery.

REMEMBER!

1. Interrogatories should be the first discovery tool you use.
2. You force the opposition to work for you—free of charge.
3. Use interrogatories as an inexpensive substitute for investigation.
4. Use it to uncover static facts:
   Who
   What
   Where
   When
5. The opposing party is bound by the answers to interrogatories.
6. You have the opportunity to frame the questions in your own style.
7. You are not limited to facts directly related to the lawsuit but can inquire into matters that will lead to such facts.

AN ILLUSTRATION OF THE ABUSE OF DISCOVERY

We were discussing, a few moments ago, a theoretical accident in an Otis elevator located in a department store. If we may disgress for a moment from a discussion of proper discovery we can use that example to demonstrate an abuse of discovery that is becoming quite prevalent. Suppose the department store contained additional elevators manufactured and installed by, let us say, Westinghouse Corporation. Now if you decide to interrogate as to the Westinghouse elevators in the same manner as you did concerning the Otis elevators, a serious, practical, ethical problem is created. Certainly you have no reason to believe that the Westinghouse elevators had anything to do with the accident in which you are involved, or that they are constructed the same way or are the same design as the Otis elevators. (You can legitimately inquire if this is true if you have doubts in the matter.) Nonetheless if you ask the questions you may be able to convince some judge that maybe—just maybe—there are significant similarities that justify your probing. This puts the judge in an uncomfortable position; even though he really doesn't believe it, nonetheless he doesn't want to restrict discovery if you think it's important. He isn't close enough to the facts to draw fine distinctions, so, applying the liberal construction rule, he lets you proceed. You may well force the defendant to spend many man-hours searching through old and current records and interviewing its maintenance men—and all for naught. You know, opposing counsel knows, and the department store knows that even if a prior accident on, or defect in, the Westinghouse equipment is found, it isn't going to help you. This is the kind of thing that brings discovery into disrepute. There is a certain discipline required of lawyers to avoid this sort of thing.

All of the above-mentioned strictures can be ignored if we just change the facts a little bit.

Suppose that the accident occurred because of a defect in the power source to all the elevators, or a breakdown in some master control panel. That one little change could make a world of difference; now it might well be necessary and appropriate to make inquiry about stoppages, breakdowns and accidents involving all the elevators—both Otis and Westinghouse.

As you can see, much depends on the factual basis with which you are confronted. Conduct that is justified under one set of circumstances is completely improper under a different set of facts. Attorneys have fine minds and habitually make discriminating judgments, and it is appropriate that they do so in deciding just when discovery reaches the boundary of proper conduct and begins to step into the forbidden zone of behavior that may not be malicious but is deliberately miserable.

FORM INTERROGATORIES—HELP OR HINDRANCE?

I am slightly cynical about human nature and happen to believe in the adage that the less one has to do the less one does. If you take the fact that preparing interrogatories is hard work to begin with and throw in the enticement of a set of forms lying around the office, I will wager, and give odds, that the average person will use the forms every time even if half the questions have nothing to do with the lawsuit. I know this to be so. In Assumpsit cases I've received form interrogatories that asked questions about "prior medical treatment to the same part of the body involved herein," and in a trespass case involving a baby I've seen extensive questions about employment, wages, marital status, dependents and taxpayer's ID number. Let's fact it—forms are a lazy man's way of doing things. We start off with the best of intentions: let's draw up a set of basic questions for different kinds of cases and then for each specific case we will simply add the precise, pertinent questions relevant to that case. It sounds good, but it never works out as well as it sounds.

I believe that Interrogatories have to be expressly designed for the individual case—from scratch—and that you are only deceiving yourself if you think you can prepare forms that will do a creditable job in every case or, more importantly, that you will seriously and diligently add specific, searching questions to your forms.

The only justifiable exception to this rule is the large, high-volume law office that lives by forms or drowns in a sea of pleadings. This type of operation has to have forms, but the very reason for the need—a lack of time to give individual attention to each case—implies that even if specific questions are supposed to be added they probably won't be, or only a few will be tacked on in a slap-dash manner. As an individual attorney you should enjoy seeing form interrogatories come to your office from opposing counsel; it is a clear signal that the lawyer is too busy to pay significant attention to this one case and that he or she is susceptible to some important blunders. It's just a little matter to keep in mind.

I suspect that plaintiffs' attorneys are a little more inhibited in designing forms than are the defense attorneys. This is mainly because a plaintiff's lawyer is searching for facts regarding liability (which doesn't easily fit into categories) while a defense attorney is after facts pertaining to both liability and damages, and the latter can be categorized. Injuries and losses are relatively fixed items and therefore fit easily within the orbit of form interrogatories.

Despite my admonition some readers are going to opt for forms. So be it. If you are going to use them, let's decide what they should contain and then look at some sample forms, although the actual preparation of forms has to be a do-it-yourself project tailored to your specific needs and desires. Their scope and content will depend on:

> The type of case you habitually handle (i.e., medical malpractice, automobile cases, sales of goods and merchandise, entertainment contracts);
>
> Your personal attitude (do you want a lot of details or not?); and
>
> Your goals (are you inquisitive about general background information or do you want to zero right in on the significant, vital issues?).

Another problem is that we tend to categorize our cases—Trespass and Assumpsit—according to "liability" or "type of incident" standards. Thus we speak of a "gas explosion" case, "medical malpractice," and an "intersection collision" in the field of personal injury law. The same is true of contract law: we refer to a financial transaction or a case involving defective goods or a breach of service contract. These terms identify the case in terms of "what happened," and that relates directly to questions involving liability.

As you can imagine, a plaintiff's attorney is very much restricted in preparing a form that will apply to all or several of these different causes of action; there just isn't much similarity between an airplane accident and a medical malpractice case. The only thing he can do is to analyze his volume of each type of case, and if the numbers indicate that there is a steady repetition of a particular class of cases, then he can prepare a set of form interrogatories for that style of action.

The defense attorney is in a little different situation; in every personal injury case a plaintiff has been injured, has received medical treatment, incurred bills for same, lost wages and, frequently, suffered a disability. This is true whether the loss occurred due to the collapse of the landing gear on an airplane or the slip of a surgeon's knife. Thus defense counsel can prepare a good set of form interrogatories encompassing matters of injury and loss to the plaintiff. On the liability side, however, he is in no better position than the plaintiff's attorney.

Since there are such a variety of types of lawsuits, let us try to categorize the information in terms of some other standard—need, perhaps. Thus in every trespass case—no matter what it is—we want to know about *Witnesses* and *Investigation* and *Documents*. A set of standard interrogatories for use in every such case for both plaintiff and defense counsel could be these:

I. Witnesses

1. Identify by name and address each and every person known to the (opposing party) who witnessed the accident (incident) involved in this lawsuit.
2. Identify by name and address every person known to the (opposing party) who was a witness to events immediately preceding the accident (incident) involved in this lawsuit.
3. Identify by name and address every person known to the (opposing party) who was a witness to events immediately subsequent to the accident (incident) involved in this lawsuit.

This will serve to identify the witnesses—those who were at the scene when the accident occurred, the ones who came running up after the event, and those who just happened to be in the area beforehand.

Now let's get some information about the witnesses:

4. As to each person named in answer to interrogatories 1–3, identify those who were either a friend or relative to the (opposing party).
5. As to each witnesses named in answer to interrogatories 1–3, identify those persons from whom a written, or tape-recorded, statement has been taken by any person or organization to the knowledge of (opposing party) or on his behalf by his counsel, insurance carrier, investigators, family or friends.

6. As to each person identified in answer to Interrogatory No. 5, set forth:

   a. the date the statement was taken;

   b. The name and address of the person taking the statement;

   c. Whether the statement is in writing or was tape-recorded.

   d. The name and address of the person who presently has possession of the statement or tape;

   e. Whether the witness was paid any money, for whatever purpose, in connection with, or relating to, the giving of the statement.

These last two questions—Interrogatories No. 5 and No. 6—raise a question about you and your relations with the other members of your Bar and the style of practice in your community. Is it relaxed and friendly or hostile and hypertechnical? The difference could affect the way one phrases these questions—and others like them. The questions refer to a "written statement" or "tape recording."

There are other ways to collect information. An investigator could prepare a summary of his conversation with a witness—that's not necessarily a written statement; a telephone call could be made to a witness and notes made of the conversation or a stenographic transcript made of the conversation—that's not a tape recording. In my jurisdiction the Plaintiff's Bar and Defense Bar are composed of excellent lawyers who dispute mightily over the issues but who do not bother with minutiae or split hairs in matters involving discovery. I know that the questions, as framed, would draw forth from opposing counsel an answer that would include whatever information he had, however secured. He knows what the questions are driving at and he is willing to produce the data. That may not be true in your jurisdiction. In certain areas hypertechnicality, hair-splitting and nitpicking are a way of life. That's unfortunate. If you must practice in such an area then you have no alternative but to go on with questions 7, 8 and 9 (possibly 10, 11 and 12) to cover every possible device that your opponent may have used to collect the information from a witness. At least, once you have prepared a set of standard questions designed to cover all known means of securing a statement from a person, you know you won't have to do it again.

Along this line I call your attention to the fact that the Pennsylvania Supreme Court recently amended a Discovery Rule which requires the production of "statements" upon request. It felt obligated to define "statement" as:

1. A written statement signed or otherwise adopted or approved by the person making it, or

2. A stenographic, mechanical, electrical or other recording, or a Transcript thereof, which is a substantially verbatim recital of an oral statement by the person making it and contemporaneously recorded.

You will note the specific devices mentioned in subsection (2); I assume that was put in for the benefit of Philadelphia lawyers (since it was not in the least bit necessary for the practitioners in Pittsburgh).

You will simply have to be guided by conditions existing in your jurisdiction.

But let's get back to witnesses. The principal reason that you want data about statements and tape recordings is that by the time you secure a case, get it filed and begin to invoke discovery a witness could be ill and unavailable, have moved, or have died, and thus the statement would be the only thing available to you. You can get it from opposing counsel without too much trouble, but first you have to know that he has it. Second, it's always good background information and, depending on circumstances, you might want it produced at a deposition or at trial. Once again, if you don't know that your opponent has it you'll never demand it.

II. Investigation

1. Identify by name and address any person who was employed by (or retained by) Plaintiff (Defendant), or his counsel, or a representative of Plaintiff (Defendant), to conduct an investigation into the facts and circumstances of this case.
2. Set forth the identify of the person who retained or employed the investigator.
3. Identify the period of time during which investigation was conducted.
4. Identify by name and address all persons contacted by the investigator.
5. Identify all documents secured by the investigator.
6. State whether any Report of Investigation was filed and, if so, where a copy of same may presently be found.

While these questions are acceptable you may run into problems when you try to follow up the answers with a Request for Production of, let us say, the Investigation Report. Immediately you will be confronted with an argument that the information is privileged—having been secured at the request of counsel and for his or her benefit and guidance. The objection is valid, but sometimes you will learn that the investigation was done at the request of a third party—the insurance company involved, a relative of the Plaintiff or Defendant, or, in the case of a corporate Party, by a parent corporation or subsidiary organization.

Then the claim of privilege becomes decidedly less clear and may evaporate altogether.

At the very least, however, these questions will help you to learn who your adversary is talking to, what documents he is collecting, and in what period of time he has been busy investigating the case. Finally, if the investigator talked to a witness who has since died, or secured a document that is presently unavailable, then (1) you know that fact and (2) you have a strong argument for securing the witness's statement or the document from opposing counsel. Once again, if you haven't asked the question you'll never know the answer.

III. Documents

Documents, of course, can range from photographs to maps, textbooks, construction drawings, hospital records, work records, weather reports—one could categorize a seemingly endless list of written materials. Naturally your Interrogatories will zero in on the specific type of document that is involved in your case. To this extent, at least, even form Interrogatories will have to be tailored to the situation. For illustrative purposes let us assume that you are interested in photographs of the scene of an accident. The Interrogatories would be as follows:

1. State whether (opposing party) has any photographs of the scene of this accident, whether taken before, on the day of, or after the accident involved in this case.
2. Identify:
    a. The date the photographs were taken.
    b. The person who took the photographs.
    c. The number of photographs.
3. Set forth in whose possession the photographs may presently be found.

We can now assemble a basic set of Form Interrogatories which should be useful to both Plaintiffs and Defense Counsel in almost every case:

Example 1: Basic and Standard Form Interrogatories

1. Identify by name and address each and every person known to the (opposing party) who witnessed the accident (incident) involved in this lawsuit.
2. Identify by name and address every person known to the (opposing party) who was a witness to events immediately preceding the accident (incident) involved in this lawsuit.

3. Identify by name and address every person known to the (opposing party) who was a witness to events immediately subsequent to the accident (incident) involved in this lawsuit.

4. As to each person named in answer to Interrogatories 1–3, identify those who were either a friend or relative of the (opposing party).

5. As to each witness named in answer to Interrogatories 1–3, identify those persons from whom a written, or tape-recorded, statement has been taken by any person or organization to the knowledge of (opposing party) or on his behalf by his counsel, insurance carrier, investigators, family or friends.

6. As to each person identified in answer to Interrogatory No. 5, set forth:

   a. The date the statement was taken;

   b. The name and address of the person taking the statement;

   c. Whether the statement is in writing or was tape-recorded;

   d. The name and address of the person who presently has possession of the statement or tape;

   e. Whether the witness was paid any money, for whatever purpose, in connection with, or relating to, the giving of the statement.

7. Identify by name and address any person who was employed by (or retained by) Plaintiff (Defendant), or his counsel, or a representative of Plaintiff (Defendant), to conduct an investigation into the facts and circumstances of this case.

8. Set forth the identify of the person who retained or employed the investigator.

9. Identify the period of time during which investigation was conducted.

10. Identify by name and address all persons contacted by the investigator.

11. Identify all documents secured by the investigator.

12. State whether any Report of Investigation was filed and, if so, where a copy of same may presently be found.

13. State whether (opposing party) has any photographs of the scene of this accident whether taken before, on the day of, or after the accident involved in this case.

14. Identify:

    a. The date the photographs were taken.

    b. The person who took the photographs.

    c. The number of photographs.

15. Set forth in whose possession the photographs may presently be found.

These Interrogatories can apply to any case—personal injury, assumpsit, landslide, divorce, etc.

However, if one is a defense attorney in a personal injury case there are additional basic questions that have applicability in every case. They all relate to the Plaintiff's medical history, work record, and bills and expenses. Example 2 represents a good set of this type of Interrogatories.

Example 2: Defendant's Basic Interrogatories Directed to a Plaintiff in a Personal Injury Action

1. Set forth the following information as of the date of the incident set forth in the Complaint:
   a. Your exact age
   b. Birthdate
   c. Height
   d. Weight
   e. Social Security Number

2. For the past ten years set forth your various residence addresses and give the approximate dates during which you resided at each of such residences.

3. Have you ever been known by any other name? If so, set forth the name or names by which you have been known, and if you are a married woman please give your maiden name. Please set forth the date or dates when each of the names was used.

4. Identify by name and office address all physicians, osteopaths or chiropractors or other licensed medical practitioners, who have examined, treated or attended you for the conditions or injuries alleged in the Complaint.

5. As to those persons named in Answer to Interrogatory No. 4 who treated you, set forth:
   a. The dates and periods during which you were under the care of each such person;
   b. The nature of the treatment given;
   c. As to those persons who only conducted an examination give the date of each such examination.

6. Set forth in detail all injuries sustained by you as a result of the incident referred to in the Complaint.

7. Set forth the name and address of each hospital or institution at which you received treatment on account of the injuries complained of in your Complaint and further set forth:

    a. The nature of the treatment received.

    b. The date or dates on or between which you were confined and/or received treatment at the institution.

    c. Whether you were treated as an inpatient or an outpatient at the hospitals or other institutions.

8. Set forth the amount of the bills of each of those persons listed in Interrogatory No. 4.

9. Set forth the amount of the bills of each of the hospitals or other institutions identified in Interogatory No. 7.

10. State whether you received nursing care or household help as a result of the incident identified in the Complaint. If so, set forth the following:

    a. The nature of the services rendered.

    b. The name and address of each person furnishing such services.

    c. The beginning and ending dates during which each of such services was rendered.

    d. The rate of pay.

    e. The total amount owed or paid to each person rendering service.

    f. Set forth which of the persons identified herein have already been paid and which have not.

    g. State which of the persons have rendered written invoices to you for services.

    h. State whether any of the persons are related by blood or marriage to you or your spouse, and if so identify such persons.

11. Other than the medical bills or other bills identified in preceding Interrogatories, list every other bill incurred to date as a result of the incident set forth in the Complaint and set forth:

    a. The nature or purpose of the charge.

    b. The amount.

    c. The name and address of the payee.

12. Were you confined to your home? If so, give the dates when such confinement began and ended.

13. If you were confined to your home as a result of the incident set forth in the Complaint, further state whether you were confined to bed at your home. If so, give the dates when such confinement began and ended.

14. Was it necessary for you as a result of this incident to purchase and wear any surgical appliances? If so, set forth:

   a. The nature of the appliance.

   b. Where purchased.

   c. The date of purchase.

   d. The cost thereof.

   e. By whom ordered or prescribed.

   f. The date or dates during which such appliance was worn.

   g. The frequency with which it was worn during such period.

15. With regard to your claim for pain, suffering and inconvenience, set forth:

   a. The nature or type or other appropriate description of the pain, suffering and inconvenience.

   b. Whether you received any medication for pain and suffering and if so the identity of the medication and the dosage thereof and the frequency of application.

   c. The duration of the pain, suffering and inconvenience.

16. Have you completely recovered from any of the injuries sustained in the incident alleged in your Complaint? If the answer is ''yes,'' set forth:

   a. An identification of the injuries from which you have recovered.

   b. The approximate date of the recovery.

17. If you have not recovered at the time of the answering of these Interrogatories from certain of the injuries which you allege to have sustained in the incident described in your Complaint, set forth in detail those injuries from which you have not recovered.

18. State the degree of any disability to any part or parts of your body which you claim resulted from the alleged incident set forth in your Complaint. In addition, state whether such disability is claimed to be temporary or permanent in each instance.

19. During a five-year period prior to the date of the incident here involved, state whether you have ever been confined to any hospital. If the answer is ''yes,'' set forth the following:

   a. Identify the hospital by name and address.

   b. Set forth the date at which you received treatment or were confined to the hospital.

    c. Identify the injury, illness or condition that required the hopitalization.

    d. Identify by name and address the physician who was primarily in charge of your treatment.

    e. Set forth whether you have made a recovery from the condition, illness or injury that required hospitalization.

20. State whether subsequent to the date of the incident here involved, you have been confined or treated at any hospital for conditions not related to the incident involved in this lawsuit. If the answer is ''yes,'' set forth:

    a. The identity of the hospital by name and address.

    b. The date at which you received treatment or were confined to the hospital.

    c. The injury, illness or condition that required the hospitalization.

    d. The name and address of the physician who was primarily in charge of your treatment.

    e. Whether you have made a recovery from the condition, illness or injury that required hospitalization.

21. Identify all physicians, chiropractors or osteopaths who have attended you for any condition during the five years prior to the date of the incident here involved and further set forth the following information:

    a. The date or dates of your examination and/or treatment by said physician, osteopath or chiropractor.

    b. The diagnosis of said physician, chiropractor or osteopath.

    c. The nature of treatment that was required.

    d. The result of the treatment that was rendered.

22. Identify any physician, osteopath or chiropractor who, between the date of the incident involved in this lawsuit and the present time, has attended you or given treatment for any condition not related to injuries received in the incident involved in this lawsuit, and further set forth:

    a. The date or dates of your examination or treatment by said physician, osteopath or chiropractor.

    b. The diagnosis of said physician, chiropractor or osteopath.

    c. The nature of treatment that was required.

    d. The result of the treatment that was rendered.

23. Have you been involved in any accident or accidents either prior to or subsequent to the incident alleged in the Complaint filed in this case? If the answer is ''yes,'' set forth the following information:

   a. The date or dates of the accidents.

   b. A brief description of the accidents.

   c. The identity of any other parties involved in the accidents.

   d. The nature of any injuries that you sustained in the accidents.

   e. The names and addresses of any hospitals or physicians who examined you or treated you as a result of any injuries you sustained in said accidents.

   f. Whether you made any claim against any insurance company or other person as a result of injuries or losses sustained in such accidents.

   g. The identity of the insurance company or other person against whom you made a claim and the date upon which you made the claim and whether any payment was received by you.

24. Subsequent to the incident alleged in your Complaint, have you been disabled either partially or totally as a result of sickness or accident other than any claimed disability arising from the incident involved in this lawsuit?

25. If the answer to the prior Interrogatory is "yes," set forth the following:

   a. The date of such disability.

   b. The nature of the disability.

   c. The cause of the disability.

   d. The extent of the disability.

26. Have you ever filed an application for life insurance or health and accident insurance that was rejected by the company to which you applied by reason of your health? If the answer is "yes," please set forth:

   a. The date of such application.

   b. The name of the company to which you applied.

   c. The name and address of the insurance agent through whom you made such application.

   d. The date of rejection.

   e. The cause of rejection.

27. Prior to the incident complained of in this Complaint did you participate in any sports activities? If the answer is "yes," set forth the following:

   a. The identity of the sport or sports.

   b. Whether your participation was on an organized team basis and if so the identity of the team or league.

   c. The names and addresses of the other team members with whom you played.

28. Since the incident set forth in the Complaint have you participated in the sports identified in the preceding Interrogatory? If the answer is "yes," identify the sport and the nature and extent of your participation.

29. Set forth the degree of impairment of earning capacity which you claim resulted from the incident set forth in your Complaint. Further set forth whether such impairment is temporary or of a permanent nature.

30. If you are claiming any loss of earnings or impairment of earning capacity as a result of the incident set forth in the Complaint, set forth in detail the following:

   a. The names and addresses of your employers for the ten years immediately preceding the incident and the name of your immediate supervisor in each job or position.

   b. The length of time of each such employment.

   c. The nature of your job or position immediately prior to the incident here involved.

   d. As to each employer, the amount of your weekly, monthly or yearly earnings.

   e. If self-employed, state the amount you claim as loss of earnings; your net income for the three years prior to the date of the incident here involved.

31. Identify by name and address each person or firm by whom you have been employed subsequent to the accident here involved. Further set forth:

   a. The periods of such employment.

   b. The nature of the duties you performed.

   c. The amount of the hourly, daily, weekly or monthly income you received from such employer.

   d. The name of your immediate supervisor during each period of employment.

32. Did the injuries you allegedly received from the accident here involved prevent you from attending your employment with any of the persons or firms named in your answer to the last two Interrogatories? If your answer is "yes," set forth as follows:

   a. The specific dates or periods of time in each instance in which you were unable to work.

   b. Your rate of pay for each period of time during which you were unable to work.

c. The total amount of lost earnings that you are claiming to date.

33. Set forth whether you received any money from any employer between the date of the happening of the accident here involved and the present time, and if so set forth:

   a. The amount of money you have received.

   b. An identification of the nature or purpose of the payments to you.

   c. The period of time during which you have received payment from your employer.

34. State the total amount of income earned by you during each of the immediate five calendar years prior to the happening of the incident here involved.

35. State the total amount of income earned by you during each calendar year since the happening of the accident here involved.

36. State whether or not you are receiving any disability compensation from any source. If the answer is "yes," set forth:

   a. The identity of the person making payments.

   b. The amount of the payments.

   c. The nature of the payments.

   d. The date the payments began.

   e. Whether the payments were received by you on a weekly, monthly, or other similar basis.

37. Have you filed Federal, state or municipal income tax returns during the three years prior to the date of the accident here involved? If the answer is "yes," identify the person or organization or office which whom the returns were filed for each year.

38 Have you retained copies of the income tax returns referred to in the next preceding Interrogatory for the years involved? If so, please attach copies of those returns to the answers to these interrogatories or attach authorizations to obtain copies of the various income tax returns that you filed.

Respectfully submitted,

_____

INTERROGATORIES FOR AN EXPERT WITNESS

Another set of Form Interrogatories that you might prepare and keep on file would be a set directed to an expert witness. In the nature of things you will have learned the identity of this person through either the answers to a previous set of interrogatories, a prior deposition, or the production of a report. Knowing that your opponent is going to use an expert, you will often find it expedient and appropriate to serve interrogatories directed to that expert. Of course this should be done prior to deposing the expert (if you intend to use that procedure) so that you have some detailed knowledge about the individual which can be of invaluable help as you begin to outline your questions for the deposition. In addition, having these answers in advance does help shorten the time required in taking the deposition although, in general, that is not a factor of great importance.

A more significant matter to be considered—and one that can be of serious concern to your client—is the desirability of utilizing interrogatories in lieu of a deposition. Here the basic consideration is the cost factor. Most attorneys worry about the cost of litigation and legitimately have to spend some time evaluating the question of cost versus gain. We don't all work in large law firms to whom money is (or appears to be) no problem, nor do we all have well-heeled clients who can finance extravagant discovery procedures. Deposing one or more expert witnesses can often qualify as an "extravagant" discovery procedure. Many times—in fact almost always—the expert will be an out-of-towner, and you will have to pay the cost of his or her transportation expenses, hotel accommodations, taxi fare or car rental, and meals, if you bring him or her to your office for a deposition. In addition, whether the witness is an out-of-towner or a local person, *every time* you are going to have to pay an expert witness fee, and every expert witness I have ever run into has a sufficient ego to believe that he or she should command a very substantial figure. Frequently this will amount to $1,000 to $2,000 per day if the witness is from out of town, and it will usually amount to $500 to $1,000 per day for an expert in your own city. If you have not paid an expert witness fee recently it might be appropriate to make a few phone calls to friends who have; you may be quite startled to learn of the going rate for architects, engineers or medical doctors who are willing to review a file, write a report, and be prepared to testify in Court. When you add up the total cost of fee plus expenses you may well learn that the expense of bringing the expert to your office for a deposition (completely aside from the deposition itself) is extremely high, and possibly prohibitive. It can easily amount to $2,000 or more. That amount of money is a significant sum if you are the one advancing the payment or you have a client who is struggling to finance the cost of his or her lawsuit.

Is the deposition worth this expense? Frequently not. It is very difficult to break down a good qualified expert in a deposition. These persons are retained because they are "pros"—they have been deposed or given testimony in court many times and are thoroughly familiar with the intricacies of legal interrogation. It is easy enough to elicit information from them in a deposition (the gist of which you can secure just as easily from their reports on a Motion to Produce or otherwise), but you're not going to easily get them to change their minds or their opinions. Such experts are well aware of the fact that they have a right to stick firmly to their opinions and will be sufficiently facile and glib to justify their beliefs. Unlike a defendant expert, the expert witness is not emotionally involved in the lawsuit (which is very important and explains why you can often "break down" the defendant expert), and this person is not the doer of the conduct complained of and which is the subject of detailed scrutiny. The expert witness is simply there to express an opinion which he or she will do— unshakably.

Under these circumstances, you might well opt in favor of Interrogatories to the expert, and frankly I would recommend this procedure. There is far less expense involved and you can get almost all the information you need. Under the Federal Rules, and many State Rules, the Court will determine and approve the expert's fee, and you can rest assured that the fee will be much more modest than it will be for a deposition. In my jurisdiction, for example, the fee is generally $200–$400 for a routine set of 20 interrogatories or so.

It is true that you lose some advantages by not taking a deposition—not the least of which is the ability to meet the witness and to appraise him or her as a person—but, on balance, the likely gain does not justify the cost. Interrogatories will supply all the important background material you need and will often give you ammunition for cross-examination or will provide a hint or clue as to a specific area in which you might want to cross-examine.

Under all the circumstances it is my recommendation that you serve the interrogatories upon the expert witness and let the matter rest with that. Example 3 is a basic set of questions that you can use as a guide. Obviously these are specific for a medical expert, but they are sufficiently general that by the change of a word or two they can be used for an engineer, architect, chemist, nuclear physicist or what have you. I might mention that since nearly everyone is insured these days for professional negligence or liability, questions about the insurance carrier and claims made against the expert or his company are appropriate.

Example 3: Interrogatories Directed to an Expert Witness

1. Identify any book acknowledged by Dr. C. A. Jones as a recognized authority on the subject of Pulmonary Emboli, setting forth the name of the book, the author, the publisher and the date of publication.
2. Identify any book in the office or in the home of Dr. C. A. Jones dealing with the subject of Pulmonary Emboli and further set forth the title of the book, the author, the publishing company and the date of publication.
3. As to Dr. C. A. Jones, set forth the following:

a. The manner in which he became involved in this lawsuit.

b. Whether he is a friend of the defendant and if so:

 1. Whether he is a personal, social or professional friend of the defendant.

 2. For how long the friendship has been in existence.

 3. Whether he was contacted by the defendant to be a witness in this matter.

c. Whether Dr. Jones has performed any services for the law firm of Smith & Brown in the past, and if so set forth:

 1. Whether he has been consulted by the members of the law firm and if so the number of times in which he has been consulted.

 2. Whether he has submitted reports to the aforesaid law firm and if so the number of cases in which he has submitted reports.

 3. Whether he has ever testified for any member of the aforesaid law firm and if so the number of cases in which he has testified.

d. Whether Dr. Jones has performed any work or services of any nature whatsoever for the ABC Insurance Company and if so:

 1. The number of occasions in which he has been contacted.

 2. The number of cases in which he has done work.

 3. The number of cases in which he has testified at the instance of the aforesaid insurance company.

e. If Dr. Jones has performed services for either the law firm of Smith & Brown and/or the ABC Insurance Company set forth:

 1. The amount of his fee in each instance in which he performed services for the law firm of Smith & Brown.

 2. The amount of his fee in each instance in which he performed services for the ABC Insurance company.

 3. The amount of his fee in the instant case.

f. In the instant case and as to this physician set forth:

 1. The date in which he was first contacted by any person acting on behalf of the defendant or the defendant himself.

 2. The number of occasions and the dates thereof in which he has consulted with the defendant, the defense attorney or any representative of the ABC Company.

 3. The identity of the person or persons with whom he consulted on the dates set forth immediately above.

4. From the initial contact with defendant's attorney until the date of answers to these interrogatories, list all reports, letters or written communications that you have directed to defendant's attorney.

5. List all material that you have reviewed before arriving at the opinions expressed in your reports of April 30, 1980 and March 23, 1981.

6. With regard to your medical education and training, state:

   a. The name of the medical school graduated from, the date of graduation and the nature of any honors received.

   b. The name and address of the hospital where your internship was served and the dates of the internship.

   c. The names and addresses of the hospitals where residency programs were served, the dates served, the type of programs, and the nature of any honors received during the programs.

   d. If in the service, state the years and nature of medical work and training in the service.

   e. The nature of any additional formal medical training and education and the years thereof.

7. State the nature of your professional work from the time you graduated from medical school until the present time, giving dates and titles of various positions and employment.

8. Have you been associated with any hospitals during your professional career?

9. If the answer to Interrogatory No. 8 is "yes," for each hospital, state:

   a. The name and address.

   b. Nature of association.

   c. Dates of association.

   d. The positions held.

10. Have you ever had hospital privileges suspended or revoked?

11. If the answer to Interrogatory No. 10 is "yes," for each such suspension or revocation, state:

   a. Name and address of the involved hospital.

   b. Whether a suspension or revocation.

   c. Reason for suspension or revocation.

   d. Effective dates of suspension or revocation.

12. Have you ever been denied privileges at a hospital?

13. If the answer to Interrogatory No. 12 is "yes," for each such denial of privileges, state:

    a. Name and address of involved hospital.

    b. Date of denial of privileges.

    c. Reason for denial of privileges.

14. Have you authorized or published any articles or textbooks?

15. If the answer to Interrogatory No. 14 is "yes," for each article or textbook, state:

    a. Name of articles or textbooks published and citation for publication.

    b. Date of publication.

16. State the names of your medical malpractice liability insurance carriers during your professional career. For each carrier, state the dates of coverage.

17. Have you ever had any medical malpractice claims submitted against you?

18. If the answer to Interrogatory No. 17 is "yes," for each claim, state:

    a. Names and addresses of persons or patients submitting claim.

    b. Date of treatment in question.

    c. Nature of claim.

    d. Disposition of claim.

    e. Identity of your liability insurance carrier handling the claim.

19 Have any medical malpractice actions been filed against you in arbitration or in a court of law?

20 If the answer to Interrogatory No. 19 is "yes," for each such action, state:

    a. Names and addresses of persons or patients filing action.

    b. Date of treatment in question.

    c. Nature of action.

    d. Disposition of action.

    e. Caption indicating court or tribunal number and term.

    f. Identity of your liability insurance carrier defending action.

These three sets of basic interrogatories are all you need to get started in nearly every kind of lawsuit. They represent a beginning—something upon which to build by adding the questions that are specific for your particular case. You must use your imagination and inquire for detailed information, and don't forget—ask too many questions, not too few.

HOW TO HANDLE DELAY AND STALLING ON THE PART OF YOUR OPPONENT

In every jurisdiction the time prescribed for answering interrogatories is either 20 or 30 days, and that is never enough time. In view of the realities of the situation one cannot help but wonder why the procedural rules comittees of the several courts have not extended the time to 60 days, which is more reasonable. Nonetheless, they cling to the 20 and 30-day periods. Inevitably the deadline passes and the answers are not filed. Sometimes opposing counsel will call you and ask for an extension of time, but usually that does not happen. The question is: what do you do now?

One thing is certain—you have to take some action, and promptly. If you permit it to happen, months will go by while you wait for the answers and your discovery is effectively blocked. You can't go ahead with additional investigation because you don't have the names of witnesses; you can't file a motion to produce documents because you don't know what is available or who has them; you shouldn't proceed with depositions because there are too many gaps in your case, or you lack certain background information that you need in order to prepare your questions properly. In short, you're stuck.

You cannot permit this state of affairs to last very long. There are two ways to bring this matter to a head:

1. Call the other attorney and secure from him or her a firm, definite date by which the answers are to be filed. Put this in the form of a Stipulation of Counsel, have it signed and file it.
2. File a Motion to Compel Answers to Interrogatories and let the Court set a date in an Order.

Whichever procedure you adopt, the important point is that a date certain is now officially of record, and if the answers are not filed by that date you are in a position to move for sanctions.

Above all, do not rely on telephone assurances that the answers will be filed "soon," "shortly," "in a few days," or "in a little while." Someone should enshrine in Famous Last Words the phrase, "I just need a little more time." If you fall for that there's a bridge in Brooklyn that I can sell you, cheap. It may be that you will get the answers—someday—but only when opposing counsel gets around to it. There's no reason for your lawsuit, upon which your livelihood depends, to be subject to the whimsical delays of your opponent. If you let him or her get away with it you have no one to blame but yourself.

HOW TO HANDLE EVASIVE ANSWERS TO YOUR QUESTIONS

First of all, be suspicious. What is he or she trying to hide? Why the evasion? Have you struck a very sensitive nerve? These must be the first thoughts to come to mind. Your suspicions may be justly amplified if most of the other questions are answered directly and concisely but only a very pertinent few contain a vague or a verbose response. The only way to handle this situation is to file an appropriate motion to compel a direct answer to your question. You will find that the average judge can read between the lines and if he or she is satisfied that the question is clear while the answer is a "masterpiece of subterfuge," your opponent will be compelled to file a new and proper answer.

In addition, be sure to note the subject matter of the question as one area in which you intend to do some probing when you take depositions. Usually the vague answer to a pertinent question sticks out like the proverbial sore thumb and invites lengthy interrogation at depositions.

CHECKLIST FOR PREPARATION OF INTERROGATORIES

1. Review the pleadings. Note the factual matters that are contested.
2. Study your investigation reports and data secured from client. Locate the gaps in the information available to you.
3. Define the issues and determine the facts you need to resolve them.
4. If appropriate, discuss the case with an expert to learn information that you might inquire about.
5. Prepare the questions specifically for the facts and issues involved in your case. Try to avoid form interrogatories.
6. Use the interrogatories primarily as an investigative tool.
7. Be sure to ask some questions that relate to key issues which, if answered favorably, can lead to a prompt settlement.
8. Ask too many questions, not too few.
9. Make certain that the answers are submitted in a timely manner.
10. Force your opponent to answer directly. Do not permit vague and evasive answers to go unchallenged.

4

Rummaging Through a Litigant's Files: The Successful Use of Motions or Requests for Production of Documents

"Put it in writing." That age-old challenge is alive and well today, and because its admonition is so often followed much of the evidence you need will be composed of written materials. This chapter deals with the question of where to find them and how to get them.

WRITTEN MATERIAL IS ALWAYS THE VERY BEST EVIDENCE YOU CAN GET

There is no doubt that nearly every person holds to the belief that whatever is written is automatically (1) true and (2) binding on the parties. Conversely, if one is reluctant to "put it in writing," one's word is suspect and the integrity of any agreement one is trying to reach is in jeopardy. Every lawyer knows that this old canard is an exaggeration of the truth, and that every written document is not, per se, honest, accurate and important. There have been popular dissents expressed by the adage, "Figures don't lie but liars can figure," which, in a sardonic fashion, casts doubt on pages of statistics, tax returns, corporate annual reports, and some financial statements. Another warning is contained in the saying, "Believe ten percent of all you hear and fifty percent of all you read," which certainly tends to diminish the veracity of the printed word even as it elevates it above the oral statement. Nonetheless the world pays respect and obeisance to the written word in a way that it does not to a verbal statement.

MOST IMPORTANT MATTERS ARE REDUCED
TO WRITING

With the possible exception of a proposal of marriage, nearly every important matter in the lives of people and businesses is reduced to writing. Some of these documents are meant to be permanent and retained—a deed, will, baptismal certificate, family portrait; others are intended to be transient and temporary—a letter, the daily newspaper, a calendar, and that picture of her current boyfriend on the desk of your teen-aged daughter. But they all represent an object that is deemed important and one that is more accurate than human memory and more truthful than the tongue of man (or woman).

As a rule, these objects are retained, in private as well as in business life—so much so that it's a standing joke about periodically ''cleaning out the attic,'' and a whole industry has sprung up to help government and business dispose of some of its old records.

In terms of preparation of a lawsuit, it is extremely valuable to secure documentary evidence, and there are all sorts of documents that you should think about—letters, statistics, contracts, deeds, manuals, books, drawings, photographs—the list is endless. Most of the time it is the document itself that will be helpful to you, but do not forget that very often it has no value in itself, but can lead you to information that you must have. To illustrate, very simply, a hospital record, in and of itself, may not be a lot of help in ascertaining negligent conduct, but it contains the names of nurses who were on duty when the significant event occurred, and you need those names for the purposes of depositions—and the nurses' notes to give you leads in preparing your areas of inquiry.

Many of the documents you need are frequently and necessarily in the hands of your opposition. They can range from a love letter (useful in a divorce case), to business income statistics (necessary to prove a loss in a breach of contract case or to lay a foundation for punitive damages), to construction design drawings (required to prove a case of engineering negligence in a trespass case), to checks and deposit tickets (which are needed to trace funds in a fraud case). The other party has them and may not want you to see them. That is when a Motion or a Request to Produce becomes an invaluable right.

HOW DO YOU LEARN THAT THE DOCUMENTS EXIST?

There are five sources available to you in ascertaining the existence of necessary documents—your client, your investigator, depositions and interrogatories, an expert, and your own fertile imagination.

1. Interrogate Your Client Regarding Documentary Evidence

The client is your most obvious source of information. Except in an accident case where the parties met only briefly and violently, your client usually has had a significant period of contact with the opposing party and has some idea concerning the documentary evidence that does, or might, exist. Certainly that is true of a spouse, a business partner or associate, an employee of a company, and the executives of corporations. The executives at Chrysler have a pretty good idea of the kind of documents Ford keeps, and the staff at Westinghouse know pretty well the things you need that General Electric is sure to have. The same thing applies to smaller companies who are in competition with one another, or even those who complement one another. A subcontractor to a major company knows the kinds of records that company keeps in its particular area of specialization. It's only natural; months or years of contractual dealings inevitably lead to the kind of knowledge and information you need as you begin to inquire about documents.

2. Educate Your Investigator to Be Alert Concerning Documents

The investigator spends most of his life mingling and mixing with witnesses, and as he takes his statements and gathers data, he should always be sensitive to comments about documents the other side has, or may be collecting. Thus from one witness he will learn that a defendant's insurance company took pictures of the scene of the accident on the day that it happened; while interrogating a document clerk at a hospital he will learn that the hospital records were changed, and who has the original pages; and over a friendly beer with a carpenter he will learn who, of several employees of subcontractors, has possession of the blueprints you need. A good investigator is literally worth his weight in gold; the prime reason for this is his ability to learn more than he sets out to know and to always be alert to the miscellaneous type of data he thinks you might need.

3. Depositions and Interrogatories Are Prime Sources of Information

These discovery tools were expressly designed to help you find out "who has what." They are a natural in helping you learn of the nature and type of documents the other side possesses and the identity of the person who has them. You can have a lot of fun asking questions such as "What records do you have pertaining to..?"; then make sure such questions are a standard part of your repertoire. When the party mentions the types of records it has, always follow up with more questions about the precise nature of these records and in whose possession they may currently be found.

Do you remember the source of the infamous Nixon "Watergate Tapes"? It was a perfectly routine interrogation—a deposition in effect—of a relatively minor administration figure who suddenly blurted out that all conversations in the Oval Office were taped—and Leon Jaworski was on his way! That happens more often than you think. In one case I remember, a routine deposition of a nurse revealed that an Incident Report had been prepared by a hospital, followed by a more extensive internal investigation—both of which proved quite damaging to the defendants; in another case, during a deposition an engineer from a company only peripherally involved in the lawsuit mentioned that he had seen certain important documents in a report prepared by the company who was a party to the case. These things pop up most often during depositions, often as a casual statement or an afterthought, simply because it is a conversation or a dialogue. People talk without thinking sometimes and other times they throw out little asides without realizing how important they are. This is the great advantage of depositions. It hardly ever happens when you serve interrogatories. Here the answers are prepared carefully, critically reviewed, and are sometimes deliberately evasive. You will never see a slip of the tongue in Answers to Interrogatories.

4. Consult an Expert

A fourth source of information about documents is the expert whom you retain. Because of his specialized knowledge he can tell you what the other side "ought" to have and can help you prepare interrogatories in which you delve into areas you never heard of or thought of. If you are working on a serious case involving the faulty construction of a building you have to sit down with architects, structural engineers, metallurgists and other specialists who will soon have you preparing interrogatories in a language you never even heard of before and inquiring about the whereabouts of documents you didn't ever dream existed. *They* know they're out there somewhere; *you* would never have known it.

5. Use Your Own Imagination

Finally, you have to use your own imagination and experience. If a plaintiff in a personal injury action is claiming a loss of earnings or impairment of earning capacity, you just know you have to get wage records and/or income tax returns. If the lawsuit involves payment for coal delivered during a certain period of time, you know that you are going to have to get a copy of the records of the railroad or barge line that transported the coal. Certain things are obvious, though it may take a little reflection to decide just exactly how to identify what you want.

SOURCES OF INFORMATION
CONCERNING DOCUMENTS YOU NEED

1. Turn first to your client.
2. Warn your investigator to be alert regarding documentary evidence.
3. Ask questions about documents in interrogatories and depositions.
4. Go talk with an expert.
5. Use your vivid imagination.

AFTER YOU LEARN WHAT YOU WANT, AND WHO HAS IT, HOW DO YOU GET IT?

It is at this stage that the Motion or Request to Produce comes into play. Initially, it must be stated that a motion or a request applies only to the opposing party. You cannot use it if a third person, such as a bank, a hospital or an employer, has the documents. These organizations are not directly involved in the lawsuit, and your method for procuring documents from them is generally by a deposition with a subpoena duces tecum to produce records for inspection and/or copying. The discovery motion with which we are involved is directed solely to a party to the lawsuit.

USING A "REQUEST FOR PRODUCTION" RATHER THAN A MOTION

Under Rule 34 of the Federal Rules of Civil Procedure one does not file a Motion to Produce. Instead, a "Request to Produce" is served upon the other side. The Supreme Court of Pennsylvania only recently adopted a similar rule; you will have to check your own discovery rules to determine which procedure is in use in your state. The differences between a Request under the Federal Rules and a Motion under the practice of some states is quite significant. Utilizing a Request, one merely asks for the production of certain documents and the burden is cast on the opposition to object and to give good reasons for the objection. In the usual motion practice—and this may be true in your state—the burden is on the moving party to justify his (or her) demands. As you can see, the burden of sustaining one's position is distinctly opposite in the two forms of practice, and clearly the Federal procedure is slanted in favor of the one seeking the documents. It seems to me to be just one more step forward in favor of open disclosure and requiring, in effect, each side in a lawsuit to have every opportunity to learn about its case, and the position of its opponent, prior to trial. Whatever the intent, that is the result. It is to be hoped that this open disclosure further facilitates the amicable resolution of cases by settlements.

Whether called a Request or a Motion, your problem remains the same in terms of knowing what you need or want, where to seek it, how to ask for it, and how to review the documents after you have them.

For illustrative purposes let me alternate Motions and Requests to give you an idea concerning the preparation of each. A typical petition, or motion, would be the following, directed to the Defendant Hospital:

```
Mary Jones,          )
    Plaintiff,       )
        v.           ) CA 12345
City Hospital,       )
    Defendant.       )
```

MOTION TO PRODUCE DOCUMENTS

Now comes the Plaintiff by John Smith, Esquire, her attorney and does respectfully submit as follows:

1. The Plaintiff has instituted an action in Trespass against the Defendant alleging negligence in the treatment of Plaintiff during an admission of June 15–30, 1981.

2. That in order to properly prepare this case and pursuant to the provisions of Rule 4009 of the Pa. Rules of Civil Procedure, counsel for Plaintiff desires to inspect and/or copy certain correspondence, records, and manuals in the possession of Defendant.

3. That the documents requested to be produced are the following:

   a. Operating Room Log for June 15, 1981;

   b. Letter from Samuel Smith, Administrator, to Dr. James Brown dated July 25, 1981;

   c. Incident Report dated July 23, 1981;

   d. Any directive or manual utilized by the Defendant concerning Operating Room procedures and regulations as of June 15, 1981;

   e. Any manual, directive, or regulations pertaining to the operation and functioning of the Emergency Room on June 8, 1981;

   f. All rules, regulations, directives or manuals which relate to the summoning of additional medical and nursing personnel to the hospital in emergency situations.

4. Counsel for Plaintiff believes that his examination of the aforesaid documents is essential to the proper preparation of this lawsuit and Defendant has advised that it will not voluntarily produce them.

WHEREFORE, Your Honorable court is respectfully requested to enter an Order directing Defendant to produce the documents, at a time convenient to counsel for the parties, for inspection and/or copying by counsel for Plaintiff.

Respectfully submitted,

_____

John Smith
Attorney for Plaintiff

In this case Plaintiff's counsel knew of the existence of the various documents by virtue of investigation (the Incident Report), a deposition (the letter to Dr. Brown), and his general knowledge of hospital policies and procedures (the Operating Room Log and Manual, and the Emergency Room Manual).

If you have served interrogatories and secured information about documents, your Motion can explicitly refer to the documents identified in the Answers to Interrogatories, in this fashion:

Caroline Black, et al.	)
Plaintiff,	)
v.	) CA 4589-1981
White Pharmaceutical	)
Co., Inc.,	)
Defendant.	)

*REQUEST FOR PRODUCTION AND INSPECTION OF
DOCUMENTS*

To: Defendant and Paul Smith Esquire, its attorney.

Pursuant to the provisions of rule 4003.4 and Rule 4009 of the Rules of Civil Procedure, counsel for Plaintiffs requests as follows:

1. A copy of any statement made by those persons identified in Answers to Plaintiff's Interrogatories Nos. 22 and 23.

2. To inspect and photograph the portion of the catheter referred to in Answer to Plaintiff's Interrogatory No. 1, together with the container and labels referred to in Answer to Interrogatory No. 3.

3. The written material referred to in Answer to Interrogatory No. 8.

4. The Notice of Recall referred to in Answer to Interrogatory No. 12.

5. Any written complaints, suggestions, letters, memos, or documents, received by the Product Evaluation Committee of Defendant between 1980 and 1981, from any physician relating to the catheter involved in this case.

6. A copy of any statement made by an officer of the Defendant to the public media which relates to the subject matter of this lawsuit.

7. It is requested that this material be reviewed and/or copied at the office of Defense Counsel on Tuesday, August 14, 1981, at 10:00 A.M.

Respectfully submitted,

_____

John Brown
Attorney for Plaintiff

TRY TO AVOID BEING TOO SPECIFIC

There is a constant battle raging between the person who wants a document and the person who has it, especially if it is damaging. The possessor will demand that you be extremely precise in identifying the document, and should you err in any respect which he or she can claim is significant, that person will deny that he or she has the document or will not produce the document you really want. The argument, always, is that your opponent should not have to "guess" which letter, memo, drawing, etc., you really want if there are several, even though both you and your adversary know damn good and well which document you are interested in and that the objection, or denial, is really in the nature of "games people play." Unfortunately, it's a legitimate game. Here, as in so many other areas of a lawsuit, much depends on your relationship with opposing counsel. If you get along well, if you have been fair in your past dealings with him or her, you will get the document you want. If you have been hypertechnical and obstinate in the past, you had better be precisely correct—very specific—in identifying the document you want. This is one occasion when your past can come back to haunt you.

In general, however, try to avoid being too specific in your request for documents. Quite often you honestly do not know all that your opponent has, and if you can frame your motion to include something like "all correspondence between Sam Jones and ABC Corporation during the period of April 1–May 31, 1981, pertaining to the appearance of Jones at the Broadway Theater on July 4, 1981," you are far better off than you will be if you only demand specific letters. When you get "all" the papers, you may well find some gems you never knew about. As you can realize, you could never have identified specific letters, in a Motion or Request, if you didn't even know about them! Interrogatories might have identified the letters but people make mistakes when they answer interrogatories. That's why you should always ask for *all* the documents you think the other party may have, and try to avoid specificity. A good illustration of this is one in which a building was damaged while two other buildings—one beside it and one across the street from it—were being constructed. Plaintiff's counsel consulted architects and engineers who gave him a long list of the documents they wanted to see and assured him that these would number in the hundreds! There was no alternative but to prepare a motion such as this:

IN THE COURT OF COMMON PLEAS OF ALLEGHENY
COUNTY, PENNSYLVANIA CIVIL DIVISION

Cathedral Church,	)	
Plaintiff,	)	
v.	) CA 89245	
Universe Corporation,	)	
Jones Pile Company,	)	
Smith Drilling Company,	) IN TRESPASS	
Brown & White	)	
Architects, and ABC	)	
Engineering Company,	)	
Defendants.	)	

MOTION FOR PRODUCTION OF DOCUMENTS
To the Honorable, The Judges of Said Court:

And now comes counsel for the Plaintiff above named and does hereby respectfully submit as follows:

1. Interrogatories were served on Universe Corporation, the Answers to which reveal that it possesses records concerning matters essential to the trial of this case. These records were utilized in the construction of the Universe Building and include the following:

   a. Deflection design drawings;

   b. Retaining wall drawings;

    c. Subsurface explorations;

    d. Foundation investigation reports;

    e. Test borings;

    f. Subsurface studies;

    g. Retaining wall studies;

    h. Design drawings;

    i. "As-built" foundation drawings;

    j. Photographs;

    k. Soil studies;

    l. Blasting records.

2. The experts retained by counsel must review these records in preparation of their reports concerning the cause of the damage to Cathedral Church.

3. The records are voluminous in nature and cannot be identified specifically.

4. It is necessary that all documents in the categories mentioned in paragraph 1 be produced for inspection.

      WHEREFORE, Your Honorable Court is respectfully requested to enter an Order requiring the production of the aforesaid documents for inspection by counsel for Plaintiff and his expert witnesses.

                            Respectfully submitted,

                          _____

                          John A. Black
                          Attorney for Plaintiff

      Most of the time the Court will grant a Motion of this nature despite the fact that it is pretty general. However, if there is an argument you can use the occasion to force opposing counsel to tell you what data is pertinent—either in terms of dates, or category or area of construction—in such manner that even though your Order will be narrower than your motion the net result is that you zero in on the most crucial documents. That helps, because, after all, you have to read these things and it's a lot better to look at 200 pertinent sheets than at 1,000 pages of which you may pull out only 200 documents—and this, after several weary hours. Also, at the argument, be certain that you have one of your experts in the courtroom to guide you when the opposing attorney and the Court begin to try to get you to narrow the scope of your Motion.

      You will find that there is a constant tug-of-war going on between attorneys in this area, the one trying to be as general as possible in his or her demands and the opposition trying to be as specific as possible in his or her response. Let your approach be that you want "everything" the other party has, or that you think they have, and therefore make your Motion or Request as all-inclusive and non-specific as you can.

WORK WITH YOUR EXPERT BEFORE YOU FILE YOUR MOTION

As an illustration I call your attention again to the material requested in the Cathedral Church case. How many trial lawyers know enough about engineering to realize that there are such things as "deflection design drawings"? An attorney, thinking about it, might have guessed that there would be "test borings" and "blasting records," but it would be the rare lawyer who, without experience, would conjure up "retaining wall studies." These are matters that are completely foreign to the ordinary lawyer but well known to a construction engineer or a soils engineer. When you get a case like this it is essential that you have lengthy meetings with persons who know the matter thoroughly and can tell you what they need to form an opinion on the subject of causation and to give testimony. Without their expertise to guide you, you will soon be hopelessly lost. Worse—in ignorance, you won't realize the important matters that you are completely missing.

When I first began handling medical malpractice cases I tried to "make do" initially by ordering only the cover sheet, discharge summary, operative reports, consultation reports and progress notes from the hospital record. A doctor-friend pointed out that I was really missing a lot by not requesting the Physician's Order Sheet, which details the doctor's instructions for the care of the patient, and that it was penny wise and pound foolish to ignore the nurses' notes and laboratory data. In short order I found that I was winning cases solely on the basis of documents that, in the past, I never even requested. My experts were finding negligence by comparing the nursing notes and the doctor's orders or by checking the progress notes against the laboratory data. This is illustrative of the type of instance in which it doesn't help much to say, "Gee, I didn't know that!"

Make it a point to consult with experts before you prepare a Motion to Produce Documents.

GO TO WHERE THE DOCUMENTS ARE LOCATED AND LOOK AT THE ORIGINALS

Funny things can happen to copies—both innocently and maliciously. As you know, you can put a blank sheet of paper over a portion of an original, make a copy, and, if it is skillfully done, one would never know that the copy was an incomplete replica of the original. Scandalous? It happens from time to time when a party to a lawsuit gets desperate or is highly emotional. That it can happen is one good reason to review the originals yourself and either have the copies made yourself or have them made while you have the original to compare.

Leaving your office and going to wherever the originals are located may be a nuisance, but it has to be done and it is worth the effort. Normally you will go to the office of the opposing party, especially where the documents are voluminous in number or bulky; otherwise you will go to the office of opposing counsel.

When you review the originals you will notice that they are clearer and much easier to read than copies, especially if there are small notations made on the page. In addition you will be able to note that some entries have been made with different colored pens, usually blue, black, or green, that do not show up on the copies. This may well raise the suspicion that they were made by different persons—or, if the handwriting is the same, at different times. Depending on the nature of your case, this discovery may be quite important. You may also observe that some writing is in pencil and some in ink—again, a matter you may not be able to discover in a copy.

These differences or variations sound trite as you read these pages, but in practice they are not. In reviewing documents it can be important to notice that a person who made all prior entries with a blue, ball-point pen suddenly makes a particularly important entry in pencil. One has a right to ask why. As you seek the answer, in a deposition or otherwise, bear in mind that you would never have known of this had you not seen the original document.

Then, there is the matter of substituted pages. Every once in awhile, when leafing through some dull-appearing, smudgy, slightly torn pages, suddenly you come across one that is bright, crisp and obviously new. Look at it. Once again you have a legitimate right to wonder, and to ask why this new page is here and what happened to the old one? It may be a perfectly innocent substitution (someone tore the old page accidentally and a new one was typed up as a substitute), or it could be a tip-off that shady and suspect activities are going on. Once again—had you not seen the original you would never have known.

Finally, if you are reviewing these documents at the place of business of a party, you will have a chance to look around and check out some aspect of the organization. Perhaps there are library shelves in the room and you can glance at the books to see if there is anything helpful. After all, if a matter of expertise is involved in the case, and a book of recognized excellence sits on a shelf, the party will be hard put to deny that the book is an authority in the field. If the book contains material that helps you, your glance paid off.

Likewise you may see other documents stored in the room—neatly indexed and identified. It's possible that, now that you've seen them and know that the party has them, they could be the subject of a new Motion to Produce. The other party is hardly in a position to say he doesn't have them! There are all sorts of things you might learn if you will force yourself to go to the other person's place of business and review the original papers. Granted that luck, good fortune, and pure chance play a role in this—still it cannot be denied that if you don't go you will never give Chance an opportunity to help you.

DON'T BE IN A HURRY WHEN YOU REVIEW DOCUMENTS—AND DON'T LET ANYONE RUSH YOU

Going through papers is a laborious process, but this is one time when the old adage applies that "if you're going to do it, do it right!" Look over every sheet of paper that you asked for and take your time when you do so. Don't be in a hurry. It takes time to study a page and assimilate its contents and it cannot be done quickly. In like manner don't let anyone rush you, or set a time limitation. If people try to do so it can only be because they do not want you to study the papers before you. At least you can assume so.

Finally, do not engage in conversation while you're trying to review documents. An ordinary person cannot read and talk at the same time. If another person wants to converse, then either put down the papers and talk, resuming your study afterward, or ask that person to leave the room. You can't do both and do a good job at either.

**REMEMBER THESE RULES WHEN
SEEKING AND REVIEWING DOCUMENTS**

1. Make your request as general as possible; try to avoid being specific.
2. Work with an expert before filing your motion.
3. Be sure to go to the place where the documents are kept.
4. Always look at original papers.
5. Do not be in a rush and never let anyone hurry your review.

USE A REQUEST, OR MOTION, TO INSPECT LAND, MACHINERY OR BUILDINGS

Very often attorneys get so terribly involved in the preparation of their cases that they spend all their time working with pleadings, discovery, and the gathering of "things" (photographs, engineering drawings, demonstrative evidence of all kinds) for presentation in a courtroom. They forget that, for their own benefit, one of the most important things for them to do is to actually go to the scene at which an event occurred. If your case involves a huge steel ladle which spilled some molten steel, maybe you'd better get into the steel mill and watch the men and machines at work. If the case involves a fire in a hotel, you had better go to that hotel and look around at the rooms, hallways, stairwells, fire extinguishers, and location of the alarm signals and sensing devices. If it involves an incident in an operating room at a hospital, possibly you ought to see that operating room and learn for yourself how the equipment and fixtures are situated in the room.

Usually these areas are strictly off limits to outsiders and the initial reaction to your informal suggestion for a visit will be a curt "no."

If these sites are important to your lawsuit, the discovery rules of every state provide some means of access for you, and the pertinent rule is nearly always tied in with the rule pertaining to discovering documents. Sometimes lawyers forget this, so it is good to be reminded of it from time to time. On-site inspection is vital to your appreciation of "what happened and why." In addition, while you are there you might view the area with the idea of possibly bringing the jury to this scene if you think it will enhance their understanding— and help your case.

Remember that a Motion to Permit Entry upon Land (or a Request for same) is an integral part of Motions to Produce Documents in most states and should be used as often as appropriate, and probably more than you do at the present time.

11 RULES TO REMEMBER REGARDING PRODUCTION OF DOCUMENTS

1. Written material has a charisma of its own in the popular mind: if it's written it is accepted as both true and binding.

2. As a practical matter most important matters are reduced to writing.

3. To learn about the types and kinds of documents that the other side has, or may have, rely upon your client, your investigator, depositions and interrogatories, consulting Experts, and your own vivid imagination.

4. Under the Federal Rules and possibly those of your State one files a Request for Production, and the burden is on the other party to object and explain his reasons for so doing; if your State relies on more traditional practice one files a Motion to Produce and the moving party has the burden of justifying the demand.

5. If there is an objection, use the argument in Court as a process to determine what your opponent has that you need, then narrow the scope of your Motion or Request.

6. Make your Request or Motion as general as possible, encompassing all documents that you can think of; avoid being too specific.

7. If the case requires expert and specialized knowledge, consult with your Expert to find out what he or she needs and what documents the other side ought to have.

8. Try to review the documents in the place that they are ordinarily kept.

9. Always look at the original documents.

10. Take your time when you review documents; do not let anyone hurry you.

11. Use a Request or Motion to secure entry on land or into a building so you can see for yourself the conditions that exist at the scene of the incident.

5

Depositions: Your Most Powerful—and Versatile— Discovery Tool

DEPOSITIONS DEFINED: A REMINDER ABOUT THE NATURE OF A DEPOSITION

A deposition can be briefly described as a legal procedure in which a person is summoned to your office and interrogated by you about the subject matter of the lawsuit so that you can learn some things that you don't know. That's it in a nutshell. It is the most important of the battery of discovery tools created to help you to learn more about your case.

As you might expect, there is much more involved than mentioned above:

- Reasonable notice is required in every instance.
- The Deponent, if a party to the lawsuit, will come to your office because your Civil Rules require it; if he or she is a witness, and not a party, a subpoena will have to be used to compel attendance.
- The deposition is usually held in your office, but on occasion some room in a courthouse building may be used, and at other times you will go to the office of the deponent.
- The deponent will be placed under oath, so that you may receive sworn testimony.

75

- The opposing lawyer must be invited to be present (note: he need not attend), and the witness is entitled to bring his or her own lawyer.

- Your interrogation may utilize leading questions and you are not restricted to the subject matter of the lawsuit; you may inquire into areas that can lead to evidence which is within the ambit of the subject matter of the lawsuit.

- Objections are generally restricted to complaints about the form of your questions, but you may run into objections that you are inquiring into matters that cannot possibly relate to the case at hand.

- At the conclusion of the deposition, the witness has a right to read it and correct obvious errors (though not change the testimony), sign it, or waive reading and signing.

- Finally, a transcript is prepared and sent to the attorneys or filed in Court as your Civil Rules provide.

CONSIDER IT AS ESSENTIALLY A SERIOUS CONVERSATION BETWEEN YOU AND THE WITNESS

A deposition is a conversation: you ask the questions and the witness gives the answers. If you don't understand an answer or some aspect of your case you may ask for an explanation and the witness gives it. The opportunity to have this "conversation" is an extremely versatile discovery tool. It is the only discovery technique that enables you, easily, to receive an answer and then frame a new question based on that answer or to inquire into subtleties and nuances involved in the answer. In addition, you can change the subject and later return to it from a different perspective, and inquire in depth concerning a specific matter. You can utilize the tactic of surprise. It is especially helpful to subpoena documents with the witness and use the occasion to go over those documents and get a thorough understanding of them. It has all the advantages of cross-examination and more; your scope of inquiry is broader and you are not faced with objections based on technical rules of evidence.

However, there are a few cautions about approaching a deposition as a pleasant conversation:

1. Take Charge of the Deposition

In a very literal sense, the deposition is in your hands to do with as you please. It's your baby. You are the one who is to provide direction, select the subject matter, and determine the length of time that will be involved. You set the tone of the proceeding—whether it will be casual or formal, serious or good-humored, general or detailed. Since you have this authority, use it. Don't let either the witness or another attorney usurp your prerogative in this matter.

2. Do Not Engage in Debate with the Witness

He or she is there to answer your questions, not vice-versa. You are searching the mind of the witness; the witness is not there to find out what you know.

Sometimes the informality of the setting and your initial good-natured questions mislead a witness into thinking that he, or she, can respond with questions and not with answers. If that happens, disabuse the witness of that understanding very promptly.

3. Do Not Permit the Procedure to Degenerate into an Argument

Many times you will touch on sensitive matters that will provoke an emotional response. You must never respond to these outbursts in kind. Remember that it takes two to argue. If you will just remain calm, permit a long pause to give the witness a chance to cool off, perhaps change the subject for a few minutes, and then proceed with your interrogation in a professional manner, there will never be an argument.

4. Avoid Too Much Conviviality and Idle Conversation

It is always a good idea to put the witness at ease by engaging in a few light-hearted comments about sports, politics, or a recent humorous occasion. However, if such talk goes on for too long, it will distract the witness; what you want is serious concentration and a determined effort to recall facts. In addition, idle conversation deceives the witness into thinking the whole affair is not very important that it can be taken lightly, and you may well encourage facetious and frivolous answers. While you want the witness to be relaxed, you certainly don't want him or her to regard the deposition as a game or merely a pleasant visit.

REMEMBER THESE CAUTIONS!

1. Be certain that you are in control of the deposition.
2. Do not engage in debate with the witness
3. Do not permit the deposition to degenerate into an argument.
4. Avoid too much conviviality and idle conversation.

THE TRIAL LAWYER MUST TAKE THE DEPOSITION

This is the one discovery technique that must be handled exclusively by the trial lawyer. Remember that success in the preparation and trial of a lawsuit is as much as a result of intuition, judgment and "feelings," as it is of reason, logic, law and facts. The subjective nature of the matter is not often discussed by experienced trial lawyers, but it is recognized under the guise of "experience" and it is important. Accordingly, the person who is in charge of the case and who will eventually try it is the only person who should take a deposition. This will be the means by which he or she not only gets facts but also makes a judgment and appraisal of the person who testifies to the facts. Many times that instinctive feeling (often called a "gut reaction") is as important as the fact itself, and doubly so when the witness testifies to information that one doesn't particularly like, or the witness cannot remember facts that he or she should know. Don't we all recognize that sometimes "it isn't what you say but the way you say it" that is important. If the trial lawyer does not take the deposition it is obvious that he, or she, will never observe and thus have the chance to evaluate "the way" the witness says things. The lawyer will be the one who loses if this opportunity is missed.

Another factor that compels the presence of a trial lawyer is the requirement that some one person must know everything about the case that it is humanly possible to learn and absorb. This is for the purpose of guiding preparation, conducting settlement negotiations, and, where necessary, trying the case. It simply will not do that the person in charge of the case know only certain aspects of it, that the assistant know other information, and that a paralegal have the sole knowledge of a different aspect of the case. One person must be able to "put the pieces together."

On a trip to England some time ago with members of my Bar Association we were appalled to learn that under the English system the Barrister, who has to try the case, relies entirely on his Solicitor to visit the scene of an accident, crime, or other event, interview witnesses and gather documents. The Barrister goes into court with purely secondhand information. In the nature of things, he is bound to be at a tremendous disadvantage if his opponent has personal knowledge of the facts, has met with the witnesses and gathered information about the documents.

The same thing applies in taking depositions. The lawyer who is present asking the questions, thinking of new ones based on the answers given, and evaluating the witness as the deposition proceeds, is way ahead of the lawyer who relies solely on a naked transcript.

TREAT A DEPOSITION AS A MINI-TRIAL

The primary function of a lawyer in court is to interrogate witnesses. A good lawyer will not go into Court unprepared. The sole purpose of a deposition is to interrogate a witness to gain facts and opinions—and one should not begin a deposition unprepared.

First of all, an attorney should approach a deposition just as he, or she, would a trial. It should be considered a mini-trial and should be conducted with the same serious purpose and careful preparation as an actual trial would be. Thus, the attorney should review and study all materials that have been collected to date. If others have worked on some phase of the case they should be consulted to secure their thoughts and ideas with regard to the information one hopes to gain from the witness to be deposed, and the approach that might be taken with the particular witness. In addition, the investigation folder should be studied and pertinent documents or photographs extracted from it. The attorney will have to go through the Answers to Interrogatories and Answers to Requests for Admissions and note those particular ones that may be of value either because they provide essential background information or because they constitute the subject matter of the questioning of the witness to be deposed. One must also read the transcripts of prior depositions to determine whether they contain information that might be helpful during the interrogation of the proposed deponent.

Second, after the file has been reviewed, one comes to the problem of deciding the precise purpose of this deposition. This is in the category of "knowing what you are doing," and I am sorry to say that many depositions are taken when the lawyer does not know what he is doing. The result, at best, is a waste of time and nothing is gained from the interrogation; at worst, the lawyer gets tangled up in matters that don't really concern him or gets some nasty answers to his questions and his opponent's case is bolstered as a result. There is no need for this. It is your job to decide why you are taking the deposition. Are you taking it to establish a particular fact? Are you groping for documents and an explanation of them? Are you deposing a party with the intent of trying to win the case right there and then? What are you doing? A deposition has to have a purpose, goal, or destination. One cannot proceed without it. To do so is to literally grope in the dark. Remember that you are going to be asking a question of the witness and there is no hope of getting a helpful answer if you don't have a clear understanding of what you are looking for. If you are certain of your goals, your questions will be clear and direct and the witness will answer definitely and helpfully. On the other hand, if you are not sure what you are after your questions will be ambiguous, general, hazy, uncertain—and so will the answers. Having a clearly defined goal or purpose when taking the deposition is certainly one of the critical matters to be considered beforehand.

Third, an outline should be prepared to give cohesion and direction to the deposition. An outline to an attorney is like a map to a driver: it tells you where you have been, where you are, where you are going, and the alternative routes that are available to you if there is a detour. Without an outline, there is every likelihood that you are going to forget to ask questions in one or two areas that you had hoped to cover with this witness. During the deposition an answer may well lead you into an area of inquiry that you did not anticipate, and after you have interrogated the witness for ten or fifteen minutes in this new and unexpected area it is easy to forget to go over another matter that may be important, though more mundane in nature. Later you may want to kick yourself for having forgotten to ask the witness about these mundane matters—but it will be too late. This can be avoided if you will only prepare an outline. Then when you get led off onto an interesting detour and have concluded that matter to your satisfaction, you will have a guide to get you back to the main road, so to speak.

Finally, if there is any doubt about your ability to remember specific matters of importance, the actual questions should be prepared. Sometimes the exact phrasing of a question is crucial, and for those instances the questions should be written out beforehand. I have seen many excellent attorneys come to a deposition with an outline which they place on one side of their desk and many pages of prepared questions which they place to the other side. They will begin working from the outline but from time to time turn to the prepared questions and check them off as they are asked. This leads to a thorough deposition, and certainly all those present know that the lawyer is prepared and is taking the matter very seriously. It certainly gives the opposition grounds for worry if they have not prepared as diligently.

THE GOALS AND PURPOSES OF SUCCESSFUL DEPOSITIONS

Since it is critical to decide in advance the specific purpose for which you are taking the deposition, it is well to take a look at what some of those goals might be. In a broad sense, one takes a deposition for two good reasons:

1. To win the case, and
2. To gather information.

CHECKLIST
YOUR PREPARATION FOR
A GOOD DEPOSITION

1. *Review* Investigation Folder.
2. *Read* Answers to Interrogatories and Request for Admissions. Note pertinent material.
3. *Read* Transcipts of Prior Depositions.
4. *Discuss* the case, the witness, and possible goals of the deposition with others who have worked on the case.
5. *Decide* on a specific purpose of the deposition.
6. *Prepare* an outline
7. *Write out* the important questions you want to be sure to ask.

Most depositions are taken for the second reason—to gather information that you don't have and need. There is not enough attention given to the first reason for taking a deposition—to win the case. Naturally, this can be done conclusively only when one deposes a party to the lawsuit; it can be done indirectly however, by soliciting damning testimony from a key witness. Unfortunately, most attorneys lack faith in the possibility of winning a case by way of a deposition and do not try to do so—at least not very hard. We will discuss this at greater length in a moment.

Returning to the question of the various purposes for which depositions are taken, the phrase "to gather information" is both broad and general. It can be refined—and perhaps, in so doing, we can arrive at some goals that you have not thought of before.

Being more specific, we can delineate six principal objectives of depositions:

Objective No. 1: To win the case.

Objective No. 2: To find and prove an essential fact.

Objective No. 3: To block a defense or theory of your opponent.

Objective No. 4: To secure documents and to gather information about them.

Objective No. 5: To prove your damages for settlement purposes.

Objective No. 6: To develop facts needed to file a complaint.

Having these objectives before us, we can see that by knowing why we are taking the deposition, we can alter our preparation, attitude and approach in each instance. For example, if one is going to try to win the case, one needs a party as a deponent, the deposition will be lengthy and detailed, the attorney must prepare himself carefully and extensively, and at the deposition he must utilize every skill to go for the jugular. However, if one is deposing a witness to establish a particular fact (a weatherman, about the amount of rain on a particular day; a city engineer, about when a particular traffic light was installed) the deposition can be direct, brief, will require relatively little preparation, and can be taken in a relaxed manner. The first deposition may require several hours of time; the second, ten minutes.

There is also a difference in scheduling the various types of depositions. Usually a deposition taken to win a case will be scheduled a considerable time after a lawsuit has been filed. This is also true of a deposition taken for the purpose of proving the damages to the satisfaction of a skeptical claimsman or insurance adjuster. On the other hand, depositions taken for the purpose of discovering additional parties who might be joined in a lawsuit, or for the purpose of developing facts needed to file a complaint (where permitted), are necessarily scheduled very early in a case.

So there are important differences in timing, approach, and preparation depending upon your objective in taking the deposition. Let us look more closely at these objectives.

PART II—OBJECTIVES

NO. 1: TO WIN THE CASE

Every discovery technique has, as its ultimate goal, victory in the lawsuit, but it is only in taking a deposition that one is reasonably likely to accomplish this goal. And it can be done! If you will combine the principles of a good knowledge of the case, detailed preparation, and a diligent application of skill—all of which are within your capabilities—you can win the case in the quiet of your office by the simple and economical means of a good deposition. If you will do some hard work now, and follow the principles laid down in this book, there will be no need for five or seven days of trial, two weeks of preparation, high experts' fees, worry about witnesses not showing up in court, and legitimate concern about how your client will hold up under cross-examination or how the judge will rule on some serious questions of evidence.

Remember that, to accomplish this purpose, you must be deposing a party to the lawsuit (either the individual Plaintiff or Defendant) or a critical witness, or, if it is a corporation, a senior officer whose word can bind the corporation.

Look at some illustrations of cases in which this was done.

Case History 1: A Products Liability Case: Entry Door of Store Falls and Crushes Patron's Hand

A woman patron began to enter the front, swinging door of a department store. As she pushed, the door suddenly broke loose and began to fall toward her. As she tried to hold the glass door her hand slid to the right and was crushed between the right edge of the door and the frame. The defendant claimed it had no notice of any defect in the door, and proclaimed that it was mystified as to the cause of the accident. Then the day came that a deposition was taken of the independent (and thoroughly honest) repairman who fixed the door. Portions of the transcript of his testimony include the following:

Q: Okay. did you later that day go out to Smith's Department Store?

A: That's correct.

Q: *And what did you find upon your arrival?*

A: *A broken bottom pivot.*

Q: *What is a broken bottom pivot?*

A: *The bottom pivot was completely broken off at the threshold.*

Q: Is the pivot–is that a solid piece of metal that goes up inside that door that permits the door to turn?

A: Basically, that's it. It is a bearing mounted on a solid piece of metal, and the portion that is–that portion is attached to the threshold. The portion inside the door is attached to the door and has a small catch that holds it in place.

Q: Okay. And when you got there, you indicated that that was broken?

A: That's correct.

Q: So the door had not popped off. The pivot had actually snapped?

A: That is correct.

Q: Where had it snapped?

A: Where it attaches to the metal plate that attaches to the threshold.

Q: And the threshold is the steel plate that runs along the floor that the doors sit on?

A: The aluminum plate, yes, sir.

Q: Okay. In this instance, the pivot has broken off at the point where the pivot meets the thin steel plate?

A: That is correct.

Q: And was it a clean break completely through?

A: Yes. The reason the door would fall off is when the bottom pivot breaks, if the door isn't high enough, the top arm isn't clamped tightly to the operator that is actually above the door. By raising it, I can get a better grip on that spindle for the operator and prevent the door or attempt to prevent the door from falling off if the bottom pivot is broken again.

Q: Okay. So this door is attached both on the bottom with a pivot—

A: That's correct.

Q: —and at the top with a spindle?

A: Yes.

Q: Okay. Now, the closer holds the door at the top; is that right?

A: The spindle of the closer is a one-half inch metal–square metal spindle. It is a part of the internal workings of the closer and would–up inside, it's attached to cams and the mechanism that meters the closing of the door. The arm that clamps onto it is a square cutout that slides over that half-inch square spindle and has two bolts that bolt a metal clamp to the back side of it.

Q: Okay. Now just so I understand–and if I get this wrong, straighten me out–if the door is high enough, close enough to the spindle of the closer, when the bottom pivot breaks, the door will not fall?

A: If the door is not high enough, instead of getting the full depth of the approximately half inch that the spindle comes down, you may only have an eighth of an inch grip there, which, whenever the bottom pivot breaks and the door slides forward, it will pull it right off of there. So what I would do is add shims underneath the door portion between the door and the portion of the pivot to bring the door up higher, as high as it would go and still not scrape to give a better bite on the spindle so that if the pivot broke in the fututure, it is less likely to fall off.

Q: Do pivots periodically break?

A: They do.

Q: How frequently?

A: That depends on where they are. *At this particular store, very often.*

Q: How many times did you replace the pivot prior to December 20, 1985?

A: Replacing that pivot, I wouldn't know if I ever replaced it before. What happens is if someone hits the back edge of that door hard, it breaks the pivot off. This happens more frequently in the summer at that particular store, because they will have sidewalk sales, and the merchandise is taken out through two 30-inch doors on a large pallet. *The weight of the pallet and the merchandise when brought through rapidly knocks the pivots off. There have been occasions where I've replaced a pivot in the morning and gone back there that night at closing time and replaced the same pivot because it was broken off on the way back in.*

Q: You would have records, then, of repairs at the Smith's Department store but not of specific doors?

A: As this particular service report indicates, I tried to show that specific door. I replaced the broken pivot, the broken bottom pivot. . . .

Q: Did you have additional pivots in the car, or in the truck?

A: Yes. I always have them with me.

Q: That's the kind of part that you keep with you at all times?

A: That is correct.

Q: *It's a frequently breaking part?*

A: *Yes, it is.* Again, that depends on the use that it gets from the store that it's in.

Q: Does it break more frequently with increased use?

A: It breaks more frequently with the type of use it gets, *such as I described, bringing heavy loads in and out and using the pallet or the dolly that the weight is on as a means of opening the door.* If you took the door and pushed them open and blocked them, then you could walk right through without any damage. *But if you're going to use that pallet to force the doors open, you're going to break the pivots.*

Q: That's a lot of pounds per square inch pressure, a heavy load on a pallet hitting a door. Does it take a significant amount of force to break one of those pivots?

A: I wouldn't know how much force it would take, but it could be broken off with a shopping cart if you hit it hard enough.

Q: What about somebody just opening and closing the door? That's not going to break the pivot?

A: No. That would be normal use. If you had them on your doors here at this building, they would probably last a very long time, and they would wear out. The door would slowly lower and start dragging on the threshold as opposed to them breaking off.

Q: To break off, there has to be abnormal use?

A: That is correct.

Q: Incidentally, when you were asked the question whether, "the Smith's store is pretty good about keeping the doors in good operating condition?" You hesitated before you answered. Could you explain the hesitation, what you were going to say.

A: You're putting me in a position where I'm passing judgment on how my customer maintains their buildings, which is going to cost me a customer. *I have, on occasion, sent proposals to Smith's to have repairs made that I felt were necessary, and they did not act on them. Smith's will call me to replace a pivot if it is broken.*

Q: *But they won't call you to inspect, to maintain, to do preventative maintenance; isn't that right?*

A: *That is correct.*

In this one deposition we learn that:

- A broken pivot caused this accident;
- Such breakages occurred so frequently that the repairman always carried extras in his truck;
- Defendants' employees usually caused this by banging pallets loaded with merchandise through the door;
- The repairman had made recommendations about this matter to Smith's managers and these were ignored; and
- While he was frequently called to repair broken doors, he was never called to conduct routine inspections or maintenance.

That's a lot of information to get from one deposition! And all of it is *crucial* information, and it was dispositive of the liability side of this case. Since the seriousness of the injuries and the extent of the damages were never at issue, this case was settled, but only after that excellent deposition.

The important point is that the deposition was planned and the questions thought out in advance. Success in this case just didn't happen as a matter of luck or because the attorney happened to spontaneously think of a question.

This calls to mind a quotation I read somewhere of the very famous lawyer, Louis Nizer, who was asked about the role of luck in his success, to which he is reported to have responded something to this effect: "Oh, Lady Luck visits me all right, but somehow she always appears at 2 A.M. when I'm working in my library. She never shows up when I'm out on the golf course."

Just so in this instance. The file had been reviewed, interrogatories served and answered which gave the name of this witness, and considerable thought was given to what he might say and the questions that could be asked. And it was all worthwhile. There was no need for a trial here—thanks to a good deposition.

Outline for Deposing an Expert to Win the Case

1. *Education, Training and Experience*

   An introduction. For background only. You probably won't get anything significant from this. Touch lightly and move on.

2. *Professors and Recognized Texts in the Field*

   A former teacher might disagree with the conduct of his student.

   The texts are important. You may well find material that will prove helpful in cross-examination.

3. *Prior Claims or Lawsuits*

   This may be helpful. don't spend too much time on it. Remember that if there are any—however the outcome—it is unsettling for the deponent to discuss them.

4. *Verify and Interrogate About Documents the Deponent Helped Prepare*

   Hospital records, engineering drawings, real estate appraisals, blasting records.

   This is the time to strike hard— unnerve the witness.

   This is the first time to press the witness; bear down hard.

   You should know these documents better than the witness does. Watch for errors.

   Sharp questioning—detailed and lengthy. This is a good place to set the stage for questions that will win the case.

5. *Relations with Assistants and Subordinate Personnel*

   At this point try to avoid aggressive questioning. Let the witness relax for a few moments.

   Back off from tough questioning; let the witness relax.

   Inquire about "Who did what?" Includes medical residents, junior attorneys, draftsmen, laboratory personnel.

   Will the witness accept responsibility for their work?

   To what extent did he supervise them?

6. *The Incident*

Win the case now! Come down very hard on the witness.

Win the case
here and now!
Your most aggressive and adroit questioning.

Take all the time you want.

Demand admissions of liability.

Be pointed and detailed in your questions.

7. *Compliance with Statutes, Decisions, Standards, Regulations, Custom in the Industry*

Don't accept "substantial compliance." What wasn't done?

Be sure you know what the standards are.

Go into detail only if there appears to be noncompliance.

Case History 2: A Two-Vehicle Head-On Collision

In this instance the accident happened on a two-lane road, at night. There were no witnesses. The Plaintiff had no recollection of the accident. The Defendant driver had a passenger—his girlfriend—who was asleep at the time of impact. Most of the debris was slightly to the Plaintiff's side of the center line. The significant part of the deposition was substantially as follows:

Q: You picked up your girlfriend at 11:15 at her place of business, is that right?

A: Yeah.

Q: I understand she promptly went to sleep on you.

A: Yeah, she was tired.

Q: Tell me, as you drove along Blackburn road, did you ever glance at your girlfriend to see if she was all right?

A: Yeah, a couple of times.

Q: What was her position in the front seat?

A: She was in the corner of the seat and the door and her head was against the window.

Q: You say you glanced at her to see if she was all right. How many times did you do this?

A: Two or three times.

Q: Was one of those times just before this accident?

A: Yes.

Q: Tell me, in glancing, did you ever lean toward her to check more closely on her condition?

A: Yes.

Q: How much time would this leaning over and looking at your girlfriend take?

A: A few seconds.

Q: When you are driving and you lean to the right of the seat—whether to roll up a window, check on your girlfriend or whatever reason—do you notice a tendency of your left hand to turn the steering wheel to the left?

A: Yes.

Q: As you recollect this accident, do you think you turned the steering wheel to the left when you leaned to the right to check on your girlfriend?

A: Yeah.

Needless to say, that was the end of that case.

Outline For Deposing a Driver in an Automobile Accident Case

	1. Training and Experience
	General background.
Background.	Don't expect too much unless a new driver.
	2. Prior Accidents and Motor Vehicle Violations
Touch and go.	Four or five speeding tickets, two or three prior intersection accidents might open the door to serious questioning.
	3. Conduct and Condition of Driver
Spend a lot of time with this.	Tired? Drinking? Long day? In a hurry? In ill health? Medicated? Any physical disabilities? Any distractions—children, noise, many passengers? Disturbing conditions on road—much traffic, road surface, accident, animals?
	Spend some time with this subject.
	4. Conduct and Condition of Vehicle
Usually cautionary questions.	Brakes OK? Lights? Last inspection—any problems? Windshield wipers, steering mechanism, tires.
	Unless there is an obvious defect—which you should already know about—this questioning will be cautionary in nature.

5. *Circumstances Preceding the Accident*

Step up the pace and intensity of the questions.

Now is the time to start to bear down on the witness. Detailed, aggressive questions.

What did he, or she, see? Speed. Distances.

What was the witness doing. Alertness for danger signs— children playing near road, traffic ahead beginning to slow down.

6. *The Accident*

Use all your skills at this point.

Win the case here.

What did the driver do and why?

Take your time.

How could this accident have been avoided.

Try to get admissions of poor judgment, distractions or excessive speed.

Try to get the witness to draw a sketch; it is often incorrect and damning.

7. *Post-Accident Circumstances*

General questions— admissions.

Position of vehicles

Witnesses

Police and ambulance

Try to use the deponent as a condition witness to the plaintiff's injuries.

Admissions at the scene.

8. *Violations of Statutes, Regulations, Motor Vehicle Code*

Usually routine.

Be sure you know the applicable ones. Run through them.

Touch lightly and move on unless non-compliance is shown.

Case History 3: A Products Liability Case Involving a Defective Printing Press

The operator of this large machine had the duty of wiping off the rolls (two of which turned toward each other) from time to time. At one time he reached for a rag located near the rolls, the end of the rag caught in the rolls and pulled his hand into them, causing a severe crush injury to the hand. Other employees stated that after the "Stop" button was pushed, it took 20 to 30 seconds for the machine to stop. Incidentally the machine was less than eight years old, a fact that became highly significant as will be seen. The Theory of Liability rested on the twin assertions that:

1. There should have been a guard at the rolls tied into the power source so that, when the guard was lifted to clean the rolls, the machine would stop; and

2. The braking mechanism was defective.

The deponent was the chief engineer for the defendant and had helped to design the machine. A synopsis of this deposition tells us the following:

Q: Is the model X-23 produced specifically for a particular customer, or is that a standard design?

A: It's pretty much a standard design for the stock forms industry.

Q: And was the X-23 model a standard design back in 1982?

A: Yes.

Q: You indicated that the design of the X-23 model dry offset press was an evolutionary process?

A: Yes.

Q: When was the original design completed?

A: I think it was about—oh, 10 to 15 years ago.

Q: So, late seventies is when the original design?

A: Approximately.

Q: Subsequent to that, were there design modifications made?

A: Small changes, no real major changes.

Q: How about the safety features? Any modification with respect to safety features over the years?

A: There have been additional guards added.

Q: What additional guards have been added?

A: Area guards over the printing unit and over the processing units. It's a punch and perforator unit.

Q: Those were the area guards over the printing unit—

A: Yes.

Q: Those were not part of the original design, but were subsequently added?

A: Yes.

Q: When were those guards added?

A: I believe that the guards for the perforating and punch unit were added, oh, probably five years after the thing, after the presses were started, which would have been '82, '83.

Q: Okay. How about the area guards over the printing unit?

A: They came along maybe five or six years ago.

Q: So, they would have come along in—

A: '86, '87, in that area.

Q: And the area guards over the printing unit, that would have been after the sale of the dry offset press to the employer corporation that's involved in this case?

A: Yes.

Q: I'd like you to take a quick look at the photograph I place in front of you, and ask if you can describe that for me.

A: It's a photograph from the operator's side, looking in between the mill roll unwinder and the printing unit of the press.

Q: Is the area shown by the rolls—do you see the rolls in the photograph?

A: Yes.

Q: Is that area the section that is now, or beginning in '86 or '87, covered by area guards?

A: Yes.

Q: And who designed those area guards?

A: I couldn't say; I don't recall. It was just an evolutionary thing, we were adding guards.

Q: Okay. Again, staying with this photograph, if I were to buy an identical machine today, the area depicted by the rolls would be covered by a guard; is that correct?

A: Yes.

Q: Yes, it would?

A: Yes.

Q: Could you describe the nature of the guard.

A: It would be a solid aluminum piece of sheet metal, and hinged at the top.

Q: Why was the printing unit guard developed?

A: It was just evolutionary feedback from customers, that some of them requested it.

Q: Do you know why they requested it?

A: Just to add additional guards. *I think some of them maybe came from OSHA inspections in their plants.*

Q: *So you had some suggestion that OSHA did not approve of the machine without the guard, and wanted the guard put on?*

A: *Yes.*

Q: *And is that the motivation for your company in designing the guard?*

A: *Yes.*

Q: Okay. Getting back to the printing unit guard, is it a fixed guard or is it tied in electrically to the operation of the equipment?

A: The ones today have an electrical interlock switch on them.

Q: Okay. *So that today the guard has an interlock switch?*

A: *Yes.*

Q: *So that if I lift the guard, the machine will shut down; is that right?*

A: *Yes.*

Q: Originally back in '86 or '87, it was just a fixed guard without the interlock; is that right?

A: It was a pivoting guard.

Q: Could you describe it?

A: It had a hinge at the top and you could lift it up.

Q: But the machine would continue to run in the event you did lift it up?

A: Yes.

Q: Okay. When was the interlock added?

A: About three years ago.

Q: Could you describe how the interlock system works.

A: It's a cam-actuated switch on the pivot end of the guard so that as soon as the guard is lifted, it actuates the stop circuit in the press.

Q: Does it operate a brake, or does it cut off power to the press?

A: Operates a brake.

Q: So that it affirmatively stops the press rather than just let the press wind down by cutting the power?

A: Yes.

Q: *Was any effort ever made to retrofit machines that were sold prior to 1988 or 1989, when you first developed the printing unit guard?*

A: *No.*

Q: *Were customers who had purchased machines prior to '88 or '89 ever told about the guard?*

A: *No.*

Q: *Were there any mailings sent out to them, advertising brochures saying, "Hey, folks, you can buy this thing?*

A: *No.*

Q: Was it added to all of the X-23 model dry offset presses after '88, '89?

A: We had a guard on after '88, '89.

Q: On all of them?

A: Right.

Q: Okay. All new models?

A: Yes.

That information is quite helpful. The interlocking guard mechanism was available before the accident date, but no effort was made to retrofit old models of the press or to advise former purchasers of this new safety device. All this despite the following knowledge on the part of the company:

Q: Are you aware of any claims that were made against your company for injuries in the area shown by the photograph in Exhibit 1?

A: Not in X-23 presses.

Q: In other types of presses?

A: Yes.

Q: Is there any difference between the X-23 presses and the other types of presses, as far as the rolls shown by that photograph are concerned?

A: Different arrangement of the rolls.

Q: But the principal, the rotating rolls, rolls rotating towards each other would be the same?

A: Yes.

Q: Those problems, were they people getting their hands caught between the rolls?

A: Yes.

Q: Were you aware of any lawsuits that have been filed against your company with respect to people getting their hands caught in the rolls?

A: I was involved in all of them, I think, the lawsuits that were filed, but I can't date them.

Finally, inquiry was made about the statements of fellow employees that the press failed to stop for up to 20 or 30 seconds after the "Stop" button was pushed:

Q: Going back to the stop buttons—I'm going to have to tell you, there's been some testimony that Joe Jones, when he got his hand caught in the rolls, he hit the stop botton but the machine didn't stop; instead it wound down. And there's been some talk that it took as much as 30 seconds for this machine to wind down after the stop is pressed, after the stop button is pressed. First of all, does that sound right to you?

A: No.

Q: *It should stop faster than that?*

A: *It certainly should.*

Q: Does that indicate to you some sort of problem?

A: Could you repeat that?

Q: Well, is it supposed to work like that?

A: Is it supposed to take 30 seconds to stop?

Q: Right.

A: No.

Q: Okay. *Now, assuming that it does take 30 seconds to stop, does that indicate to you that there's something wrong?*

A: *Yes.* It would indicate to me that there was something wrong either with the mechanical electrical brake itself or the control for the brake. But the stop button would have functioned because all it does is operate a relay, and obviously the relay worked because the press did stop.

Q: You gave me two possibilities there and I only wrote the first one down. There was something wrong with the mechanical brake?

A: Or the electrical control.

Q: What is the brake control?

A: It's a control that is operated by a relay which applies voltage to the electrical mechanical brake, to apply the brake itself.

Q: Okay. If the brake control was not functioning, would that be an electrical malfunction?

A: It could be an electrical malfunction or *it could be a setting of the brake. There is a potentiometer to control the amount of voltage that's applied to the brake.*

Q: How about if there's a problem with the mechanical brake? What types of problems would the mechanical brake have?

A: Maybe just severely worn, would be the only thing I would know.

Q: I'd like to show you a document that was provided to me pursuant to a

Q: request for production. It's a field service report—how can we identify it—and seems to be signed off by Bill Brown, production manager. Do you see that down at the bottom?

A: Yes.

Q: On the second page, could you flip that? That begins a typewritten report, doesn't it?

A: Yes.

Q: And it's called a trip report?

A: Yes.

Q: Do you see the name in the upper left-hand corner as Bill Brown?

A: Yes.

Q: Is Bill Brown an employee of your company?

A: He was at that time.

Q: *What's the problem that he is—Mr. Brown in his report is describing in the third paragraph?*

A: *It indicates that he adjusted the potentiometer, which I previously described, on the dynatorque brake control.*

Q: *Why did he do that, from the report?*

A: *Because it was not stopping the press soon enough.*

Q: Take a look at the last paragraph on that same page, the third page—do you see the complaint Mr. Jones is reporting there?

A: Yes.

Q: What is that complaint?

A: That the—according to the operator, sometimes the line shaft brake does not stop the press when the stop button is pushed; instead, the press appears to coast to a stop.

Q: It continues onto the next page. Do you see that Mr. Brown is reporting that relay contacts and z relays were found to be badly burnt?

A: Yes.

Q: What would cause the relay contact and the z relays to be badly burnt?

A: I don't know.

Q: Okay. It also indicates, last sentence, mechanically, the brake itself appears to need refurbishing. Do you see that?

A: Yes.

Q: What's the life of the brake mechanism?

A: I'd say normally they will last eight to ten years.

Q: And it would have to be replaced, then, every eight to ten years?

A: Approximately, depending on the usage.

Q: And to be on the safe side, maybe a little short of that?

A: Usually, they will go eight years.

Q: *Did you make any recommendations to your customers about how often they should replace the mechanical brake?*

A: *No.*

Q: *Did the company issue any warnings to customers that the life of one of those brakes is eight to ten years?*

A: *No.*

For all practical purposes this case was over at the conclusion of this deposition. The chief engineer knew about lawsuits involving people getting their hands crushed in these rolls, devised a guard and interlock system to prevent that, but never notified old customers. Finally, we have a brake system that was supposed to be effective for eight or ten years and wasn't.

What could defense counsel do? Where was he to turn for support of his case? There was nowhere to go. This case was settled for a substantial sum in large part due to this deposition.

These case histories are given for the sole purpose of illustrating the fact that you can win your case by taking a good deposition. This is not a rare event. It happens often—if the attorney is well prepared and knows what he is after.

IS IT ALL A MATTER OF LUCK?

Many lawyers truly believe that getting a damaging answer from a witness is simply a matter of luck or a pure mistake on the part of the witness. The argument goes that, after all, when you come down to essential questions the witness knows what you're driving at and will answer negatively, or evasively, just to protect himself, or herself. This is absolutely wrong.

To begin with the vast majority of your deponents are completely honest people. They are under oath and they will respond with a direct and candid answer even when they know they are hurting themselves.

Second, you assume too much if you believe that the average person knows what is and what is not a crucial question. Many times he or she does not know why you are asking certain questions or where you are leading him or her. Certainly the witness doesn't know the law as well as you do so that he cannot frame answers to comply with particular legal standards.

In addition, the witness will not know as much about the case as you do. Your questions can be designed around facts and ideas about which the witness has little specific knowledge even though he has some very precise information that you must have. In short, sometimes he doesn't appreciate that what he is telling you has great significance and that, inadvertently, he is, in effect, giving the case away.

Finally, deponents are nervous and do get tired. One does not begin a deposition by asking, "Were you negligent?" or, "Did you understand what you were doing when you signed this contract?" Of course one will get a "bad" answer if one goes about questioning in this fashion at that time. Crucial questions should come at the middle or near the end of a deposition, not at the beginning. Also, one does not ask blunt questions suggesting that a witness has done something wrong, stupid or foolish. Instead, one leads up to the critical questions and asks them in as innocuous a manner as possible. You may recall the words of a popular song of not long ago: "A little bit of sugar makes the medicine go down." So it goes with your questions in a deposition. The witness is put at ease, a rapport is established, routine questions are asked, and when the witness responds promptly and with candor the attorney works his way to the vital and sensitive material and then asks his questions at a time and in a manner he deems most suitable to get the desired answer.

Luck doesn't have much to do with the manner. You can get the answers you want—and need—without the help of a fickle Dame Fortune. Hard work and skill are the keys to success.

**REMEMBER: SKILL, NOT LUCK
DETERMINES SUCCESS IN A DEPOSITION**

1. Most witnesses *will answer honestly.*
2. The average person *does not realize* what is, or is not, a crucial question.
3. The deponent *does not know the law.*
4. Usually the witness *will not know all the details* of the case that you know.
5. The witness is *nervous, gets tired, and is unaware* that you are asking a "crucial question.

NO. 2: TO FIND AND PROVE AN ESSENTIAL FACT

In every case there are a multiplicity of facts that are essential to prove in order to win the case. Naturally, you will use investigation, interrogatories, and Requests for Admissions to gather many of these. There are some facts, however, that cannot be established by these procedures and as to those you will have to take depositions. Many times—in fact, usually—the deponent will not be the other party to the lawsuit or an officer of a litigant corporation. Also, and usually, the deponent is one who will not talk to an investigator for personal or business reasons.

A good example of this is the policeman standing on a corner who witnesses an accident but who, because of the internal rules of his department, cannot give a signed statement. He may have heard a party explain, "It was all my fault," but it is not in his report. This is a person who will have to be deposed to elicit, under oath, that most damaging statement of the party.

A second example is the traditional bank officer. You know how banks are when it comes to divulging details about their customers' accounts and transactions. They generally won't do it, or do it reluctantly and carelessly. If it is important to you to know that a specific transaction occurred on a particular day, then you will have to depose this witness.

Finally, there is the instance in which a witness is stubborn or frightened and refuses to give a statement to your investigator. This usually happens in the case of automobile accidents or other similar instances in which the witnesses are bystanders or passersby who give their name to a policeman but thereafter just don't want to get involved. A good investigator will get them to talk to him but they won't give a signed statement. This makes a deposition essential.

A typical example is the following extract. Here a former manager of one of the divisions of a corporation was suing the company for salary, bonus and other benefits that had not been fully paid. In September and October of the year he left the company he called the head of the Compensation Payment Division and inquired about payments to him and payments to others who had occupied positions similar to the one he had, and voiced his personal complaints about the whole matter. In the course of the lawsuit those telephone calls became very important. Did he make the calls? Did he apprise the head of the Compensation Payment Division of the nature of his complaints? Notice to the company was important.

Since the proposed witness would not talk to anyone about the matter, a deposition was essential.

Take a moment to consider your approach to this deposition. There are only two important elements: (1) were the calls made on certain dates and, (2) did the caller complain about specific matters?

Note the matters that *are not* important in this deposition but which most attorneys simply cannot resist asking:

- Do you care about the education of the deponent?
- Do you care about his marital status, the number of children he has and what they are doing?

- Do you care about how long the deponent was with the company or his prior work experience?
- Do you care if the witness either likes or dislikes your client?
- Do you care about anything except the two essential facts?

The answers are no, no, no, no and no.
Therefore, why go into these matters at all?

The deponent is an older, experienced man who is either going to tell the truth, "won't remember," or will simply lie about the affair. The subject matter is devoid of emotion, it does not concern either the deponent or his department. In 99 percent of these instances, either you will get the truth or the witness honestly will not remember.

So, why fool around? Get directly to the heart of the matter. This is the way it went:

Q: May I have your full name, please.

A: John P. Smith.

Q: And who is your employer?

A: Jones Express Corporation.

Q: What is your present position with them?

A: Director of Compensation Payment.

Q: What are your duties, Mr. Smith?

A: In general, it's to develop corporate policies and procedures pertaining to the compensation of the exempt personnel in this company and to help the organization units in implementation of those policies and procedures.

Q: Mr. Smith, are you acquainted with Mr. Sam Roberts?

A: I've met Mr. Roberts a time or two and we talked on the phone a time or two.

Q: All right. I direct your attention, Mr. Smith, to the period of October through November, 1980, an approximate two-month period. Do you recall first of all meeting Mr. Roberts during that time span?

A: No.

Q: All right. Do you recall talking with him on the telephone during that period?

A: Yes.

Q: Right. To the best of your recollection, about when would that have been?

A: October '80, he called once. In November '80, we talked.

Q: That would be two separate occasions?

A: Correct.

Q: All right. First of all, did you make any memoranda of the phone call?

A: I took some notes, yes.

Q: Do you have them with you?

A: No.

Q: I see. As best as you can recall, what was the substance of the phone call?

A: Which one?

Q: Well, let's take the October one.

A: He said that he had been offered the job of division manager by Bob White at a salary of $38,000 a year, and he said he asked Bob for a guaranteed bonus, and he said that Bob told him he would be eligible for a salary increase at the end of six months and every month or every year, thereafter. He would be eligible for a salary increase in the order of eight percent. He said that he talked to Bob several times about salary increases and got no satisfactory response and talked about bonuses and got no satisfactory answers as far as he was concerned. Then he said there were several meetings then over a period of a few months, some involving Mr. Bingham, who was then the chief executive officer, and then he became disabled and unable to work.

Q: What did Mr. Roberts say his meetings with Mr. Bingham were about?

A: The only thing he told me was Mr. Bingham said that he, Mr. Roberts, had done everything he, Mr. Bingham would have done under those circumstances in terms of running the division, phasing it out.

Q: Did he, during this conversation, mention to you any claim for bonuses and salary increases?

A: Yes, he did.

Q: And what was the reference at this time?

A: He simply referred back to our earlier conversation but not in any significant detail and wanted to know if there was anything that would be done about that.

Q: From the conversations that you had in October and November, did you gather or feel or believe that Mr. Roberts was requesting payment or submitting a claim or pressing a claim for salaries and bonuses?

A: Yes.

Q: What did you gather from your conversation as to Mr. Roberts' purpose in mentioning these things?

A: I think he was relating to me a misunderstanding between him and Mr. White.

Q: Pertaining to salaries and bonuses?

A: Yes.

Q: Now did you receive a telephone call from Mr. Roberts in November of 1980?

A: Yes, I did.

Q: What was that call about?

A: It was almost a repetition of the October one. Same subject matter.

Q: Thank you, Mr. Smith.

Note that the witness answered honestly and thoroughly, that he really gave more information than expected (it was now known that he had memoranda of the telephone calls), and all of this was accomplished in a 12-page deposition. The deposition should have taken eight pages but the attorney just had to ramble a little bit at one point.

Since the deponent is nearly always an administrative person (medical record librarian at a hospital, department head at a university or private corporation, governmental employee) who is not in any way directly involved in the case, there is no need for a lengthy deposition. The witness can be relied on to give you honest and complete responses since he or she is not personally involved and the subject matter is dispassionate in nature. Under these circumstances, you can get directly to the point. Establish the fact you need and close the record.

There are many examples of this type of deposition:

Policeman: Was the traffic light red or green for the Plaintiff (Defendant) Driver?

Air Traffic Controller: Was the airplane at the altitude and on the course its flight plan indicated?

University Department Head: What are the specific criteria for securing tenure at your school? Is homosexuality a specific disqualification?

Civil Engineer: Is there a regulation of the Department of Labor and Industry regarding the shoring up of the walls of ditches and trenches?

What does it require in the case of a trench twelve feet deep, and five feet wide and 50 feet long?

Describe the shoring you saw in the trench involved in this accident.

None of these depositions should run over ten pages. You know what you're after, you can rest assured that this witness will give it to you if he, or she, can—so get on with it.

NO. 3: BLOCKING A DEFENSE OR
THEORY OF YOUR OPPONENT

After a lawsuit has been filed and some discovery has been invoked, it soon becomes obvious that your opponent may have several theories of liability or defense. As long as he is permitted to encumber you with this shotgun approach, your time and talents are going to be diverted and diluted because you must prepare for, and work on, each of the separate contingencies. This can lead to a great deal of very unnecessary work.

The best way to control this situation and to compel your opponent to settle on one or two theories is to deliberately plan to block the others by discovery—and chiefly through depositions.

Since by definition we are dealing with "theories" and your opponent is no more sure of the end result of his approach than you are, the burden is on you to take the offensive. If you do nothing, the other attorney will keep his multiple approach going to the time of trial. So—smoke him out.

If, in an automobile accident, the plaintiff takes the position that your driver was negligent in the way he handled the car and also that the brakes on the car were defective, you might depose a passenger or bystander to block negligent driving, or a mechanic who worked on the car to block the "defective brakes" approach.

In an assumpsit action for the late delivery of defective goods you might well depose the freight carrier who delivered the material to prove that the delivery was on time (or was late through no fault of your client—snowstorm, bridge out, wildcate strike), thus leaving you free to concentrate on the issue of whether the goods were defective.

As in the case of Objective No. 2, the depositions often involve neutral third parties who have no reason to do other than tell the truth and the whole truth.

Unlike those in Objective No. 2, however, such parties may have freely talked to you in detail, given signed statements—in fact cooperated in every way. You could wait to the time of trial to use them—but why? Why burden a trial, and the rest of your preparation of the case, with needless testimony. If you can satisfy your opponent, in advance, that his "theory" is going absolutely nowhere, he is going to drop it and try to get on to better things. If he won't agree to do so, your depositions can be used to support a Motion for Summary Judgment as to that aspect of the case and you'll probably win.

In Chapter 9 I discuss a very dramatic deposition in which a neurosurgeon negligently severed a nerve root while doing lumbar disc surgery with the result that the patient was left with a permanent "foot drop."

A very unusual event happened there; after the operation, the neurosurgeon went away on vacation and the patient was referred to a specialist in physical rehabilitation. This doctor never talked to the neurosurgeon and of course, in the hospital record at the time, there was no reference to a severance of the filaments of the L-5 nerve root.

The other specialist then made a diagnosis of "peroneal nerve palsy." Very interesting, except that peroneal nerve palsy is quite different from a severed nerve (or nerve filaments). So is its cause. Where peroneal nerve injury immediately follows surgery, the finger of suspicion points to the O R Personnel and the charge that they failed to properly pad the patient by placing pillows at those points where the dead weight of the body will put pressure on (and damage) nerves that run close to the skin. The peroneal nerve, running along the outside of the leg near the surface of the skin, is one of those that require padding.

One might say that the plaintiff's attorney had the best of both worlds—a clear case against the hospital and against the neurosurgeon. Actually, it's a bad position to be in: one is caught in the crossfire between the two defendants and their insurance companies and two markedly different etiologies of a "foot drop." This can cause real headaches and the case will go to trial unnecessarily. Besides, the Plaintiff's attorney was sure that the neurosurgeon was correct and the physical medicine specialist was wrong. What's to be done? Before the attorney for the neurosurgeon joined the other doctor as a Third Party Defendant it was decided to take the deposition of the Rehabilitation Specialist and try to get him to admit that he was wrong. This is a little bit delicate but it can be done. Somehow, you must provide the doctor with an "out"—a good explanation. This is how it went in a 19-page deposition (again, too long). When the doctor proved cooperative, the attorney went on to discuss the problems associated with a "foot drop":

Q: Let me show you, Doctor, a letter dated June 21, 1979, and I ask you is that your signature on the letter?

A: No, that is my secretary's signature.

Q: Did you dictate the letter?

A: Yes.

Q: And is that letter true and correct?

A: Yes.

Q: Doctor, there is a diagnosis there of "left peroneal palsy." Is that your diagnosis?

A: That was Dr. Lang's diagnosis, my assistant. The other diagnosis was "status post lumbar laminectomy."

Q: Did you make a diagnosis of peroneal nerve palsy in this case?

A: I felt that he had a little more weakness than just the peroneal nerve, so I didn't feel that that was the correct diagnosis.

Q: What diagnosis do you think is correct?

A: It appears from the weakness, from one of my previous reports, the patient had more weakness in muscles that are not innervated by the peroneal nerve.

Q: What is peroneal nerve palsy?

A: Peroneal nerve palsy is impairment of the peroneal nerve and the muscles that it innervates.

Q: What causes peroneal nerve palsy?

A: Peroneal nerve palsies are most directly seen secondary to pressure.

Q: Where does the peroneal nerve run?

A: It runs from the posterior part or back part of the knee, splits off the main trunk of the sciatic nerve, splits into the peroneal nerve and the tibial nerve.

Q: So there was pressure on the right side of the leg, if one is talking about the right leg, or the left side of the leg if one is talking about the left leg. That can produce peroneal nerve palsy?

A: Yes, sir.

Q: Now, is that to be guarded against during an operation, that is, pressure on the peroneal nerve?

A: I imagine they do.

Q: And the precaution would be padding or pillowing between the extremity and a hard surface to avoid pressure. Is that correct?

A: It could be that.

Q: And lacking that padding, you could develop a peroneal nerve palsy. Is that correct?

A: If there were pressure for an extended period of time.

Q: Do you think that an hour or two hours of constant pressure would be enough to produce it?

A: That would probably give him numbness and weakness, yes.

Q: Would it produce the nerve palsy?

A: It could, yes.

Q: Doctor, you state that you don't agree with the diagnosis in that letter, Exhibit 2.

A: Yes. I think he had more than peroneal nerve palsy.

Q: Yes, you do agree or yes, you don't agree?

A: We have status post lumbar laminectomy, which I agree with.

Q: But you don't agree with the peroneal nerve palsy?

A: Yes, sir.

Q: Doctor Marks has previously testified in this case that he avulsed a filament of the L-5 nerve root? Would an avulsed filament of the L-5 nerve root produce the condition that you have observed in Mr. Grimes?

A: Well, I think that the tibial nerve or a filament from the—there is some problem with the nerve root along the spinal cord or spinal column.

Q: Let me read from Dr. Mark's testimony, Page 34. He is referring to—the question is: ''Dr. Marks, what is causing the foot drop from which Mr. Grimes suffers?'' He concludes, ''The reason that he is unable to move his foot properly is because of damage to the nerve that goes to the foot.'' Question: ''What nerve?'' Answer: ''That would be the L-5 root.'' Do you agree with that?

A: Yes.

Q: And that is the reason that Mr. Grimes is unable to move his foot properly?

A: Yes, sir.

Q: So the diagnosis of peroneal nerve palsy is incorrect, is that right?

A: Right.

As you can see, the doctor followed the questions along, changing his diagnosis, and effectively removed peroneal nerve palsy from the case.

Taking a deposition to block a theory of one's opponent should be done more often, but it's not. This seems to be difficult to explain where disadvantage lies in permitting a party to proceed with multiple theories of liability, or defense, clear up to the time of the trial when, by effective and judicious use of depositions, you can knock out one or more of these theories and concentrate on a single theory of liability or defense.

NO. 4: TO SECURE DOCUMENTS AND
GATHER INFORMATION ABOUT THEM

This is an important use of depositions and, almost by definition, it usually requires a good bit of time. The first job for the attorney is to find out the answers to the question: ''Who has the documents?'' That is easily enough done through the use of interrogatories. The second step is to subpoena the person in charge of the documents with the requirement that that person bring the documents to your office or produce them at his office. Your state law will provide you with the correct procedure.

Once the person appears with the papers your work begins. The documents first have to be identified, and then explained and discussed. If there is a small group of documents you might have the witness identify each one for the record, initially, and then go back over them for your discussion. This becomes unworkable, however, in the case of a large number of papers. As to these, it is best to identify and interrogate as you go along.

SCAN A LOT: READ A LITTLE

If you try to read every document that is produced it will soon become obvious that the deposition will drag on interminably. This is a waste of your time and that of everyone present. Now, admittedly, you won't know exactly what the witness will bring with him, but you must have a pretty good idea of the particular documents in which you are interested. A bank officer may bring signature cards, statements, checks and correspondence regarding a mix-up in an account at one time. You should know in advance that you are primarily interested in a few checks and the bank statements relating to those checks. Accordingly, you can scan everything else very quickly, setting aside only those documents that have special interest and reading them carefully. This will go a long way toward reducing the time involved in the deposition.

Another problem you may run into is that of the witness who knows most of what you are after but cannot answer, in detail, questions about some of the documents. This is normal and poses no problem. Just ask him to identify the person who does have the knowledge and plan to schedule that person for a deposition at a later date.

ALWAYS MAKE COPIES

Anytime you find a document that strikes you as "interesting" or "possibly helpful"—in addition to those you recognize as "necessary"—be sure to make a copy of it. It is surprising how often intuition tells you to copy a paper that seems innocuous at the time but that turns out to be important later on. You can always throw it away if you don't need it, whereas if you don't copy it you will be amazed how often you will remember that you once had the paper you now need but can't remember where you saw it or when you had it. Nonetheless, use good judgment and don't let this admonition be your justification for copying everything. Don't become a paper-collector.

INQUIRE IN DETAIL CONCERNING EVERY PERTINENT DOCUMENT

When you do uncover written material that is of value be sure that you interrogate as exhaustively as necessary about it. This is no time to be slipshod or in a hurry. This witness is the person who can tell you about the document, so ask about it.

A good illustration, necessarily shortened somewhat, is the following excerpt from a deposition of a witness suppoenaed to produce documents in a landslide case:

Q: Let me show you a group of documents that have been marked as Deposition Exhibit No. 20, and then you tell me what that is.

A: This is data related to the inspection and later, repair, of the Parkview Avenue Landslide, File No. 891011 for Bliss Township.

Q: Again, when you say "The Parkview Avenue Landslide" does that refer to the one that you previously mentioned?

A: Yes, it does.

Q: The same slide?

A: Yes, it does.

Q: What does the exhibit contain?

A: Quantity calculations, typical stabilization trench details, survey information, geometric calculations and, apparently, volumetric calculations associated with the Parkview Avenue Landslide project.

Q: Is there anything further in there?

A: Yes, it has correspondence, engineering drawings, and inspection reports.

[By Mr. DeMay:]

May I have the folder, please. I would like to take a moment to review these various documents.

[Mr. DeMay reviews folder-exhibit 20.]

Q: Now, Mr. Riley, the reporter has marked this letter as Exhibit 20-A. Will you look at it please. That letter appears to be signed by Mr. James Smith. Do you know Mr. Smith?

A: Yes, I do.

Q: Is the signature appearing on Exhibit 20-A that of Mr. Smith?

A: Yes, it is.

Q: This letter questions some of the calculations that were made regarding the stabilization trench, does it not?

A: Yes, it does.

Q: The calculations are contained in a series of documents, which I will have the reporter mark as Exhibit 20-B. Look at them please; did you prepare those calculations?

A: Yes, I did.

Q: Was Mr. Smith retained by your company as an independent consultant?

A: Yes.

Q: In the letter, Exhibit 20-A, Mr. Smith obviously disagrees with some of your calculations. Let's review them item by item.

*   *   *   *   *   *   *   *   *   *

[And later, by Mr. DeMay:]

Gentlemen, I would like to have copies made of the engineering drawings, Exhibits 20-D, E and F; the letter, Exhibit 20-A; and the calculations, Exhibit 20-B. There is nothing further in Exhibit 20 that I need. Mr. Brown, I will have copies made for you.

Quite obviously the important aspect of this deposition was the conflict between the engineer who made the calculations and the independent consultant. In this kind of situation you must take all the time you need to explore the matter in great detail. This could well be the crux of the lawsuit, and your careful examination of this engineer may result in your winning the case right then and there.

In this connection it is appropriate to bring up one matter about deposing persons who are specialists of one kind or another.

BE SURE THAT YOU KNOW AS MUCH AS THE WITNESS DOES ABOUT THE PRECISE MATTER UNDER DISCUSSION

This is a *must* if a deposition is to be truly effective. Gathering this knowledge is not impossible or even difficult, though it can be time-consuming. For example, you don't have to be a pilot—with a pilot's vast knowledge of flying, aerodynamics, navigation, mechanics, airplane structures, and FAA rules and regulations—to know all that can be known about one single flight maneuver that happens to be involved in your case. Similarly, in a short time, with effort, you can learn all that a medical doctor knows about the little finger of the right hand. Or, consider the proper use of high explosives; it may be an esoteric and complicated subject but if you narrow the subject matter to one explosive used under a precise set of circumstances you can match wits with any demolition expert. The key is to limit the scope of your inquiry as much as possible, read voraciously every book and article you can find on that subject, and confer with a friendly expert, absorbing all that he or she can tell you. Thus primed, you can handle any witness in a deposition. Just remember that a good definition of an expert is "one who knows a great deal about very little." Your duty is to become an expert. (As an aside, this is one of the great joys about being a trial lawyer. You learn a little bit about everything under the sun and get the opportunity to meet fascinating people. One minute, for an assumpsit case, you're trying to learn how the value of a race horse is determined and a little later, because of a botched abortion, you are studying gynecology. You will meet with a soils engineer for a landslide case, and learn the "rights" and "wrongs" of politics for a slander action. It is fascinating work, and at every step of the way you have the opportunity of becoming an expert—of learning a great deal about a very little bit of the world's affairs. It's fun, and you can be thankful you selected the law as a career.)

NO. 5: PROVING YOUR DAMAGES FOR SETTLEMENT PURPOSES

The principal obstacle in settlement negotiations is the question of liability. Perhaps it would be more apt to say that until the liability question is resolved there won't be any settlement discussion. One side has to be in the position of saying: "Look, within reason, the odds are against your winning this case. Let's talk settlement." If there is agreement on this from the other attorney, the negotiations get under way. If the damages and losses are relatively fixed as in a death case, or are easy to ascertain as in most breach of contract matters, or if they are simply not in dispute then, usually, the case settles.

There are many cases, however, in which settlement is held up because some aspect of the damages claim cannot be accepted by one side and will not be given up by the other:

1. An injured mechanic claims that despite his recovery, medically, he cannot work as long or as well as he did before the accident.

2. A self-employed building contractor suffers the loss of his business in a fire. He claims that his business would have escalated in volume during the time he spent rebuilding or reestablishing himself elsewhere.

3. A plaintiff department store claims that non-delivery of football memorabilia and trinkets caused it to lose money because it had to cancel a Super-Bowl promotion.

4. An actress claims to have lost lucrative roles due to the negligent scarring of her face by a plastic surgeon and the necessity for a new operation and a long recovery period.

The common theme running through these claims is genuine doubt, or legitimate concern, that the plaintiff did lose anything because of the event for which defendent concedes liability. Would the actress have gotten one of those juicy roles? Would any shoppers have come to the department store because of the Super Bowl promotion? Why would the business of the building contractor have theoretically increased during the months it took him to get back into business?

These are legitimate questions for any defendant to ask. If they are not answered satisfactorily there may well be no settlement.

Unfortunately many plaintiffs rely solely on the statement of their clients and a lot of shouting to resolve the issue. Quite obviously the defendant—or his insurance company—will not accept the word of the plaintiff and as for the shouting—that's always a waste of time.

The simple solution is to take the deposition of those persons who can cast some light on the problem and bring it to a quick resolution. You will have to produce these people at trial in any event; why not do it now to convince the other side that the claim is valid and get the case settled? Take our actress—if you will depose the casting director or producer you will find out directly whether, if she were to have auditioned, she would have gotten the roles. In the case of the injured mechanic, depose his co-workers, and especially his boss, to prove that he is working at only about 60 percent of the level that he had attained before the accident. As far as the building contractor is concerned, he must belong to a trade association and the executive director of that organization can probably give you facts and figures to prove that your client lost work in one of the best six-month periods of the decade. Take his deposition!

When the opposing side holds a transcript of testimony, given under oath, and the witness having been subject to examination by his own attorney, which states that your claimant has really suffered a loss, there is no longer any good reason for denying the claim. At this juncture there can be no good argument that the Plaintiff is exaggerating the loss or that the loss cannot be proven. The transcript answers all of the questions.

In like manner if the transcript is filled with negative comments to the effect that the actress had only a slim chance to get one of the roles, or the builder overlooked the effects of a strike in the lumber industry during the months his business was closed, then it is time for the Plaintiff to reappraise his position.

Either way the settlement process is helped and an obstacle is removed from a sensible approach to the negotiations.

The key to success is the use of depositions. You must remember that sometimes you take a deposition *not to gain* facts for yourself but *to tell* facts to the other side.

CHOOSING THE CORRECT WITNESS

If your purpose is to convince a skeptical opponent that your damages are valid, you had better give a little thought to the type of person you are going to depose. If your client is the injured mechanic who claims that he cannot work as well or as long as he used to, don't bother trying to prove this through a relative or a buddy. Their comments will receive no respect. Instead, use a co-worker who is not a close friend, the foreman, and, possibly, the plant manager or division supervisor. The word of these men will be believed. If your client was the owner of a small business, try to use a competitor to testify to the great season your client was obliged to miss.

The key to success is choosing those witnesses who can be objective and knowledgeable. These are the people your adversary will be most inclined to believe and who will have the most influence with the personnel at the home office of the insurance company.

KEEP THE DEPOSITION BRIEF AND TO THE POINT

This is another instance in which you can forego miscellaneous and background questions. It matters not at all how many children the deponent has or whether he or she is married. The witness' educational background has nothing to do with the issues and it makes little difference whether he or she drives a car or is in good health. Don't ask these mundane, routine, boring, irrelevant questions that simply drag out the deposition and add to the cost (unless the reporter is a good friend who has come on hard times and needs the money). Concentrate, instead, solely on the experience of the deponent in the job or business involved in your case, his knowledge of your client, and his awareness that your client suffered the claimed loss. Probably no deposition of this kind should take more than 20 minutes unless records or statistics must be gone into.

Remember—keep it brief and to the point.

NO. 6: DEVELOPING FACTS FOR THE PURPOSE OF FILING A COMPLAINT

Many states do not permit Notice Pleading, and in those jurisdictions the Plaintiff's attorney has always been in a difficult position in terms of filing a complaint. He doesn't know enough facts to file a detailed complaint and yet there is no legal process provided wherein he can learn the facts before filing a complaint.

Some states have addressed this problem by permitting the Plaintiff's attorney to invoke discovery—and especially depositions—for the purpose of gathering the facts needed to file a Complaint.

This authorization permits the Plaintiff's attorney to engage in what is essentially a legitimate "fishing expedition." There is no other term to describe it.

The attorney knows many facts through his conferences with his client, and others by virtue of investigation. But there will be many gaps in his knowledge and these can be filled through the judicious use of depositions.

This is a salutary procedure which not only helps you to build your case but sometimes even reveals that you don't have a case and should not file a complaint at all.

There is no special technique or approach that is specific to this objective; indeed you will be taking depositions for all the reasons that have been previously discussed—i. e., to gather documents, to learn very specific facts, and even to depose the opposition and possibly win the case before you have even filed a complaint. These depositions will be for a fact-gathering purpose, and all of the admonitions previously mentioned must be applied to each deposition.

SUMMARY

It is crucial that you have a specific purpose, a goal, an objective in taking a deposition. Only then will you be able to prepare an outline and frame your questions carefully and with purpose. Take the time to analyze your case, keeping in mind that the deposition will be a waste of time unless you have the objective squarely before you.

Remember the following points:

The Six Major Objectives of a Successful Deposition

1. *To Win the Case*
   This deposition must be lengthy, detailed and carefully planned. You must know every aspect of the case.

2. *To Learn Specific Facts*
   The deponent will be an objective person. Keep the deposition short and to the point. Get the information you need and quit.

3. *Blocking a Theory or Defense of Your Opponent*
   The witness may be a party or an outside observer. Take your time, know

your opponent's theory well and direct your questions to knocking it out of the case.

4. *Searching for Documents and an Explanation of Them*
   Usually this is going to be laborious and time consuming. Don't rush. Make everything an exhibit, scan them quickly, question on the important one.

5. *Prove Your Damages for Settlement Purposes*
   You're trying to convince a skeptic—your opponent. Try to use objective witnesses who have no axe to grind. Get to the point. Avoid irrelevant, routine questions.

6. *To Learn Facts for the Purpose of Filing a Complaint*
   This goal is going to combine attributes of each of the five objectives outlined above.

———————— PART III—SETTING THE SCENE ————————

SOME HELPFUL ADVICE CONCERNING WHERE A DEPOSITION SHOULD BE TAKEN

It may come as a surprise to some to learn that the place at which a deposition is taken is a very important part of the procedure. Many lawyers feel that the setting is insignificant—a trifle. In this they are wrong. While the matter may not be monumental in nature, it *is* significant. Consider the large number of deponents—doctors, corporate officers and governmental bureaucrats—who insist that the deposition be taken in their office. The reason is simple: they are in familiar surroundings; you are not. They are lounging in their comfortable chairs while you squirm in a straight-backed one. They can lean confidently across their own desks while you are forced to apologetically clear away a corner of it on which to place your tablet. When your questions become embarrassing, or deal with sensitive subjects, they can always think of some important matter to justify excusing themselves and leaving the room for a few minutes to collect their thoughts. If they were in your office under identical circumstances, where would they go? Then there is the matter of the telephone and the secretary. Both spell interruptions and trouble. In every case the interruption is an "important" one. Strangely there are never any trivial telephone calls received during a deposition, and secretaries never interrupt for routine matters. The call is always urgent and the interruption necessary. The tip-off is when the secretary steals into the room, disrupts your questioning respectfully and whispers in a husky voice: "Doctor, it's Mrs. Jones on the phone and I really think you ought to talk to her," or, "Mr. Smith, it's Mr. White in London calling." You might damn the hypocrisy and phoniness of it all, but blame yourself first for getting into the predicament. Why did you let it happen?

Under the Civil Rules of most jurisdictions, and as a matter of practice nearly everywhere, depositions are taken in one of two places:

1. In the office of the attorney scheduling the deposition, or
2. At the courthouse of the county in which the deponent resides.

If anyone is going to be relaxed, comfortable and in friendly surroundings, let it be you; on the other hand, if the surroundings are to be strange and difficult let it be so for everyone.

Insofar as possible let the deposition be taken in your office. That is your home, so to speak, and is the place where you control the secretary, the telephone and, since for them it is an unfamiliar area, the movements of the other persons present.

Since it is your desk you can spread out your papers wherever you please and can arrange the furniture as you will.

PLAN THE SEATING ARRANGEMENT

There are certain things to remember—for example, the seating of the court reporter. That good person has to be in a position to hear well. Can you imagine anything worse than to have elicited a crucial answer only to have the reporter speak up, "I didn't get that," and then have the witness realize that he committed an error, and fudge on the answer when he repeats it? Don't let this happen. Place the reporter somewhere between you and the witness so that he or she can clearly hear both of you.

Second, place the witness directly across the desk from you if you can. If you are in a room in the courthouse, for example, don't get either too far away or too close. If the witness is immediately beside you, or very close by, a chummy atmosphere is created which makes it difficult to ask intimidating or embarrassing questions.

It's just as hard to be at the end of a 10- or 12-foot table with the witness at the other end. Here one loses contact with the witness and there is endless repetition of, "I didn't hear you," or, "What did you say?" Usually those questions are asked only to give the witness time to think of an answer, but the distance provides a convenient excuse.

The ideal is to be about four or five feet away. At this distance you are close enough to observe the witness' facial expressions for tell-tale signs of evasiveness or lying; you hear clearly and yet you are far enough away so that you are not shy about asking tough questions.

The remainder of those attending can sit almost anywhere else as long as they do not get between you and either the witness or the court reporter.

Finally, in general, no two witnesses should be in the room while the deposition of one is taken. This is not too important if they are to testify to entirely independent unrelated matters, but if, to any degree, they are to testify about the same subject matter, they must be separated.

THE "HOWs" AND "WHYs" OF ASKING QUESTIONS

The phrasing of a question is always important in the sense that the witness has to understand what you are after. It is doubly important if you are trying to force the witness to give a damaging answer. Therefore, you have to devote some time and thought to determine how and when you are going to ask critical questions.

In most depositions, those whose objective is only to nail down a specific fact, to interrogate about documents, to prove an item of damages, or to block a defense or theory of the other side, your concern is to be clear and understandable. The questions in these depositions will come easily to you and you can follow a logical sequence of moving from fact to fact as the situation requires until you have completed your examination.

However, when you are deposing for the purpose of winning the case, or are confronted with a witness you know will be hostile, some definite skill and planning are called for. Let's think about this for a few moments:

HOW WILL YOU APPROACH THE WITNESS?

Remember that you set the tone of the deposition. You can be witty, make a pal of the witness, and get him to "confidentially but frankly" admit that he was wrong. On the other hand you can be formal, somewhat indignant, and, metaphorically, bludgeon the witness into admitting his actions were incorrect or improper. Third, you can use a pedantic approach and from the position of a teacher vis-à-vis his student secure an acknowledgment that as a matter of logic the acts of the witness were indefensible.

The keys to the selection of the appropriate attitude on your part are the personality, education and character of the witness. A frightened, nervous, uneducated witness will often succumb to very sharp, angry, direct questioning—but don't try that on the president of a substantial corporation. Most experts—architects, engineers, doctors, automobile mechanics—will respond favorably to a scholarly approach, provided you know what you are talking about and the evidence is reasonably clear that they are in the wrong. The friendly, cheerful approach works best with anyone who is calm and relaxed and with whom you can establish a rapport very quickly. Salesmen, most women, lawyers—gregarious people—fall into this category. Your task is to appraise the witness during the few minutes that you meet before the deposition begins and with your first series of questions. After you get a "feel" for the type of person you are dealing with, then you can adjust your approach to secure the most favorable responses possible.

SELECT THE RIGHT TIME TO ASK THE MOST DEVASTATING QUESTIONS

Timing is a very important element in securing answers that will win your lawsuit. They should never—well, hardly ever—be asked at the beginning of the deposition. Nearly all your crucial interrogation should be presented in the latter one-third of the deposition. The beginning questions should be used to gauge the character and personality of the witness. Then there should follow a series of questions designed to gather facts and to begin to narrow the ring. You should build up to the probing questions yet to come. At this point you will have a clear idea of the type of person you are dealing with and you can begin to needle him with some tough interrogation. Following this you might back off a little or change the subject and resume collecting facts that aren't too important. Let the witness relax and lower his guard for awhile. Then, come back strong with the sharp, decisive, rough and tough questioning. This should be about two-thirds of the way through the deposition, and literally it's a now or never situation. If you are ever going to force and secure a damaging answer, this is the time it is most likely to occur.

BE BLUNT AND FORTHRIGHT WITH YOUR CRUCIAL QUESTIONS

The general public always worries about trick questions from lawyers. If they have a place at all in legal proceedings—and that is debatable—the place is the courtroom setting. It is only there that the unintended, damaging answer, and the confusion surrounding a trick question (objections by your opponent, attempted retraction by the witness), can have their intended dramatic effect.

This doesn't work well in a deposition. There is no jury present. The testimony is going to be transcribed, and when the opposing attorney and the witness get together to review it they will be able to figure out all kinds of ways to evade, or minimize the effects of, the answer you get to a trick question. In addition—insofar as settlement is concerned—no one on the other side is going to be impressed with the answer. You are going to be met with nothing but argument about your tactics (or ethics) and there will be precious little discussion of the facts that you elicited. Don't use this technique.

If you want a solid damaging answer that you can really use either in court of for settlement purposes, then ask a blunt, direct question that will draw forth the answer. Don't be cute, be candid.

This is the time to say:

Doctor, didn't you err when you prescribed this medication?

Mr. Architect, aren't your calculations mistaken regarding the strength of that steel beam?

Mr. Jones, isn't it true that you were looking at a sexy billboard, and not the road, when this accident happened?

Mr. President of ABC Corporation, since the profits of all your competitors dropped during the six months in questions, isn't it reasonable to conclude that your profits would have decreased in the same period?

You need the answers to these questions if you are to be successful, and there is no nice, easy, sugar-coated way to ask them. If you have done your job in appraising the witness and in "setting him up" for these tough questions, then you stand a very good chance of getting the answer you want. It might be that you will ask the question very quietly, or you may slip it into the general run of interrogation in a surprising manner, but, one way or the other, ask the question in a frank manner.

REMEMBER THESE CAUTIONS

1. Plan Your Approach to the Witness.

   Be a pal; or

   Be formal, tough, angry; or

   Adopt the role of a teacher vis-à-vis a student.

2. Select the Right Time to Ask Tough Questions.

   Do so in the middle or the latter portion of the procedure.

   Study the witness.

Build up to a climax—ask sharp questions, then back off.

Come back hard with the crucial question.

3. Let Your Critical Questions Be Blunt Ones.

Avoid trick questions

Don't try to sugar-coat the pill.

Get clear, definite answers to tough, positive questions.

PART IV—SUMMARY

- A deposition is your most powerful, and versatile, discovery tool.
- You must plan it carefully—treat it as a mini-trial.
- Take charge of the deposition from the beginning.
- Know your objective in taking the deposition:
  1. To win the case.
  2. To prove an essential fact.
  3. To block a defense or theory of your opponent.
  4. To secure documents and gather information about them.
  5. To prove your damages for settlement.
  6. To develop facts needed to file a Complaint.
- Prepare an outline and write out important questions.
- Remember that a witness:
  1. Does not know the law;
  2. Does not know all the facts that you know;
  3. Is nervous, apprehensive and uncertain;
  4. Will answer honestly.
- Develop only the information you need; don't ramble.
- Take the deposition in your office.
- Watch the seating arrangement.
- Plan your questioning:
  1. Appraise the witness.
  2. Vary your approach with the character of the witness.
  3. Select the right time to ask tough questions.
  4. Make your crucial questions blunt and direct ones.

If you will follow these rules you can win your cases with depositions. Alternatively, if you are not completely successful, you will develop a substantial quantity of facts and documents that will help you to win the case at trial—and a trial that can be substantially shorter in time than would otherwise be necessary.

6

Requests for Admissions: Forcing Your Opponent to Admit Crucial Facts

Pursuant to the provisions of Rule 36 of the Federal Rules of Civil Procedure, *you* are requested to admit the following statements of fact:

1. You have not filed Requests for Admissions once in the past five years.

   Answer: _____ ?

2. You have never tried to win a case by using Requests for Admissions in conjunction with a Motion for Summary Judgment.

   Answer: _____ ?

3. You have not used Requests for Admissions to establish the authenticity of Documents.

   Answer: _____ ?

4. You have not tried to use Requests for Admissions to establish facts that will be laborious to prove at trial.

   Answer: _____ ?

Of the readers of this book, fully 95 percent will have to answer each of those Requests with the answer "Admitted." That is wrong. It's hardly a consolation to know that you have plenty of company. The failure to use Requests for Admissions is a tribute to lethargy and a lack of imagination on the part of most lawyers. Don't go with the current—change it! Use your imagination and a little effort and with this important legal tool win your case!

Just recently a Case Report appeared in the local Legal Journal which showed how a diligent and attentive attorney won his case through the effective use of Requests for Admission combined with a Motion for Summary Judgment.

WINNING A CASE FOR THE DEFENSE

It seems that Mr. William White was involved in an automobile accident on September 23, 1981. It was his fault, and shortly thereafter claims for property damage and personal injury were filed against him. He submitted them to his insurance company and was told that the insurance had expired. Quite outraged, Mr. White sued his agent, the Crown Agency, claiming it was all their fault. The Crown Agency then joined the Foresight Insurance Company as a Third Party Defendant, alleging that they had placed the insurance with Foresight and thereafter stepped out of the picture, that Foresight was to have billed White directly, and that all notices and correspondence were between Foresight and White.

At this point the attorney for Foresight was apparently deluged by his client with all kinds of documentary proof and they wanted out of the case! The question was how to best use the information he had and the facts that he knew to be true. He could take a deposition of White but it's possible that the gentleman could evade a direct answer and leave him without anything definite with which to get out of the case. Interrogatories were not quite appropriate since they are primarily a discovery tool and he already had the facts that he needed. Instead he elected to serve these Requests for Admissions:

REQUEST FOR ADMISSIONS
DIRECTED TO WILLIAM WHITE, PLAINTIFF

AND NOW comes the defendant herein, Foresight Insurance Company, by its attorneys, Jones & Smith, P. A., and requests that the plaintiff admit to the following:

1. That on or about January 18, 1981, the plaintiff, William White, purchased through the Crown Agency a policy of insurance written by the Foresight Insurance Company which ran from January 18, 1981 until July 17, 1981.

Answer: _____ ?

2. That the declaration sheet of said Foresight Insurance Company stated that, if renewed, each successive policy renewal period shall be six (6) calendar months.

Answer: _____ ?

3. That the plaintiff, William White, paid to Crown Agency a sum of money sufficient to cover the six (6) month premium for the Foresight Insurance Com-

pany policy which is the subject of this lawsuit, purchased from Crown on January 18, 1981.

Answer: _____ ?

4. That said policy, if not renewed, would terminate on July 17, 1981.

Answer: _____ ?

5. That on June 20, 1981, Foresight Insurance Company sent to William White, 1234 Carol Drive, Pittsburgh, Pennsylvania, a notice, offering to renew the Foresight Insurance Company policy only if the required premium was paid directly to the company before the effective date of the policy which was July 17, 1981.

Answer: _____ ?

6. That prior to July 17, 1981, William White did not pay to the Foresight Insurance Company any additional premium aside from the $190.00 paid by White to Crown in January of 1981.

Answer: _____ ?

7. That on or before July 17, 1981, William White did not pay $223.00 to Foresight Insurance Company or any other sum of money sufficient to renew said policy from July 17, 1981 until January 17, 1982.

Answer: _____ ?

8. That during July of 1981, the defendant, Foresight Insurance Company, sent to, and William White received a termination notice indicating that said policy had been cancelled for lack of payment.

Answer: _____ ?

9. That in August of 1981, Foresight Insurance Company sent to and William White received a final termination notice indicating that the policy had been cancelled for nonpayment of premium on July 17, 1981.

Answer: _____ ?

> Respectfully Submitted,
>
> JONES & SMITH, P.A.
>
> By _____
>
> Steve Smith, Esquire
> Attorney for Foresight Insurance
> Company

Upon receipt of these Requests, Plaintiff's Counsel apparently realized he had a problem. He did not answer the Requests within the original time period or an extension thereof. So the defense attorney filed a Motion for Summary Judgment arguing that the Requests must be accepted as admitted and that based on those facts Foresight Insurance Company was entitled to the Summary Judgment.

The Court agreed. It began its Opinion by stating "the facts as admitted on the record are that" and then quoted from the Requests for Admissions. It then concluded with the statement: "Based upon those undisputed facts, there is no question for the finder of fact and Summary Judgment is appropriate in this action."

Chalk up a winner for a good defense attorney and his sagacious use of Requests for Admissions.

WINNING A CASE FOR THE PLAINTIFF

Another case in which Requests for Admissions were effectively used by a Plaintiff's attorney was one in which a woman went to the hospital for a hysterectomy. Prior to the operation she was given a routine injection in the left arm. Almost immediately a large reddened area appeared at the injection site. It was noted but ignored by the hospital personnel. Suffice it to say that eventually the area became necrotic and an operation had to be performed which left her with a saucer-shaped depression in the upper portion of her arm. When her lawyer conducted an investigation he learned that the preoperative injection consisted of three medications—Demerol, Atropine, and Vistaril. If you will check the Physicians Desk Reference (PDR), which every attorney who handles medical malpractice cases must have, you will note that Vistaril is a powerful and somewhat dangerous drug. It must be given intramuscularly; if given just under the skin (subcutaneously) real troubles can occur. In the case in point, the lady had troubles.

Now at this stage consider the position of the Plaintiff's attorney. The hospital records established the injection of the drug; the PDR (a standard, recognized text) gave him his proof as to the dangers associated with the use of the drug; the obvious condition of the client plus the subsequent hospital records gave him the required proof regarding the end result.

All that was left was to prove the requisite knowledge on the part of the Defendant hospital and its personnel. One might utilize Interrogatories and a deposition of the nurse involved. The interrogatories, however, give the opposition a chance to be vague and indefinite and, as to the deposition, the nurse will either not remember the incident or will insist that she did everything right. Then the Defendant, or the insurance company, will argue that they have to "take her word" and will balk at settlement. Better to leave certain things off the record. The neat, tidy way to handle this situation is to serve Requests for Admissions and that was done:

REQUESTS FOR ADMISSIONS

Pursuant to the provisions of Rule 4104 of the Rules of Civil Procedure the Defendant is required to admit the following:

1. On April 27, 1981 Jean Riley was a patient in the State University Hospital.

Answer: Admitted.

2. She was operated upon on that date.

Answer: Admitted.

3. At 9:30 A.M. on that day she was given a preoperative injection.

Answer: Admitted.

4. This preoperative injection consisted of three medications, including Vistaril.

Answer: Admitted.

5. At 10:45 A.M. a large reddened area was noted at the site of the preoperative injection.

Answer: Denied. The operative record indicates "large reddened area, left forearm (site of preop injection) noted." The site of the preoperative injection was not, however, the left forearm, but rather the left deltoid area.

6. This defendant knows that Vistaril can cause severe irritation and local reaction which can lead to skin necrosis.

Answer: Defendant is a corporation and therefore has no "knowledge" other than the knowledge of its agents or employees. Defendant therefore objects to this request for admission because it is not directed to the knowledge of any specific agent or employee of the defendant.

7. Proper nursing procedure requires that Vistaril be injected intramuscularly.

Answer: It is admitted that P.D.R. instructions indicate that Vistaril is to be administered intramuscularly. It is denied, however, that nonintramuscular injections of vistaril necessarily imply improper nursing procedure.

8. Vistaril, given subcutaneously, causes irritation and local reaction which can lead to skin necrosis.

Answer: Defendant is a corporation and therefore has no "knowledge" other than the knowledge of its agents or employees. Defendant therefore objects to this request for admission because it is not directed to the knowledge of any specific agent or employee of the defendant.

Note the evasive answers to questions 6 and 8. You will run into this from time to time. There is no alternative but to force the issue by filing a Motion to Compel Answers which, in nearly every instance, will be granted and the answers will come back "admitted."

With this information in hand, what is left to try in Court? The nurse could testify until she is blue in the face that she definitely gave the shot intramuscularly but the facts clearly show that she did not. It is practically unheard of to give Vistaril intramuscularly and get a reaction like this. How would it extravasate back to the skin? It had to have been given—probably hurriedly and negligently—subcutaneously.

Fortunately the defense attorney did not have to face the sworn testimony of the nurse via a deposition that she had acted properly so there was no formal impediment on the record (which can sometimes be embarrassing) to his candidly admitting that the nurse had to have made an error here. Thus a very good settlement was effected—and this within a relatively short time after the lawsuit was filed. Think of the savings in time, energy and money! There was no trial here, and no waiting for two years or so to conclude the case. It took the Plaintiff's attorney a matter of hours to review the records and the PDR, to confer with an expert, to prepare the Requests for Admissions, and to negotiate with the defense attorney. Then the case was over and successfully concluded.

These two illustrations, from both the Plaintiff's and the Defendant's point of view, show what you can do with this discovery tool. To be sure, you cannnot use it effectively in every case. It has its own limitations. But you should not forget about it entirely as so many attorneys seem to do. Let us consider the manner in which you can best utilize this technique.

USE REQUESTS FOR ADMISSION WHEN:

1. You can *nail down* specific crucial facts and you intend to follow with a Motion for Summary Judgment.

2. You have *numerous documents* to be admitted into evidence and want the other side to admit their authenticity.

3. You want to *establish certain facts* that you believe to be uncontested but which would be laborious to prove at trial.

USING REQUESTS FOR ADMISSIONS TO WIN YOUR CASE

This can be done, and the effort should be made much more often than it is at present. Requests for Admissions are really in the category of a ''forgotten'' discovery technique. You should begin to think of using this device to win your case most often in Assumpsit cases, Decedent's Estates matters, Land Condemnation cases, or those involving disputes over title to land and other cases in which dates, statistics, and documents will be the primary basis for winning rather than Trespass, Custody, Support, Divorce, or similar cases in which there are wildly divergent concepts of facts and inferences to be drawn from them. Admittedly you cannot often use Requests to win a case but you have to be aware of the fact that it can be done and you have to pick and choose the case in which you attempt it. Usually these will be cases in which there is little opinion or judgment involved and those cases in which the facts, if developed and organized properly, can push your opponent into a corner from which there is no escape. Those kinds of situations most usually occur in Assumpsit cases wherein your opponent can be forced to admit certain inescapable facts because they are a matter of record somewhere or they are contained in pertinent documents. For example, one cannot quarrel, easily, about the postmark on a letter evidencing the date of mailing, monthly production figures of a foundry, a report submitted under OSHA, an itemized income tax return, employment records or a Schedule of Benefits payable under an insurance policy. Where these facts are crucial, and especially when they come from you opponent's own records by way of a Motion for Production, you had better look carefully at your case to see whether you can set up your opponent for the "coup de grace" by preparing a Request for Admissions to be followed by a Motion for Summary Judgment.

You know that many lawsuits for breach of contract exist solely because one party stubbornly refuses to look at the facts as they are rather than as he or she remembers, or thinks, them to be, and rationalizes his or her position by all manner of emotional and irrelevant justifications for refusing to pay or perform under a contract. Sometimes the client is trying to "sneak one through"; usually the client is just angry at the opposition for some irrelevant reason and refuses to abide by the terms of the contract; and finally, some clients are simply forgetful or insist, "I never received that paper in time," or "we never made that much money." If you have the data—either directly from your client or developed through other Discovery techniques—then you can prepare Requests for Admissions that go to the very heart of the case. What is the other attorney to do? He must answer, won't let the client lie about the matter, and when he confronts him or her with the facts, that person has no alternative but to admit them. This client may still insist upon placing a peculiar interpretation on these facts, but once you have the answers you can file your Motion for Summary Judgment and more times than not you will get it because the Court will construe the facts in their ordinary sense.

More usually, however, when a recalcitrant client is forced to answer the Requests—and face the facts in their starkest form—he or she will, however reluctantly, begin to be more realistic and you will be on your way to a good settlement.

Consider a case for a commission on certain insurance premiums. The arrangement was that as a bank gave loans to its customers they were to be insured through the defendant insurance company. Plaintiff, in the contract, was named General Agent for the insurance company and was authorized to solicit credit insurance on the lines of debtors of the bank. It was a great arrangement for the General Agent, who worked aggressively with the bank and began to make a lot of money. When the plan began to work smoothly and profitably, the insurance company decided to cut out the General Agent and deal directly with the bank. There was a lot of money involved here and the General Agent filed suit. The Insurance company tried to challenge the contract (by evidence outside its plain terms) and also relied on a certain Letter of Termination it sent to the General Agent which was never accepted by him. By means of normal discovery procedures the pertinent contract (and two older ones Defendant kept talking about) were secured, the Defendant's copy of the Letter of Termiantion was produced, and gross sales during the relevant time period was secured. With these in hand, counsel for Plaintiff then prepared the following Requests for Admissions:

IN THE DISTRICT COURT OF THE UNITED STATES FOR
THE WESTERN DISTRICT OF PENNSYLVANIA

CAPITAL INSURANCE AGENCY, INC.)
a Pennsylvania Corporation)
Plaintiff,)
v.) Civil Action No. 81-1234
WESTERN NATIONAL INSURANCE)
COMPANY, a Delaware Corporation)
Defendant.)

REQUESTS FOR ADMISSIONS

To: WESTERN NATIONAL INSURANCE COMPANY, Defendant, and John P. Smith, Esquire, its attorney:

You are hereby requested, pursuant to rule 36 of the Federal Rules of Civil Procedure, to admit, for the purposes of this lawsuit only, the truth of the following statements:

1. Plaintiff's Exhibits 1, 2, and 3 attached to Plaintiff's Complaint constitute the Contracts between the Parties hereto during the period December 1, 1978, and the present time.

Answer: Admitted.

2. Plaintiff's Exhibit 3 constitutes the Contract that is the subject matter of this lawsuit.

Answer: Admitted.

3. That Exhibit 3 is the only Contract in effect between the parties hereto during the period of October 1, 1979 (its effective date) and the present time.

Answer: Admitted.

4. That between October 1, 1979 and April 1, 1980, Defendant paid commissions to Plaintiff on all Life Insurance Policies and all Disability Insurance Policies written through the Southwest Pennsylvania Bank.

Answer: Admitted.

5. That the letter which is set forth below (Exhibit 4) is the only letter sent by Defendant or Southwest Pennsylvania Bank to Plaintiff relating to the subject of termination of the contract of October 1, 1979.

EXHIBIT 4

WESTERN NATIONAL INSURANCE COMPANY
784 McKenzie Avenue
Wilmington, Deleware

Capital Insurance Agency, Inc.
567 Elgin Avenue
Pittsburgh, Pa.

April 8, 1980

GENTLEMEN:

On October 1, 1979, a General Agent's Contract was entered into between Western National Insurance Company and Capital Insurance Agency, Inc., wherein Capital Insurance Agency, Inc., was granted as General Agent to solicit Credit Insurance on the lives of debtors of Southwest Pennsylvania Bank, Pittsburgh, Pa.

Under the provisions of its paragraph seven, written notice is hereby given that by mutual consent this contract is to be termined as of the first day of April, 1980.

Your written acknowledgment of this termination by signature and return of one copy of this letter will be sincerely appreciated.

Sincerely,

_____

J.R. Smith

JRS/cb
Attachment
Acknowledged by: _____
Capital Insurance, Inc.

Answer: Admitted.

6. The Plaintiff never signed, nor returned, that letter to Defendant, nor any copy thereof.

Answer: Admitted.

7. That Plaintiff has been paid no commissions by Defendant since April 1, 1980.

Answer: Admitted.

8. That Defendant, since April 1, 1980, has grossed a total of $1,285,942.80 is insurance premiums on the life insurance policies and disability policies written through Southwest Pennsylvania Bank.

Answer: Admitted.

Respectfully Submitted,

_____

Attorney for Plaintiff

I am sure the defense attorney knew the game was over as soon as he sat down with his client to prepare the answers. It was clear that Exhibit 3 was the only pertinent Contract, that it required the General Agent's consent to terminate, and that the Letter of Termination (Exhibit 4) was never signed or accepted in any way by the Plaintiff. The Insurance Company could yell, scream, be stubborn, feel "robbed," shout defiance—in short, pull any tantrum it pleased—but the facts were there staring it in the face. There was no place to go. For the Plaintiff it was simply a matter of computing his percentage of $1,285,942.80 and deciding how much of a break, if any, he wanted to give the Defendant in a settlement, and that is what happened.

Once again—there was no trial required, no lengthy delay, and no endless work on the part of counsel for Plaintiff. But it did take a conscious recognition of the fact that this case could be won with Requests for Admissions. That is the area in which many attorneys fail; they lack the "conscious recognition" of what can be done with Requests for Admission and when to use them. You should permanently lock in the back of your mind the realization that you can win a case with Requests for Admissions and constantly be on the lookout for those cases in which this device can be effectively used. They work! But you have to know your case, analyze it carefully, and decide whether this particular case is one that can be brought to a quick conclusion by this method.

USE REQUESTS FOR ADMISSIONS TO ESTABLISH
THE AUTHENTICITY OF RECORDS

In this day and age we are all getting more cases that involve large numbers of exhibits. These cases are usually class-action matters, Civil Rights cases, Antitrust actions, Assumpsit cases, and even some Support matters. Anytime one gets involved in a case in which there is a multiplicity of parties, or a case involving records of an industrial company or a financial institution or a governmental unit, one is going to have 101 pieces of paper (or 1001) that have to be admitted into evidence. It's true that at some point you could sit down with your adversary and prepare a Stipulation Concerning Exhibits, but that gets cumbersome since it means trying to arrange a meeting and toting a box of papers to his or her office and then reviewing them one by one and making a decision at that time. More importantly, perhaps, many attorneys (including your adversary?) begin to get nervous and feel that they are being put on the spot if you ask them to stipulate to the exhibits. If they agree to something and it later turns out badly for some reason, they are the ones who will catch it from the client. It is far better, in this view, to serve a Request for Admissions, attach the documents to the Request (or deliver them separately if they are bulky), and then the attorney can refer them to the client for answer. It that way it is the client who signs the Answers saying that he agrees with the Request, and the documents can be reviewed in a more leisurely manner. And, if the client obstinately refuses to admit the authenticity (or whatever) of the documents and, later, the Court imposes sanctions under the Rule, the attorney cannot be blamed for the problem.

As you can see, the choice of routes for you to follow is often controlled by the self-confidence of your adversary and his or her relationship and modus operandi with his or her client.

At any rate if you will adopt this procedure you will find that a large number of your documents will definitely be acknowledged as authentic, thus saving a considerable amount of time at trial. As to the remainder, you might be able to meet with counsel, explain your purposes in using the document, and get him to agree to some of them, and only a small balance will be left to be proven at trial.

This is a great time saver. It need not be the kind of thing you utilize solely when you have a host of papers; you can use it effectively even with a small number of exhibits and should get into the habit of doing so. Even if your documents consist only of a weather report, police report, hospital record and a few bills, it is advantageous to get the opposing party committed to their authenticity at an early stage so that there is one less matter for you to worry about. As you well know, in the preparation of a lawsuit there are so many things to do—research, discovery, directing investigation, meeting with clients and witnesses, fighting with doctors and other experts to get their reports, dealing with opposing attorneys—that the sooner you can get one matter firmly and finally in place the better off you are. Which leads to another use of Requests for Admissions.

USE REQUESTS FOR ADMISSIONS TO ESTABLISH
NECESSARY BUT UNDISPUTED FACTS

In every case there are literally a host of facts which might be described as "nuisance but necessary" cluttering up your file and your mind. Most of the time we tend not to do much about them, figuring that at trial time we will get the opposing counsel to stipulate to them or just have any old witness testify to them. Most of the time that's just the way it happens, but once in a while we forget, opposing counsel suddenly gets obnoxious (maybe because you just offended him), or the Court gets hypertechnical—and bam! you find yourself in the embarrassing position of not being able to prove some little, but important, fact. Sure, usually you can wriggle out of this jam but why get into it in the first place? There are all kinds of facts like these:

● The kind of car the opposing party was driving.
● The time an operation began and ended.
● The last date an airplane engine was inspected.
● The Social Security number of a decedent.
● The quantity of goods delivered under a prior contract.
● The Civil Action Number and date of filing of a related lawsuit.
● The price of a particular stock on the New York Stock Exchange on a certain date.
● The date a deed was filed.

I'm sure you will agree that there are dozens of facts of a similar nature that you usually don't go to any great effort to prove. Yet they have to nag at you, and I consider that one reason so many lawyers suffer from ulcers is that they don't nail these things down once and for all. That, and procrastination. It's far better—and it will ease your mind—to list these facts in an orderly manner, prepare a Request for Admissions as to them, get the other side to admit them, and then you can forget about them. It's that much less to worry about. At trial time all you have to do is to pick up the document and read the facts into the record.

A FEW "DONT'S" REGARDING REQUESTS FOR
ADMISSIONS

There are certain things that this legal tool cannot do for you. It is not a good investigation device, for example. You can't easily use Requests to search for facts or to "snoop" through your opponent's files. It lacks the inquisitiveness of

Interrogatories and the flexibility of depositions. Perhaps it's even wrong to call it a "discovery" tool since it comes into its own after discovery and is designed to summarize in a relatively concise form those facts which you already know and which are sufficiently definite that your opponent will admit them. Which leads to another point:

Don't Ask Two Questions in One.

Asking two questions in one leads to confusion and confusion leads to evasion and avoidance. For example, suppose you were to state: "The defendant was coming from a bank and was on his way to a department store."

The first part of this statement might well be true and the second part false. Don't expect your opposing counsel to do your work for you in separating the wheat from the chaff in your statements of fact. Keep them short, direct and simple. One fact per statement.

Don't Use Long, Convoluted Statements.

"On June 16, 1981, the Plaintiff withdrew $2,000.00 from Account 1234 at Jones Bank, rolled this over into a Certificate of Deposit at Smith Street Bank, deposited a small balance, and then went home."

You're wasting your time if Plaintiff left the bank and headed for the nearest bar! You're also wasting your time if he bought a Treasury Bill and not a Certificate, or if he challenges your idiosyncratic phrase, "rolled this over."

Don't Waste Your time with Statements Concerning Opinion or Judgment.

"The Defendant knew that, in removing a prostate gland, using the suprapubic technique is better than utilizing a transurethral resection."

That statement is not the proper realm of Requests for Admissions. It is judgmental in nature, and calls into question all manner of facts and opinions relating to the conditon of the patient at the time a decision was made as to "how" to perform the necessary prostate operation. If you want to establish that a medical doctor negligently used a specific surgical technique and should have used a different one, you must go to depositions wherein you have the opportunity to engage in a vigorous dialogue with the doctor.

You should try to limit your statements to ones of fact. The whole idea is to try to get the opposition to admit as many facts as possible so that a Judge, on proper motion, can give you your judgment after he draws appropriate inferences and applies the applicable law.

Your opposing counsel will simply not let his client be boxed in by admitting an opinion statement. He or she will either deny the statement, object to it, or answer in such a manner that the response is valueless to you.

Since you know that this will happen, there is simply no point in spending time drafting statements concerning opinion matters that you know will not be admitted.

If it is necessary, you can sometimes skirt around matters of judgment by phrasing a question as a fact, thus:

> In Pittsburgh, Pennsylvania, during the year 1980, the technique most used by urologists for the removal of the prostate gland was a transurethral resection.

Now that statement may well be admitted if it is statistically correct and the fact is pretty well known in urological circles. The admission of such a fact may well help you by preparing the way for a series of questions you might want to ask in Interrogatories or at Depositions, but there isn't too much more that you can develop by means of Requests for Admissions.

Remember—try to stick to facts; leave opinions as a subject matter for other discovery techniques.

A REMINDER OF PRINCIPAL POINTS TO CONSIDER IN USING REQUESTS FOR ADMISSIONS

1. Try to win your case by using Requests in combination with a Motion for Summary Judgment.
   a. Always be conscious of the possibility of doing this.
   b. Analyze your case: do you already know most of the facts and is it likely you can force your opponent to admit them?
   c. Think of this in cases that depend on documentary evidence, statistics, or facts known by independent, third parties.
   d. Consider it as most likely in Assumpsit cases, land condemnation cases or disputes over title, Decedents Estate matters, or a Support case.
   e. Use it in a Trespass case where the disputed facts are few or where they can be established by ''outside'' witnesses.

2. Where you have many documents to use at trial use Requests for Admissions to establish authenticity, identity, and possibly to get them admitted as evidence.

3. Put your mind at ease by using Requests for Admissions to prove that inevitable group of ''necessary nuisance'' facts.

4. Do not ask two questions in one; stick to one fact per statement.
5. Avoid long, convoluted, complex statements.
6. Do not waste time with statements asking for opinions or judgments.

Do use this discovery tool often!

7

The Forceful Use of Motions in Aid of Discovery

When you become involved with discovery you might just as well be thoroughly acquainted with motion practice. The two go together like the proverbial love and marriage. I think I am safe in stating that there has *never* been extensive discovery in which one side or the other did not go running into Court with a motion for something or other. The litany of Motions is long: Motion to Compel Answers to Interrogatories, Motion for More Specific Answers to Interrogatories, Motion for Sanctions, Motion for Protective Order, Motion for Counsel Fees and Expenses and ultimately, hopefully, a Motion for Summary Judgment.

Why all the motions? Because people won't do what you want them to do the way you want them to do it. They are obstreperous. This person refuses to produce a document, that one evades an Interrogatory, another refused to show up for a deposition, and a fourth shows up but won't answer certain questions. Most of the time the fault lies with a recalcitrant client, although sometimes opposing counsel is the culprit. The problems themselves are of a common, garden variety sort and the law provides these motions as a means for you to compel compliance with the rules.

Frequently there is a reasonable basis for a dispute. If you answer an important interrogatory the best you can, but not in the manner in which opposing counsel thinks you can and should, there could well be justification for an argument on the matter. A Motion to Compel Answers to Interrogatories is a good way to resolve the dispute. Perhaps you have been evasive in a matter in which you should have had a more direct answer.

When it comes to taking depositions or producing documents, there is frequently a broad area for legitimate disagreement. Many times in a deposition I have believed that the other attorney was taking advantage of the witness, or ranging far afield, and I have simply directed the witness not to answer the questions. If the other attorney wants them answered he or she can file a Motion and get a court order compelling the witness to answer. Of course my judgment (and yours) had better be pretty good because opposing counsel can also file a Motion for Counsel Fees and Expenses, and if the Court finds that my (or your) objection was frivolous or groundless we can end up with an Order directing that the witness appear and answer and, also, pay opposing counsel a fee and costs. That doesn't happen too often since one doesn't take such stern action with a witness unless one is on pretty solid ground.

EVASIVENESS AND REFUSAL TO COMPLY AS A TACTIC

You will find that some attorneys deliberately will avoid and evade your discovery procedures simply as a tactical maneuver to keep information from you. They figure that they have ''two bites at the apple'': (1) that it will be too much trouble for you to prepare a Motion, write a brief, and argue the matter in Court, and (2) they just might win the argument. To a certain degree they're right, and the tactic is a successful one. I find that large law firms adopt this tactic very often—and the basis for it is pure greed. It gives them an opportunity to bill a corporate client for an extensive brief (far out of proportion to the issues), and for an Argument. If they lose the argument they have really lost nothing for now they give you answers (or the documents) that you should have had all along. In the meantime, by a succession of these ploys they build up a substantial fee.

I'm always surprised that corporate clients put up with this sort of thing, but I take it that either they don't check the billings or the matter is justified somehow or other. Certainly it does not happen often where an individual or an insurance company is paying the bills. The individual can't bear the expense and the insurance company is too canny to put up with this nonsense.

Some individual lawyers do view this as a legitimate stalling tactic and will utilize it. The whole object is to wear you down so that you abandon or limit your discovery. It can't succeed unless you permit it to succeed. If you will be persistent, not only will you get the information you are after but also you will begin to wear down the other lawyer. Finally if this tactic can be established as a part of a pattern—occurring in relation to Interrogatories, Depositions and Production of Documents—it might reach the point where you can legitimately demand counsel fees and expenses for having to coerce the other side into giving you what you should have had under your Civil Rules.

The whole subject represents the "nasty" practice of law, is thoroughly unjustified, but is practiced often enough that you should be aware of it when it happens. You can't give in to this sort of thing just because it's the easy way to go.

BE PREPARED TO GO TO COURT OFTEN

Since most of the objections you will run into will have a legitimate basis (in the mind of adversary counsel), you must be prepared to go to Court—often. There can be no fooling around with this. You need the information—the other side has it—and you cannot let an objection stand in your way of securing the data. Since "open disclosure" is the established policy of our Judicial System, in this day, the inclination of any judge will be to require that the discovery be granted unless there is some exceptional reason why it should not. The burden is always on the shoulders of the person who objects to the discovery. You know that the rule is that you can secure not only all information that is relevant and germane to the lawsuit but also all other information that *can lead to* facts that are relevant to a lawsuit. When a judge begins to ponder the implications of that latter phrase he almost necessarily has to grant you your discovery, unless you have completely gone off the deep end. There are very few pertinent questions you can ask that cannot be interpreted as "leading to facts relevant to the lawsuit."

WATCH FOR BLANKET OBJECTIONS APPLIED TO A DOCUMENT, OR WRITING, PART OF WHICH IS RELEVANT

It will happen from time to time that a document will contain information that is helpful to you but will also have other information that is not relevant and that may be private, embarrassing, or very important to the other party. A letter, for example, might contain a valuable admission along with a personal love note. The attorney will object to showing you the letter. An income tax return may show itemized deductions that are relevant to your case but also show that the taxpayer earns part of his money by gambling—and an objection will be made.

These objections may be valid but they are no excuse for refusing to let you see the document—at least the part of it that is relevant. If you get along well with opposing counsel you can work out an agreement whereby he can cover up the personal or sensitive part of the document, make a copy, and give you the paper with only the pertinent sections showing. The same kind of agreement can be worked out with the tax return.

However, if you have any doubts go to court, demand the document, and insist that the judge review it to see whether the objectional material is as bad as it is supposed to be—and as irrelevant—or whether the objection is just a put-on.

You'll run into this from time to time: a psychiatric record reveals personal material that is not germane to the issues, love notes in a business letter, trade secrets mentioned in a report about the financial condition of a company, or income figures mentioned, as an aside, in an engineering report. You are still entitled to the document; the objectionable items can simply be blocked out and removed.

Let us look at some standard motions related to, and following, discovery:

I. MOTION TO COMPEL ANSWERS TO INTERROGATORIES, PRODUCTION OF DOCUMENTS, ATTENDANCE AT DEPOSITION, OR ANSWERS TO REQUESTS FOR ADMISSION

This is certainly the most common Motion you will be filing. It's unfortunate that we cannot devise a form you could keep in your form file, but the varieties of circumstances in which you will use this Motion are such that it is impractical. You simply have to prepare a separate, unique motion tailored to the particular facts with which you are confronted.

The motion itself should simply identify the particular discovery technique that was involved, state that the other side has failed to comply with the Rules in some particular manner or other, and ask the Court to compel the appropriate response.

As mentioned before, it is best to be able to state in the motion that you have orally endeavored to get the other side to cooperate, without success, and any letters you have sent asking for compliance with the Rules should be attached as Exhibits.

A note of caution or warning should be made at this time: you should not file a Motion like this until you have given opposing counsel a reasonable opportunity to respond to your discovery. If Answers to Interrogatories are due on May 20, I would not want to see a Motion to Compel Answers filed on May 21. The other attorney may have a good reason for the delay (he or she usually does), and it is to no one's advantage for you to rush in with a Motion. Instead, write a letter, or make a phone call, and try to solicit the discovery within a reasonable time. If, after an extension, courteously granted, there is still no reply, then file your Motion. You will have done all that can be expected of you.

If your complaint is that the other party has not fully or completely answered your Interrogatories or that the responses to Requests for Admissions have been evasive, then, in your motion, you should set forth the Interrogatory and the answer given (or Request and answer). That way the Court does not have to go through the pleadings to find your Interrogatories and then go through the

Interrogatories to find the ones you deem to be improperly answered. Thus:

> The Defendant has failed to answer, in full, Interrogatory No. 23 which reads:
>
> 23. Set forth the quantities of coal shipped by the Defendant on July 18, 1981 to:
>   a) Plaintiff's plant in Pittsburgh, Pennsylvania;
>   b) Plaintiff's plant in Des Moines, Iowa.
>
> *Answer:* 84,000 tons shipped.

Or, if the response is evasive:

> The Plaintiff has not properly answered Interrogatory No. 5. The Interrogatory, and Answer are:
>
> 5. State whether Plaintiff was driving the vehicle involved in this accident?
>
> *Answer:* Plaintiff was in the car.

In short, put the question and the response about which you are complaining up front where the Court can see it and get to it.

The following represents a typical Motion to Compel Answers to Interrogatories, which may also be used, with minor modifications, as a motion relating to the answers to Requests for Admission, or Production of Documents:

IN THE COMMON PLEAS COURT
OF ALLEGHENY COUNTY, PENNSYLVANIA

George Armstrong Custer	)
Plaintiff,	)
v.	) No. 12345
Sitting Bull, Gall, and	) *In Trespass*
Crazy Horse, Chiefs of	)
the Sioux Indian Tribe,	)
Defendants.	)

MOTION TO COMPEL
ANSWERS TO INTERROGATORIES

NOW COME the Defendants by their attorney George Crook, Esquire, and do hereby move your Honorable Court as follows:

1. Interrogatories 1-22 were served upon counsel for Plaintiff on September 10, 1981.

2. Answers to the Interrogatories were filed on September 29, 1981.

3. Three of the Interrogatories were answered in an evasive manner, to wit:

a) Interrogatory No. 4:

> Did you receive explicit warning from your scouts, while at the Crows Nest, on the morning of June 26, that a large camp of the Defendants was seen along the Little Big Horn River?

Answer: My eyes are good and I looked for myself.

b) Interrogatory No. 6:

Did you have specific instructions from General Terry to engage the Defendants on June 26?

Answer: General Terry trusted in my judgment in the matter.

c) Interrogatory No. 7:

Did you make any specific effort to ascertain the numbers of Defendant's fellow citizens encamped along the Little Big Horn River before you ordered Major Reno to charge the Defendants on June 26?

Answer: I was confident that my instructions to Major Reno were correct.

None of the answers is responsive to the questions asked.

4. Two of the Interrogatories are not answered completely and fully:

a) Interrogatory No. 9 states:

Did you at any time on June 26 send troops down to the Little Big Horn River from

(1) Weir Point?
(2) Massacre Hill?

If the answer to each of the foregoing is "no," set forth in detail, by compass direction and distances, your exact course from Weir Point.

Answer: No.

b) Interrogatory No. 15:

On the afternoon of June 26, when you sent the companies of Capt. Keogh and Capt. Calhoun in a south-easterly direction along Battle Ridge,

(1) Were you attempting to contact Major Reno and/or Captain Benteen?

(2) What instructions did you give to each Captain named above?

Answer: Yes.

Counsel for Defendants requires full and complete answers to the Interrogatories before he can engage in additional discovery by way of either depositions or additional interrogatories.

WHEREFORE Your Honorable Court is respectfully requested to enter an Order directing Plaintiff to answer in full, completely and directly, Interrogatories No's. 4, 6, 7, 9, and 15.

Respectfully Submitted,

———————————————

George Crook, Esquire
Attorney for Defendants

This kind of motion will get action from the Court and your discovery will proceed right on course.

II. MOTION FOR A PROTECTIVE ORDER

Sometimes your distinguished adversary counsel is going to do things, or ask for things, that just make you angry. He or she is simply going to go too far—either in scheduling depositions at a difficult time or place, or in serving voluminous Interrogatories (some of which are prying into personal matters and many of which have nothing to do with the case), or in demanding a document that he or she has no right to see. When you want to stop this misuse of discovery, file a Motion for a Protective Order.

In these situations you have to do something; you can't simply ignore the Notice of Deposition or the Interrogatories. Courts generally don't like your taking the position that certain discovery is, per se, improper and that you're not going to comply with it! It is possible that you are wrong and that if the other side files a Motion for Sanctions it just might be granted—and that can cause unnecessary problems.

It's far better, where you think that some discovery request goes beyond reasonable bounds, for you to bring the matter to the attention of the Court by way of a Motion for a Protective Order. It need not be lengthy and it requires no extensive briefing—just a recitation of the facts; if things are as clear as you think they are the motion will probably be granted, or some accommodation made. At least you let the Court rule on the matter instead of taking things into your own hands

Let me present an illustrative motion.

Here Plaintiff's counsel, in a medical malpractice case, gave to the defense attorney an authorization to secure three hospital records and on the very same day served a Notice of Deposition to depose the Defendant a week later. There was just no way that the defense attorney could secure the records, discuss them with other physicians and hospital personnel, go over them with his client, and be prepared for a deposition in seven days. The defense attorney could simply have refused to appear on the day set for the deposition but that would have been an arbitrary way to handle the problem. He adopted the best course by filing his motion:

IN THE COURT OF COMMON PLEAS
OF ALLEGHENY COUNTY, PENNSYLVANIA

Frank Carlton	)	
Plaintiff,	)	
v.	) No.: 6789	
Andrew Hays M.D. and	)	
City Hospital, a	)	
Corporation	)	
Defendants.	)	

MOTION FOR PROTECTIVE ORDER

AND NOW comes counsel for Andrew Hays, M.D. and moves the Court to enter a Protective Order with regard to the deposition proposed to be taken on July 8, 1981 at 10:30 A.M., notice having been served on or about July 1, 1981.

1. Counsel for the Defendant, Andrew Hays, M.D. moves that the Court order that the deposition of Andrew Hays, M.D. be taken after counsel for the defendant secures copies of all hospital records for the following reasons:

(a) Plaintiff's counsel only provided authorizations to secure all three hospital records with his letter of July 1, 1981.

(b) Counsel for the Defendant is attempting to secure the hospital records as quickly as possible.

(c) After securing the hospital records, counsel wishes to discuss the case and the hospital records with other medical personnel who were involved in the treatment of the Plaintiff.

(d) Counsel then wishes to discuss the case with his client so that Dr. Hays will be properly advised prior to his deposition.

(e) Counsel for Andrew Hays, M.D. does not believe that there are any circumstances which compel the taking of the deposition before he has been able to accomplish the foregoing.

(f) Counsel believes that he can secure the records and complete his investigations by August 1, 1981.

WHEREFORE, counsel for Andrew Hays, M.D. moves your Honorable Court to enter an Order postponing the deposition scheduled for July 8, 1981, to a date after August 1, 1981, to be selected by the Court.

John E. Brown, Esquire
Attorney For Defendant

This is clear enough to enable a judge to see the problem and rule equitably.

There will be other situations of a similar nature that will occur periodically wherein you will want to curtail the other side's discovery or change the mechanics of it. Most of the time you can, and should, work this out with the other attorney, but when that becomes impossible file a Motion for a Protective Order and secure the help of the Court.

III. MOTION FOR SANCTIONS

This motion lies somewhere between a Motion to Compel (Answers to Interrogatories or Production of Documents, etc.) and a Motion for a Default Judgment, and might be considered an alternative to either of those motions. Let's assume that you have served Interrogatories on June 1. They are not answered by July 1 so you call opposing counsel and ask that the Answers be filed. In ten days or so there is no positive response, so you write a letter—to no avail. At this point it is best to file a Motion to Compel Answers to Interrogatories, reciting the facts, and securing a Court Order directing that the Answers be filed within a certain time. If that Order is not complied with, you have a decision to make—should you apply for a Judgment by Default or ask for some lesser penalty by way of a Motion for Sanctions?

I suspect that the answer to that puzzle lies in your analysis of your Court, the seriousness or significance of the discovery you are trying to secure, and your personal relations with the other attorney.

If your Court is of such a mind that it will not grant a Default Judgment, even for a violation of its own Order, then there is no purpose in going this route. We all know that there are judges like that. They are usually wonderful persons—kindhearted and sympathetic—who will simply refuse to take drastic action against a litigant or his (or her) attorney no matter how dilatory they may be. It has been my experience that this attitude varies with the size of the community, the number of lawyers at the Bar, the number of cases in litigation, and the pressure on the court to move cases and avoid delay. Thus a judge in a large metropolitan area, with a large caseload, will grant a Motion for a Default Judgment in exactly the same circumstances in which his, or her, brother in a small community will not. So be it.

A second criterion is the importance of the discovery. If all you have done is serve a half-dozen miscellaneous interrogatories, the Answers to which are really not very important, the chances are the Court will not exact a severe penalty for failure to answer. In such event you had better settle for a Motion for Sanctions and forget the Default Judgment. On the other hand, if you have prepared a careful set of Requests for Admissions that go to the very heart of the case, and the other side refuses to answer for the simple reason that to do so, honestly, would be to ruin their position, then you can and should ask for a Default Judgment.

Finally, your judgment should consider the opposing attorney. If he or she is a decent person who has some sensible explanation for the delay, or who has a willful and obstinate client, then you might opt for the Motion for Sanctions as a spur to the client, primarily. I have seen occasions when the other attorney was actually grateful that I filed the Motion when he or she had an incorrigble client who simply would not listen to reason. By filing the motion I took the other attorney off the hook, so to speak, and he or she could tell the client that whatever happens is all the client's fault.

If opposing counsel is one of those persons who have been habitually uncooperative and miserable to deal with, and the current refusal to respond to discovery and a Court Order is but the latest example, then you might as well go for the Default Judgment. You have heard the expression, "Don't get mad, get even." Well, this is your chance to "get even."

Frankly, if it's a serious matter and you have done everything in your power to secure compliance with the Rules and the other attorney is simply "stonewalling" his or her necessary response, then there is no use fooling around; apply for a Default Judgment. If there is any indication that you will hurt the other attorney unnecessarily, then apply for Sanctions.

The following represents a typical Motion for Sanctions:

IN THE COURT OF COMMON PLEAS
OF ALLEGHENY COUNTY, PENNSYLVVANIA

American Graphics Corporation, a Pennsylvania Corporation, Plaintiff, v. Pictorial Specialty Shops, Inc., a Pennsylvania Corporation, Defendant.	))))) No. 12345) In Assumpsit))

MOTION FOR SANCTIONS

NOW COMES the Defendant, above named, by its counsel, Robert Brown, Esquire, and does hereby respectfully submit as follows:

1. A Notice of Deposition, directed to Harold Smith, President of Plaintiff, was filed on November 5, 1981 and served on counsel for Plaintiff on that date.

2. The deposition was to have been taken on November 20, 1981.

3. Harold Smith failed to appear for the deposition. No application for a continuance was ever filed and no explanation was given.

4. A Petition to Compel Attendance at Deposition was filed on November 29, 1981 and an Order of Court was entered on December 5, 1981, directing Harold Smith to appear for a deposition on December 15, 1981.

5. Harold Smith did not appear for a deposition on December 15, 1981. No request for a postponement was made nor has any explanation been given.

6. The failure of Harold Smith, President of Plaintiff Corporation, to appear and give testimony severely interferes with the right of Defendant to secure information needed to defend the allegations of the Complaint.

WHEREFORE, Your Honorable Court is respectfully requested to impose appropriate sanctions on Plaintiff (or, here name the specific sanction you desire) including attorneys' fees for the attendance of this counsel, twice, at the time and place of the depositions and the preparation and presentation of this Motion, and also Order Harold Smith to appear for a deposition on January 20, 1982, under threat of a Default Judgment for failure to do so.

Respectfully Submitted,

_____

Robert Brown, Esquire
Attorney For Defendant,
Pictorial Specialty
Shops, Inc.

When the Court signs an Order to this effect you will get compliance from the opposing party in nearly every case. It is rare to find someone who will ignore this Order, but occasionally it will happen.

At the Argument, you will have to rely on the practice in your jurisdiction in deciding whether to suggest specific sanctions or leave that matter to the Court. In either event, with a Motion like this, you are going to get some action.

IV. MOTION FOR DEFAULT JUDGMENT

A Motion for Default Judgment has all the influence of a .357 Magnum in catching, and holding, the attention of opposing counsel. It commands _respect_. Your opponent knows that he has done something that you think is seriously wrong when you are driven to the point of filing this motion.

A Motion for Default is of the ''last grasp'' variety and should never be filed frivolously. In order for a Court to consider it seriously, and to be willing to grant it, you must have filed earlier Motions to compel compliance with your discovery efforts, secured an Order of Court directing same, be able to show efforts on your part to get the opposition to respond—and to show a complete failure of all of these endeavors. Remember that Courts do not like to decide cases on the basis of pleadings or attorney dilatoriness. They would rather permit the Pleadings to be amended and discipline the lazy attorney. That is why so many Motions for Judgment on the Pleadings, for Summary Judgment, and for Default are usually denied. If an issue of fact can be found, a Motion for Summary Judgment will be denied; if the law is the least bit ambiguous or uncertain, or the Pleadings can be amended, a Motion for Judgment on the Pleadings, will be denied; and if the Court can find some excuse for the conduct of your opposing party or its counsel, your Motion for a Default Judgment will be denied.

It isn't often that you can use this legal weapon, but when you can the effects are devastating. The case ends very abruptly. There are two important prerequisites to using this Motion.

1. Always have a Court Order in existence which has not been complied with.

Any judge will want you to have made some effort to secure compliance with the Rules by gentler means. Thus, you will have to have filed a Motion to Compel Answers to Interrogatories, or to Produce Documents, or Answers to Requests for Admissions, and secured an Order of Court. That Order should state that counsel has a definite time period (30 days, for example, or "until April 21") to comply and, preferably, should contain the express words "or suffer a default," "or a default judgment will be entered." Thus both the time limitation and the threat will be clear and definite.

2. Always be prepared to show your good faith effort to secure compliance.

After opposing counsel has allowed the time limit to expire, write one or two letters asking for compliance with the court order and make one or two telephone calls. If you don't, the average judge will be inclined to give the negligent attorney "one more time." His or her mood will change if you can prove that you already gave counsel his "one more chance" and that there is no need or purpose for additional leniency. The average judge will buy that. So, with those two escapes effectively blocked, your motion stands an excellent chance of being granted.

One more thing—if opposing counsel does not have a strong explanation to justify his or her defiances of a Court Order and your letters, the filing of this Motion will probably bring a quick request for settlement negotiations, and you're going to be in an excellent position to get the highest reasonable figure for your case. Do not use this opportunity foolishly by trying to push the other attorney into a corner and asking for the "sun, moon and stars" in settlement— that will simply provoke a fight and you may end up with no settlement and no chance to get that figure in a verdict. Instead, stick with your "highest reasonable demand" and you have a good chance of getting it.

A good example of a Motion for Default Judgment is the following:

IN THE COURT OF COMMON PLEAS
OF ALLEGHENY COUNTY, PENNSYLVANIA

Lucy Jones and Henry	)
Jones, her husband,	)
Plaintiffs,	)
v.	) No. 12345
Brown Pharmaceutical	)
Company, Inc., a	)
Corporation.	)
Defendant.	)

MOTION FOR DEFAULT JUDGMENT AS TO BROWN
PHARMACEUTICAL CO., INC.

Now come Plaintiffs above named by their Attorney James B. Black, Esquire, and do hereby respectfully move for a Default Judgment for the following reasons:

1. This Honorable Court entered an Order on July 12, 1981, directing this Defendant to answer Interrogatories within 30 days or suffer a default judgment.

2. It is now 60 days later and Defendant refuses to answer the interrogatories.

3. The Interrogatories were originally served on April 21, 1981, some 5½ months ago.

4. Counsel for Plaintiff requested the Answers in letters dated August 19 and September 15, 1981, copies of which are attached hereto and marked as Exhibits 1 and 2. Defendant kept promising Answers but they were never sent. See letters of August 29, and September 21, 1981, marked Exhibits 3 and 4.

5. Plaintiff has taken every conceivable action to be cooperative. An Order of Court was secured, letters have been written, and phone calls have been made.

6. Discovery has simply come to a halt for 5½ months, as to this Defendant.

7. Plaintiff has been seriously jeopardized in terms of securing information from Defendant, in having data from which to decide who should be deposed, and in deciding whether additional, supplemental interrogatories should be prepared and served.

8. It is now 3½ months since the Order of this Court.

9. This case represents a flagrant disregard of the Order of this Court and the Rules of Civil Procedure.

WHEREFORE, your Honorable Court is respectfully requested to enter a Default Judgment as to Brown Pharmaceutical Co., Inc.

Respectfully Submitted,

_____

James B. Black
Attorney for Plaintiffs

Another example, somewhat along the same line, is this Motion:

IN THE COURT OF COMMON PLEAS
OF ALLEGHENY COUNTY, PENNSYLVANIA

Thomas W. Green and	)
Rose M. Green, his wife	)
Plaintiffs,	)
v.	) No. 26809
William C. Smith, M.D.,	)
and City Hospital, a	)
Corporation,	)
Defendants.	)

MOTION FOR DEFAULT JUDGMENT AS TO
WILLIAM C. SMITH, M.D.

Now come the Plaintiffs, above named, by their attorney, John Brown, Esquire, and do hereby respectfully submit as follows:

1. On October 11, 1981, Interrogatories 1-20 were served on Defendant, William C. Smith, M.D.

2. The Answers were due on November 11, 1981.

3. Defendant has been requested, both by letter and by telephone, to answer the Interrogatories. See Exhibit 1 attached hereto.

4. A Motion to Compel Answers to Interrogatories was filed and served on December 30, 1981.

5. On January 9, 1982, the Court entered an Order directing that the Answers be filed by January 29, 1982.

6. It is now ten days beyond the deadline established by the Court—and nearly four months since the Interrogatories were served—and no Answers have been filed.

7. The failure of this Defendant to respond to the Order of Court, and Rules of Civil Procedure, evidences a studied contempt for, and reckless disregard of, his responsibilities in this lawsuit and has caused serious harm to the Plaintiffs. The Plaintiffs have clearly been disadvantaged in the preparation and development of their case by the willful conduct of the Defendant.

WHEREFORE, your Honorable Court is respectfully requested to enter a Default Judgment in favor of Plaintiffs and against Defendant, William C. Smith, M.D.

————————————

John Brown
Attorney For Plaintiffs

These Motions are extremely effective. You can rest assured that one of three things will happen:

1. The Court will grant your motion and you will get a judgment;

2. The opposing party will be pushed into a prompt discussion of settlement;

3. You will get the discovery that initiated the whole affair.

One thing you will not get is additional procrastination from the other side—and that you can do without.

V. MOTION FOR SUMMARY JUDGMENT

Certainly this motion has to be the culmination of well-prepared, effective discovery.

By the nature of things it isn't often that you will be able to use this device. You will recall the legal maxim that a Summary Judgment cannot be granted if there is any question of fact relating to the ultimate issue in the case. If there is an issue of fact the case must be tried—whether to a jury or a judge.

Nonetheless from time to time you do elicit every significant fact from your opponent in such manner that a Motion for Summary Judgment is appropriate and can succeed.

It is necessary, when you file your motion, that it be supported by facts that are admitted under oath or affidavit. The Court will not consider matters that are not under oath nor, of course, anything de hors the record. Answers to Interrogatories and Answers to Requests for Admissions will, of necessity, be part of the pleadings but many times attorneys do not file transcripts of depositions. You will have to make certain that they are filed if you intend to make reference to them in your motion. In addition, if you have secured documents from the other side pursuant to a Request (or Motion) for Production, keep in mind that you must have these verified somehow or other—either in a deposition or by use of Requests for Admissions. Even though you secured them from the opposition they cannot, per se, be used to support a Summary Judgment. Their authenticity must be established under oath.

ATTACH IMPORTANT EXTRACTS FROM THE RECORD IN YOUR MOTION

In the Motion itself you will make reference to the location of the specific facts that support the motion, i.e., "See Answer to Interrogatory No. 12, Request for Admission No's. 3, 4, 6, 9, and 10; Deposition of Mary Smith, P. 12," but you should also include a reasonable amount of this material in the body of the motion. This has two salutary effects: (1) it heightens and dramatizes the importance of the material you have selected, and (2) it saves the Court the necessity of searching through the pleadings to find the important admissions you refer to and acts as a summary of the more important ones.

To illustrate, let's take the case of a person who agrees to become a coowner with an aged relative of a bank account so that he can physically do the banking for his uncle and also pay some of the routine bills. The lawsuit exists, of course, because the other party begins to help himself to the funds and transfers them to a Certificate of Deposit in his name alone. Now, at a deposition you effectively get the other party to agree (1) that no money of his went into the account; (2) that the money was to be used solely for the purposes of the senior citizen; (3) that this money was used to buy the Certificate of Deposit, and (4) that, in reality, it belongs to the aged relative.

Now the deposition itself may be 50 pages long, tracing the origins of the account and deposits into and withdrawals from the account. In your motion you can make such references to the depositions as you deem necessary (referring to pages), but when you come to the really vital admissions, be sure to do one of two things:

1. Quote directly from the deposition, or,
2. Attach that page of the deposition as an Exhibit to the Motion.

This is the Motion that was filed:

John Jones,	)
Plaintiff,	) Civil Division
v.	)
Frank Smith,	) No.: 1234
Defendant.	)

MOTION FOR SUMMARY JUDGMENT

Now comes the Plaintiff, above named by his attorney, James Black, Esquire, and does hereby respectfully submit as follows:

1. The Plaintiff and Defendant are Uncle and Nephew in relationship. (Deposition of Frank Smith P. 3.)

2. This action is one to recover funds given by the Plaintiff to Defendant as a matter of convenience to be used solely for the purposes of the needs of Plaintiff and at the direction of Plaintiff. (Deposition of Frank Smith P. 4.)

3. Plaintiff alleges that the funds were fraudulently and improperly transferred to Certificates of Deposit and a savings account in the name of Defendant alone and that Defendant refused to return said funds to Plaintiff. (See paragraphs 5 and 6 of Complaint.)

4. In a deposition taken on August 19, 1981, in this matter, Defendant has admitted that:

a) all of the moneys in certificates of deposit ($20,000.00) in his name and in a savings account ($3,164.44) in his name, belong solely to the Plaintiff.

b) no portion of said moneys belongs to him (the Defendant).

c) he will return said moneys to the Plaintiff.

5. The following colloquy is from Pages 28 and 29 of the deposition of defendant, Frank Smith:

Q: All right. So that at the present time you have in your name two certificates of deposit; is that correct?

A: Yes, sir.

Q: And each is for $10,000.00?

A: Yes, sir.

Q: What is it—City Bank—and what is it—Area Savings Bank?

A: Yes, sir.

Q: You also have in the Savings Account at City Bank a balance—is it approximately $3,000.00?

A: Approximately.

Q: And it is still there; is it?

A: Yes, sir.

Q: And is it your understanding that this is money belonging to John Jones?

A: It is.

Q: And do you agree to turn over this money to him?

A: Yes, sir.

Q: And likewise, the balance that still remains in the City Bank Savings Account, will you turn that money over?

A: I will.

MR. BLACK: Okay. I think that is all I have.

6. There is no other issue of fact in this lawsuit.

WHEREFORE, Your Honorable Court is respectfully requested to enter a Summary Judgment in favor of Plaintiff John Jones and against Defendant Frank Smith in the sum of $23,164.44 together with costs of this suit.

Respectfully Submitted,

_____

James Black
Attorney For Plaintiff

The little excerpt from the deposition does tend to catch one's attention and is a nice little summary of the position counsel will adopt at the Argument.

You will not want to go into too much detail in the motion—save the lengthy references to the Record for your Brief—but just put in enough material so that, upon reading the motion, the Court will see that you are very serious about this and that you have a strong case.

If you will refer back to the discussion on page 121 you will there see the effective use of a Motion for Summary Judgment based on the failure to answer Requests for Admission. The Court accepted the Requests as true, found that no issue of fact existed, and entered the Summary Judgment.

As I stated previously, it isn't often that you are going to have the basis for a Motion for Summary Judgment, but it does occur from time to time and you should always be ready to take advantage of these opportunities.

SEVEN KEYS TO THE MOST EFFECTIVE USE OF MOTIONS

1. The principal motions that you will use in aid of Discovery or following Discovery are:
   a. Motion to Compel (Answers to Interrogatories, Answers to Requests for Admissions, etc.)
   b. Motion for a Protective Order.
   c. Motion for Sanctions.
   d. Motion for Default Judgment.
   e. Motion for Summary Judgment.
2. Do not hesitate to file a motion when your discovery is unjustifiably delayed by the other side.
3. Do not take it upon yourself to refuse to comply with requested discovery; use a Motion for a Protective Order.
4. If discovery is continuously delayed, file a Motion for Sanctions. Ask for counsel fees and a date certain for performance of the desired response to your discovery.
5. Use a Motion for Default Judgment as a last resort. Before you use it have:
   a. A prior Order of court directing response to your discovery by a certain date; and
   b. Letters to opposing counsel, asking for the discovery which you can use as an Exhibit.
6. File a Motion for Summary Judgment when it is clear that your discovery has resolved all issues of fact in your favor.
7. *Remember:* Delay, evasion and avoidance can work only if you permit it to go unchallenged. *File Your Motions* and keep the discovery process moving ahead.

8

Lights, Camera, Action!
The Use of Videotapes

The advent of the inexpensive and convenient videotape camera has brought substantial changes in the preparation of a case and its presentation in court. Thanks to the combination of the camcorder, the television set, and the video-cassette recorder we can photograph a witness and simultaneously record his or her testimony on tape, set it aside until needed, bring it to court, and there produce the witness for the edification of judge and jury. For all practical purposes the witness is alive and testifying although in fact that person may be deceased or living a thousand miles away.

This device is so convenient that we all may live to see the day that "live" witnesses no longer appear in court. On the date of trial the attorneys will appear just long enough to make an opening address and drop off six or seven videotape cassettes which the judge and jury will look at and then decide the case. The attorneys can return—if they want to bother—to take the verdict. That day may come; it just is not quite here yet.

One very serious problem with this new device is that there may be too much reliance on it. Every attorney knows that witnesses hate to come to court. That obligation disrupts their orderly lifestyle, requires effort in rearranging their daily schedules and actually getting to the courtroom, and subjects them to challenging questions. In addition, a judge will be there who has the authority to force them to answer questions when they do not want to do so, and a jury and court personnel—all strangers—will be present to hear embarrassing or humiliating answers. It can be a harrowing experience.

The videotaped deposition offers a way out. Now the witness can arrange a schedule to meet his or her own desires; the location of the videotaping can frequently be at the discretion of the witness; there is no judge present and the witness has relatively free rein to be as pleasant, hostile, candid, or evasive as he or she pleases. There is no jury staring at the witness, judging demeanor, tone of voice, hesitation, or anxious glances for help—all of which can be embarrassing. In short the witness may try to do as he or she pleases believing that there isn't much the attorneys can do about it.

This is one of the great drawbacks of a videotaped deposition, and it is a problem that cannot be easily resolved. In this chapter we will discuss how to work with a witness who is being videotaped, as well as other matters that are unique to the use of this modern tool. It has such great utility for the attorney that it can, and must, be used to advantage. Let us turn to a discussion of the various ways in which we can put it to good use.

In general an attorney can effectively use videotape in five areas.

1. A deposition for use at trial,
2. Taking a statement from a witness,
3. A discovery deposition,
4. A "Day in the Life" film, and
5. Demonstrations and accident reconstructions.

Each of the usages requires a different approach even as they have things in common. For example, one might say that "a deposition is a deposition is a deposition" but that is only partly true. A videotaped deposition for use at trial is a formal, well-planned, rather deliberate proceeding. It is only a very distant cousin to a videotaped discovery deposition which is always, rambling, lengthy and frequently rather casual. The purposes are different and so are the attitudes of the attorneys. Using a camcorder to take a statement from a witness—in an office or at the scene of an accident—is vastly different from preparing a "Day in the Life" tape, which requires detailed planning and execution.

We will discuss each of these applications in considerable detail. Initially, however, attention is directed to the fact that for these videotape usages to be effective the lawyer must *learn to be a director*.

THE ATTORNEY AS DIRECTOR

In essence every time an attorney plans to videotape a witness, he or she is directing a movie. Good movies do not happen by chance; they are planned. Someone pays attention to the script, the actors, lighting, action, the quality of the sound and the location of the ''shot'' or scene. In the case of your use of a videotape camera to record an event, that ''someone'' is you. If you are the attorney who has scheduled a videotaped deposition for use at trial or a ''Day in the Life'' filming, then you must take charge of the event and see to it that it is well done.

What are some of the things you have to think about? There are several:

1. The Location

At every videotaped deposition there are going to be present, minimally, the witness, two lawyers, a stenographic reporter and the camcorder operator. There may be a need for space for a blackboard, an easel, a ''shadow-box'' to show x-rays, perhaps a table or desk to hold records, and room for the videotape equipment.

In addition the camera operator and the attorneys may have to move about from time to time, so that allowance will have to be made for easy access to and from the area occupied by the witness and/or the blackboard or easel.

This takes a little planning. The attorney must go to the place at which the videotaping is to be done and inspect it with regard to its utility for the purpose intended.

Probably every attorney has had the experience of being invited (coerced?) to a doctor's office to videotape his or her deposition, only to find that it has the area of a postage stamp. Participants end up stepping on each other, getting in the way of the camera, having no place to put documents and exhibits except their laps from which they fall to the floor in disorder. The shadow-box, necessarily placed on the desk hides the face of the doctor and one sees only a disembodied hand pointing to something on the x-ray. What a mess! What a waste of time and effort! Shown to a jury at some later date, the event becomes a farce and your case is seriously damaged as result of this ineptitude.

Don't let this happen to you.

Go to the location of the proposed videotaping and see for yourself that it is adequate. If the doctor's office is too small, use the reception room; if there is no reception room, inquire about a larger room elsewhere in the building. One way or the other you have to have adequate space in which equipment can be set up and people can function with ease.

2. Lighting

The ability of camcorders to take good film in dim lighting conditions is greatly exaggerated. This is one more matter that the director-attorney is going to have to consider. If a dying witness is to be deposed at home (in the more spacious living room and not a tiny bedroom), it may be necessary to have the camera operator bring artificial lighting. This is not something you can leave to chance; you must get to the location and see for yourself. Check to see if the room has enough windows providing natural light and, if not, whether the lamps and overhead light are adequate.

An amusing illustration of the necessity of considering lighting problems is the case in which attorneys from this writer's office went to Los Angeles to videotape the deposition of a renowned pediatric neurologist. He was a crucial expert for the plaintiff. Unfortunately he had a small office and his desk was in the corner, partly in shadow under the best of circumstances. Very unfortunately the attorneys elected to proceed under these negative circumstances. Initially the sun streaming through the window gave the doctor an almost sainted appearance. Then the sun began to move and a dark shadow covered the side of his face giving an eerie aspect to his countenance. Soon one saw one-half of a face glowing brightly and the other half in darkness. Before long, the viewer forgot all about the testimony and watched in curiosity as the expanding black shadow seemed to consume the doctor's countenance until, as the sun's rays disappeared, one heard a voice seemingly coming from a dark void. It was awful. When the attorneys finally saw the videotape, they were shocked at this sight of the play of sun and shadow on the witness. They had been so excited at the taking of this deposition and so intent on their questions that they had failed to notice this dramatic effect.

Fortunately, in that case, the insurance personnel at the "home office" only reviewed the stenographic transcript which impressed them so much that the case was settled, but they might have changed their minds had they seen the videotape. It was certainly nothing that one would want to show to a jury.

Lighting is important: pay attention to it.

3. The Operator

Many attorneys give no thought to the necessity of training, skill, or experience on the part of the camera operator. Since camcorders are so common one begins to believe that all the operator has to do is to point the camera and press a button. That is simply not true. The operator is the one who decides just what is going to appear on that tape you show in court. For that reason you had better make certain that the operator knows what he or she is doing and also knows what the attorney wants.

It is not enough that the camera be placed in a fixed position, focused on the witness and turned on. That will result in a very boring, sleep-inducing, waste-of-time production. A camcorder is designed to film action, movement, some activity that will disrupt the hypnotic, mesmerizing effect of a face on the screen droning on and on. A good operator will constantly check the quality of the picture and the sound, but will also know when to zoom in for a close-up of the witness or an exhibit, pull back for a long view of the witness amidst his or her surroundings, or pan left or right to identify the attorney who is asking a question. An adjustment will have to be made if the witness stands to write on a blackboard or uses x-rays on a shadow-box. All of these activities are designed to gain and hold the interest of the viewer, whether judge, jury or interested third party. Action of some kind is essential to keeping the viewer alert and paying attention. The operator has to know how and when to provide that activity.

Assuming that you have retained a skilled operator, the next matter is to explain to him or her just what you want done. It is for you to explain that the witness will use the blackboard at a certain point in the testimony and that it is very important that the operator zoom in on this writing and that it be clearly visible on the TV screen. The operator will have to be depended upon to advise counsel or the witness that the chalk markings on the blackboard are too light to be seen and that a different piece of chalk must be used, or that the crayon markings on an x-ray cannot be seen on the film. You, the attorney, will have to tell the operator how often you want the attorneys included in a view or how often the camera should be zoomed back to include the witness and a portion of the surroundings.

In short, there has to be a lengthy discussion between the operator and the attorney before the deposition begins, and a clear understanding between them concerning such things as:

Objects that are going to be used (model, blackboard photograph),

Action that can be expected (witness writing on blackboard or going to easel to place a photograph and then mark on it),

When close-ups are important, and

What portion of the testimony is especially critical and how that is to be filmed.

The result of this kind of cooperation will be a good videotape that will hold the viewers' interest and impress them, both visually and aurally, with the knowledge and credibility of the witness.

4. The Witness

Most witnesses have never been videotaped and don't know what to do. As a director the attorney has to take the time to explain the goal of the procedure, what the camera operator will be doing, and the various activities that the witness will be expected to perform for the camera. Thus it must be explained that after a drawing has been introduced into evidence, the attorney will place it on the easel, and then the witness is to rise, get a marking pen, move to the easel and, standing beside it, be prepared to mark on the drawing while testifying and that the camera will "zoom in" on the drawing.

When the witness knows what is expected of him or her, and when it is likely to occur, the "comfort factor" increases dramatically and the result will be a very effective film.

The witness must be impressed with the seriousness of this proceeding and that it is, in fact "just like being in court." He or she should be told that the questions are to be answered directly and courteously, and that flippant remarks and a sarcastic attitude will not be tolerated. If appropriate, a witness may be reminded that untoward conduct can be brought to the attention of the court and that sanctions could be imposed. For most witnesses "a word to the wise" is sufficient.

All of this takes time, effort, and planning on the part of the attorney. Good videotaped depositions simply do not "just happen." Somebody's hard work made them happen.

**THE FOUR MAJOR VARIABLES
IN VIDEOTAPING**

1. The location
2. The lighting
3. The camera operator
4. The witness

Make them work for you successfully!

THE USES OF VIDEOTAPE IN PREPARATION AND TRIAL

1. The Videotaped Deposition for Use at Trial

It wasn't very long ago that trial lawyers "fretted and sweated" about whether their vital medical witness would show up in court on time, or show up at all! Today that doctor can be videotaped in advance of trial, and when the testimony is needed it is a simple matter to bring TV monitors before judge and jury, and run the tape of the doctor's testimony. Attorneys breathe easier and judges are happy that there is no delay in the trial, nor any emotional plea for a continuance on the grounds that the doctor was suddenly called to an emergency.

The same thing applies to the dying witness, the one who is moving outside of the court's jurisdiction, and the lady who advises you that she will probably be delivering a baby on your trial date.

If these persons are important witnesses, their videotaped deposition are a blessing. The trial lawyer is relieved of scheduling problems and the showing of the tape is almost as good as a personal appearance in court by the witness.

There is only one small problem: if that deposition is not properly and carefully taken by the attorney it can absolutely ruin the case at the worst or diminish it at best.

These trial depositions must be carefully planned and skillfully conducted so as to maximize the possible benefits through the use of the witness.

What is the problem? One may legitimately ask this question since it should be so obvious that a deposition for use at trial is an important matter.

The answer is *no pressure*. When attorneys lack pressure, they get lazy, careless and forgetful. This attitude and conduct lead to poor results when the videotape is used in the courtroom.

Think of it for a moment: the deposition can be scheduled at any time to suit the convenience of all concerned; the deposition is an informal affair with no judge or jury present. The attorneys, the witness and the camera operator can joke, relax, take it easy, and everyone is aware that the camera can be turned on and off at will. In all honesty, haven't you heard someone say at such a deposition, ''Well, I guess it's time to stop joking and get on with this matter?'' Certainly you have. It bodes ill for the attorney for whom the deposition is important.

Certain requirements are essential for the taking of a deposition for use at trial.

Formality. To the extent possible, the scheduling attorney should make this proceeding appear to be a serious, formal matter. Most especially the witness has to be apprised of this attitude. Excessive conviviality and joking lead to a casual, flippant demeanor on the part of many witnesses, and a willingness to respond to some questions with a somewhat ''smart-aleck'' attitude. That cannot be permitted.

Start with the manner in which the witness is dressed. A lay witness may appear wearing a T-shirt and blue jeans; if the deposition is taken in a hospital the doctor may appear wearing his operating room or delivery room ''scrubs.'' Such clothing is totally inappropriate. Every man must wear a suit and tie; every woman must wear a dress or suitable blouse and slacks. It is the obligation of the attorney to see to it that this is done. It is amazing what a change of dress can do toward changing the attitude of the witness regarding the seriousness of the deposition.

The scheduling attorney must require that the location be suitable to the purpose. One does not take such a deposition in the men's lavatory! Neither does one take a deposition in a photographers salon where nude photographs decorate the walls, or in the office of a foundry where everyone must shout to be heard.

An example of the problem—having to leave the safe confines of one's own conference room—is a deposition of a doctor for use at trial which was to be held in a hotel in Miami where the doctor was attending a convention. The hotel accommodated the request of the attorney for a conference room, but upon arrival it was found that the room was a long, narrow one, with glass doors just off the lobby. If the camera operator put his back to the door and the witness sat at the far end of the table, the doctor was distracted by persons passing by in the lobby, some of whom knew him and paused to wave or watch. Of course, the camera operator could not be placed at the other end of the table because he or she would unavoidably be filming the lobby crowd behind the witness. Counsel eventually had to rent a suite and take the deposition in the living room portion of those rooms.

Finally, during a deposition, all the formality of the courtroom must be brought into play. One refers to Attorney Jones or Mr. Jones, not "hey, Joe." Exhibits are referred to by number, handed to opposing counsel, and then shown to the witness. Objections (if made) are made promptly and with an explanation of the basis for them as one would in court.

To the extent possible, the deposition must be taken with the same air of seriousness that one experiences in the courtroom. After all, the tape is going to be shown in court for the purpose of influencing a judge and jury; it ought to be prepared with that goal in mind.

Write Out Your Questions. It is crucial that the questions to the witness be thought out ahead of time and committed to paper.

If a witness is dying—and thus the purpose of the videotaped deposition—it won't do that, after the funeral, counsel suddenly discovers that he or she forgot to ask the witness an important question.

In the case of the doctor who was deposed in Miami, what good will it all have been to get back home and then discover that one "forgot" to ask about prognosis, or that one left out essential facts in the hypothetical question regarding causation? That sloppy, careless conduct can happen to anyone.

But it need not happen. Write out the questions in advance. Review them in the quiet of your room and with other members of your law firm. Make revisions. Double-check the questions (especially of an expert) against the legal requirements involved in your case. Make sure the hypothetical question is sufficiently detailed and adequate and that you can prove the facts set forth therein.

With this preparation you can take a deposition that is exhaustive of the subject and will include everything that you need for your case. The questions will be properly phrased so as to diminish objections, and they will be directly to the point instead of rambling and disjointed.

Objections. Most procedural rules require only that objections to the form of the question must be made during the deposition, leaving to the day of trial other types of objections. However, it is generally not a requirement that the miscellaneous objections await the day of trial, and it is suggested that this is not a good idea.

When one is in the midst of a serious deposition one is alert, steeped in the facts and nuances of the case, and the nature of the objection and its basis come readily to mind and tongue. That is the time and place to make good, strong objections based on relevancy, hearsay, foundation, or qualifications.

Some attorneys disagree on the basis that the objection is "tipping off" his or her opponent and giving that person the opportunity to correct an error. That much is true, but at the same time failure to object puts the court in the position that, generally, knowing that the questioning attorney cannot correct the matter, the court will lean in favor of overruling the objection. How often in these circumstances this author has seen a judge ponder the matter and heard him or her finally say, "Well, the witness is now dead and can't be recalled. The objection has some merit, but it's not completely clear, so I overrule the objection."

One can easily follow the judges' train of thought: "Counselor, you waited to this moment to make your objection. If I sustain it, your opponent is seriously damaged. The witness is now dead and gone, and since I perceive a little doubt on the matter, I elect to overrule."

On the other hand, if the objection is made during the deposition and a clear-cut basis stated, the shoe is placed on the other foot of the good judge. Now, in good conscience, a judge can say to the questioning attorney: "Counselor, the objection was made while the witness was present. You had a chance to correct the matter. You elected not to do so. Objection sustained."

It is unfortunate that some attorneys look upon "trial tactics" as an opportunity for nasty, almost meretricious conduct toward their opponent. To sandbag the other attorney is thought to be a mark of skill. It is not, and most judges don't think so. By virtue of their position they are much more concerned with abstract justice than with who wins and loses a particular case.

For that reason, when a videotape is being shown, the average judge, knowing that he or she was not present at the taking of the deposition to make rulings and to give counsel a chance to rephrase a question, will be inclined to lean in favor of the questioning attorney. The other party can appeal—for whatever that is worth. However, if the objection was made during the deposition, the judge is much less inclined to be sympathetic to the questioner and will rule more technically.

Rulings of the Court. In general there are no procedural rules describing in detail when and how the court should rule on objections. Please check the rules in your jurisdiction, and the odds are 100 to 1 that the same is true of your courts.

When we speak of the use of a videotaped deposition, we say that "it is just as if the witness was in court." Unfortunately, the witness is *not* in court. We simply pretend that he or she is.

The rule makers pretend too. Their expectation is that one will show the tape in court, objections will be made, the court will rule on the objection, and the questioning will go on "just as if the witness was in court."

These rule makers are unbelievably naive and optimistic. It never works out that way.

When an objection is made before a live witness, everything stops until the court rules. With a tape, when an objection is made, the tape goes merrily on, until the operator stops it. Then comes the backtracking—using the number counter—to the objection. Then counsels make their argument and the court rules one way or the other. If the objection is "sustained," the operator must shut off the sound and fast forward to the next question. (Frequently the operator misses the next question and has to go back and forth with rewind" and fast forward, taking "god knows how long" depending on the answer, until finally he or she gets to the proper place.) If *that* question is objected to, the mess begins all over again.

Naturally this doesn't occur with a live witness. There can be colloquy between the judge, the witness, and the attorneys. There is no answer until the judge rules.

It is the normal human communication that is missing with videotape, and rule makers never got this through their heads.

Accordingly, the attorneys have to seize the initiative and work with the judge regarding how objections are going to be handled. Every judge seems to have his or her own way of handling this matter.

The ideal method is for the judge and the attorneys, with a court reporter, to sit down one day, before trial, during a recess or at the end of the day's proceedings, and review the tape at leisure. A record should be made of the counter marker of each objection. If the objection is overruled, the operator can simply fast forward between, say, markers 1020 and 1040 and eradicate the objection. If the objection is sustained, a record can be kept of the counter markings for the answer, and the operator can fast forward from counter 1041 to 1118 and move on. If the attorneys really get along and are cooperative, they might agree to strike the question, the objection, and the answer, using the counter marker.

The purpose in all of this is to make the viewing of the deposition as smooth and intelligible to the jury as possible.

If the judge does not want to sit through the entire deposition, a second alternative is to record all objections by counter markers and then meet with the judge. The attorneys can explain to him or her the background of each question and the basis for the objection. The judge can then view only this portion of the tape and make a decision. In this manner, one can review the objections on a 60-minute tape in about 10 to 15 minutes.

Some may ask, ''What happens if opposing counsel has not made objections during the taking of the deposition?'' There are two answers. One way is for the judge and attorneys to sit through the entire tape, with the attorneys making their objections at suitable moments. Or the attorneys (alone or together) can review the tape, note by counter-marker the places where they intend to make objections, and then meet with the judge to review the selected excerpts and secure a ruling.

It is obvious that a court reporter will have to be present at the meetings with the court to record the objection, judicial ruling, and any colloquy between the attorneys and the judge.

The use of a videotaped deposition creates unusual problems that often require cooperation between the attorneys to resolve. Presumably that cooperation will be forthcoming. Trial lawyers have enough areas of legitimate dispute that they should not add to their respective burden by quarreling about matters such as this. However, if one has an especially hostile and stubborn opponent, there is no alternative to an informal meeting with the court to hammer out the details of this matter. It may be in order to file a Motion, asking for a supplemental pretrial conference or a status conference to explore the matter.

One way or the other, there should be some disposition of the problem of objections prior to trial so that the viewing of the videotape by the jury is not encumbered by interruptions.

2. The Use of Videotape In Taking Statements of Witnesses

How often has your investigator returned to your office at the end of a day with two or three signed statements that leave you bubbling with enthusiasm about the helpfulness of the statements, and which then lead to all kinds of questions about the witnesses? ''What kind of people are these men or women?'' ''What do they look like?'' ''How certain do they appear to be of the facts set forth in the statements?'' The questions tumble from your lips and the investigator can only give his or her impressions in answer. Those impressions—as you may have learned by bitter experience—are no substitute for your own.

Today there is a better way to take a statement from a witness, one that will get all of the facts concerning the incident and at the same time answer your questions about the witness. That "better way" is to videotape the interrogation.

A small, portable camcorder and a tripod should be standard equipment for every one of your investigators. These simple, inexpensive tools can enable him or her to get a much more complete story from a witness, and one in which you can now appraise the appearance and credibility of the witness. There have always been two major problems with a written statement:

1. It is a condensation of a much longer conversation between the investigator and the witness. The attorney must rely on the judgment of the investigator in deciding which portions of the discussion are important enough to commit to writing.

2. The language and words of the witness are frequently distorted by the fact that the investigator is doing the writing and uses his or her own words and manner of expression. As every experienced attorney knows, this is a major problem with written statements.

Both of these faults are corrected when the investigator videotapes the conversation.

The investigator can interview the witness in a kitchen, an office at work, a bar or the porch of a farmhouse. Thanks to the ability of modern camcorders to function in dim light and to pick up sound at a reasonable distance from the camera, the investigator can place his or her machine on the tripod, turn it on, and then leisurely engage the witness in a conversation that will cover every aspect of the accident or incident involved in the case. Thus the attorney will not only get the facts but will be able to see whether the witness makes a nice appearance, is hesitant and uncertain about some of the facts, has a sense of humor, but appears a little weak and easily led such that one could anticipate trouble on cross-examination. The attorney can make the judgment about credibility instead of relying on the impressions of the investigator.

This is a wonderful tool and should be used for statement taking as much as possible.

An expansion of this technique is to actually take the witness to the scene of the accident and to film it while the witness explains what happened. Naturally this can be done only if the scene of the accident is relatively close by and the witness has the time and willingness to go there. Whenever possible this should be done.

With this videotape available, attorneys have the chance to see the scene for themselves. They can look at the street, watch the changing traffic light, hear the children in a playground or the honking horns at a congested intersection—all the while listening to the conversation about the events that transpired there.

The benefit to the attorney is enormous.

In addition to having a visual and aural statement, the tapes can also be set aside for months until serious trial preparation begins, at which time the attorney can take them from a shelf, insert them in a VCR and, at leisure, refresh his or her recollection concerning the witness, the scene and the event.

The only drawback to the use of the camcorder is the reluctance of some witnesses to participate. Some people are willing to give a written statement but will not speak into a tape recorder, and definitely will not sit still for the use of a camcorder. One has to rely on the skill and joviality of one's investigator to break down this resistance.

Finally, we are all aware of the fact that if the incident occurred on private property there may be a problem gaining entry and taking the time to film the scene with the witness. Hospitals, manufacturing plants, airports, and grocery stores are places at which events occur that are the subject of lawsuits, and the administrative personnel at these institutions routinely say ''no'' to a request to enter and film there. Fortunately, the Discovery Rules of every jurisdiction have a built-in right of inspection, which nearly always includes the right to photograph, so that a Motion and resultant Court Order may be necessary. It is always worth the effort.

3. The Use of Videotape in Discovery Depositions

The advantage of videotaping a discovery deposition is identical to that of videotaping a statement from a witness: one has a record that shows how the person looks, speaks, and behaves. A typed transcript never shows moments of hesitation, which reveals either uncertainty or fabrication, the pleading glances to counsel seeking help before answering a question, or a strong, positive tone of voice. These are the things that make a videotape invaluable.

On the negative side, a discovery deposition, almost by definition, can be a long, laborious proceeding. Routinely one can last two or three hours and some have extended into a full day or more. One has to keep in mind that the purpose of videotaping is to have a record that someone is going to look at in the future. No one is going to look at a tape of a two-hour discovery deposition that revealed very little. Aside from the cost of the tape and the camera operator, mere storage of the tapes becomes prohibitive. And attorneys will not throw them out. By nature and training, trial attorneys are ''collectors.'' We keep boxes and boxes of papers, photographs, drawings, pieces of machinery, manuals—and scream at a secretary or paralegal who wants to throw out some of it. All this on the theory that, "Maybe I'll need that someday."

Thus videotapes by the dozens accumulate on shelves even if there is only three minutes of usable information in a two-hour tape. Sooner or later, of course, they do get thrown out, or erased for later reuse, but "not yet."

Generally speaking, the videotaping of a discovery witness is appropriate only when:

1. It is expected that the deposition will be relatively short, and;
2. It is anticipated that the witness will have some crucial information.

If the discovery deposition is to be akin to the much maligned "fishing expedition" it is probably a waste of money and effort to film it.

4. The Day in the Life Videotape

One of the most important uses of the videotape camera is filming a badly injured client to illustrate his or her difficulties in performing daily activities. It is just superb for this purpose. When one has such a client this film must be made in every case! It is invaluable for settlement since it enables insurance personnel to see an injured plaintiff trying to perform routine activities and, if a case goes to trial, a jury must be shown these activities that words could never adequately describe.

Because of the importance of this film a burden is placed on the plaintiff's attorney to plan this shoot in great detail. There will have to be careful coordination between the attorney, the client and the camera operator.

A. Working with the Client. Initially the attorney must spend a day with the client to find out which activities pose difficulties, what those problems are and how they might be filmed. A paraplegic will have trouble moving about, will probably have exercise equipment to strengthen arms and chest muscles, and may need a therapist to massage legs and back. A brain-damaged toddler may have trouble eating, may wear a football helmet at all times, may speak poorly, and may have special exercises which mother must supervise or perform daily. An arm amputee will be using his or her head and feet to perform certain functions.

The attorney has to be with the client throughout a day observing everything that goes on, and making copious notes about limitations on activities and the novel ways that the client has been trained, or developed, to accomplish routine activities.

It will not be possible to film every unusual or aberrational act; there will be too many of them. Also, some conduct may violate tenets of good taste, going to the bathroom, for example. Certain daily acts may be necessary but gross: cleaning bed sores, exposing an open wound. Why make a jury ill? They can get angry at the attorney and the client if they are unnecessarily subjected to matters better left to nurses and doctors. Good judgment and common sense come into play here. You can figure out ways to show a jury what your client has to put up with without making them sick. In the case of a colostomy, for example, one may show the stoma and a sample of the collecting bag and any plastic tubing, but *not* the client wearing a partially filled bag and demonstrating its removal, emptying and cleaning.

When the attorney leaves the client's home, he or she ought to have an extensive list of the activities to be filmed, some ideas concerning the rooms or areas in which the activities can be demonstrated, the persons who might participate (mother, wife, therapist), and the length of time each activity may involve.

B. Working with the Videotape Operator. The second meeting has to be with the person who is going to make the film. That individual will have to be appraised of the client's condition, what activities the attorney wants included or emphasized, who will be involved, what the space and lighting limitations may be, and how much time will be devoted to each activity.

Undoubtedly this will be a lively and detailed conversation involving considerable argument about what might be done and how to do it. Certainly the camera operator is the "how-to" expert, and can advise counsel of the limitations of the equipment and the manner in which seemingly distasteful matters can be filmed without offending sensitive persons.

Then there is the matter of the audio. There has to be some conversation, but who is going to say what? The attorney is the best person to act as both narrator and interrogator. He or she can guide the viewer from room to room and from one activity to another in an innocuous, unobjectionable manner, and then proceed to ask the client (parent, spouse, therapist) pertinent questions concerning the activity.

All these details must be gone over with the camera operator who will undoubtedly have comments and suggestions to ensure the fact that this is done right.

C. The Dress Rehearsal. All participants in this production will have to be gathered together for several hours to walk through the proposed shots—truly a dress rehearsal.

The camera operator will be worried about space, lighting, action, and time. Potential interference with the audio will concern him or her (shut off a noisy pump, no TV or record playing in an adjacent room, no dishwasher running in the kitchen.)

The client has to be told of each scene that will be filmed and what the client is supposed to do. Detailed explanations have to be given to mother, husband, or nurse concerning what each of them is to do.

The attorney must interact with all of these people. While counsel need not prepare a script, nonetheless there has to be a rehearsal of what questions are going to be asked and how they are to be answered.

To be certain that nothing is overlooked and that all goes smoothly, the admonition to counsel is once again, *"Write your questions!"*

Everyone should proceed through this rehearsal with the camera operator estimating the time of each shot, answering questions, and reminding people to go about their actions and "don't watch the camera."

Like anything else that is worthwhile, the preparation of a Day in the Life film is time-consuming and takes lots of effort. It is worth it. A one-hour audiovisual demonstration of the living problems of a seriously disabled person can literally be money in the bank!

5. Demonstrations and Accident Reconstructions

Demonstrations represents a very practical use for the videotape camera. In a products liability case one may be concerned with the defective operation of a large machine in a manufacturing plant. Certainly still photographs may be taken of the machine and a witness can describe how it works, but that is never a substitute for actually seeing the machine in operation. One could take the jury for a View (and they usually welcome the trip), but it is simply easier to videotape the machine at work.

It is best to do this by way of a deposition so that a witness can explain, by way of formal interrogation, how the machine works and potentially how the accident occurred or what might have been done to avoid it.

One incurs the usual problems of securing permission to enter the plant, concerns about light and noise, keeping curious onlookers out of the picture and disrupting the manufacturing process as little as possible. None of these poses a significant problem.

As in the uses previously described, the attorney will have to have lengthy discussions with the plant manager, the camera operator, and witness and coordinate the activities of all concerned. Each person will have to know what he or she is expected to do and say—and when. This can come down to such basic instructions as:

Sam, after we have described the machine, I will ask you to demonstrate its operation. At this you step forward, push the button, let the machine go through one cycle, then stop it, step back, and face the camera and I will then ask you questions about what the machine was doing.

Explicit directions are not merely courtesy, they are mandatory.

Another illustration is the situation in which the vision of a bus driver when approaching an intersection, or of an airplane pilot while taxiing down a runway or ramp, is important. These are views that a jury often does not get to see and since they are important to your case by all means videotape them. A bus driver or pilot witness can speak as he or she operates the vehicle and explain problems or events that are pertinent to your case.

All of this effort is a convenient way to give a judge and jury a "you are there" type of knowledge, so that they are in a good position to understand other witnesses' testimony and to make a fair judgment in the case.

Accident Reconstruction is quite a different matter. No one knows for certain what happened in an accident. Counsel has retained an Accident Reconstruction Expert to explore the scene, examine any material objects involved, and review statements of persons who have any information to give concerning the accident or conditions prior or subsequent to it. The expert must then come up with an opinion concerning what happened, who was negligent, and whether this conduct had a causal relation to the accident.

Reconstructing the accident and recording it on videotape are effective, dramatic, fraught with legal problems, and expensive processes.

The expense can be frightful. One may have to hire police officers while one temporarily shuts down a highway, rent heavy equipment at $100 per hour, or more, and haul it to the scene of the accident. One may have to hire operators of the equipment, secure insurance on men and machines, and pay for permits to governmental agencies. Your expert will be involved in much of this planning, and his or her charges may be very high.

Before you get into this expense you had better take a very candid look at your case to see whether its value can justify spending a large amount of money for this purpose. If there is any doubt on this matter, don't do it.

Another problem is that opposing counsel will fight everything you are doing, arguing that the equipment is not identical with that involved in the accident, the light conditions are wrong, the vehicles are going too fast or too slow, the operators are not handling the machines in the same way plaintiff or defendant did, and so on.

The objections will be unending and frustrating and, most important, may be effective unless you have dotted every "i" and crossed every "t" in your preparation of this filming.

In these reconstruction films the attorney has to rely almost exclusively on the expert to make sure that things are correct. For a change the expert will be the director and not the attorney. The expert is the one with the necessary specific knowledge, and it is his or her theory that is being demonstrated by this accident reconstruction. The attorney is relatively helpless to either change anything or add to it.

One thing the attorney must do is to have a checklist of all known facts and to make sure that the reconstruction complies with them. If the accident happened at 6 P.M., don't film at 2 P.M.; if one car was a Buick Riviera, don't use a Buick Skylark; if the vision of an operator is an issue, and one party to the lawsuit was 6 feet two inches, don't use an operator who is 5 feet 4 inches. Details are everything when one is videotaping an accident reconstruction.

If you can get over the hurdles the effort is worth the price. Assuming that the expert is credible, these video productions can be extremely effective in persuading a jury. They actually get to see the event unfold in a way that clearly demonstrates the culpability of the negligent party.

By all means videotape an accident reconstruction provided you comply with the legal requirements—and have lots of money.

SUMMARY

The videotape camcorder is a wonderful instrument to help an attorney to prepare and try his or her case. It has its drawbacks, and you have to be careful in its use. But it is of inestimable value to both counsel and the courts in saving time and in producing the testimony of a witness just as if he or she was "really in court."

To recapitulate, you will want to use video tape for:

1. Deposition for use at trial,
2. Statements of witnesses,
3. Discovery depositions,
4. "Day in the life" presentations, and
5. Demonstrations and accident reconstruction.

REMEMBER THE ADMONITIONS

1. *Be a director.*
   a. Study the location.
   b. Check the lighting.
   c. Work with the operator.
   d. Advise the witness.
2. *In videotaping for use at trial:*
   a. Make it a formal proceeding,
   b. *Write out your questions,*
   c. Make appropriate objections,
   d. Meet with the judge and get rulings on objections in advance of trial, and,
   e. Cooperate with opposing counsel.
3. As to the statement of a witness, try to get him or her to the scene of an accident and then take the statement.
4. *Use for discovery depositions only if:*
   a. The deposition will not be too long, and
   b. The witness can be expected to give important information
5. *For a "Day in the Life" videotape, you MUST:*
   a. Go to the client's home,
   b. Observe the problems and list them,
   c. Plan the shoot with the camera operator,
   d. Have a dress rehearsal, and
   e. *Write out your questions.*
6. Demonstrations and Accident Reconstructions are naturals for videotaping but can be very expensive and difficult.

9

The Use of Discovery in Medical Malpractice and Products Liability Cases

Every Plaintiff's attorney should handle medical malpractice and products liability cases. (Defense attorneys get these cases whether they like it or not.) They are financially rewarding, professionally satisfying, and just plain fun. It is a pleasure and exciting to step aside from the "blue car-red car" routine for awhile, into another person's world—that of an obstetrician or a design engineer.

In terms of earning a livelihood these cases are the best kind of money makers. If they are carefully selected your settlement negotiations and verdicts will always be in the realm of several hundred thousand dollars or higher.

Despite these advantages many Plaintiff's attorneys stay away from them. Why? Because they have had the bitter experience of spending a lot of time and money on a case, only to see it all go down the drain with a defense verdict.

It doesn't have to be that way. These cases can be the biggest and best ones that you ever work on if you will follow three admonitions:

1. Select each case carefully;
2. Win it in Discovery, and
3. Settle the case.

These are specialty cases; there can be no argument about that. They have a language of their own; doctors and engineers don't talk the way lawyers do. The cases involved scientific principles and attitudes; lawyers are used to a world of words and ideas, not test results and intricate procedures. These cases are different from those we routinely work with, and they require special effort on

175

your part in terms of education. You need to develop a new and different attitude in handling the case.

There are certain inviolable rules that apply to the initial evaluation and acceptance of these cases. If you follow them, the chances of success are good; ignore them, and the likelihood of frustration and failure is very high.

**FIVE AXIOMS FOR HANDLING MEDICAL MALPRACTICE
AND PRODUCTS LIABILITY CASES**

1. *Evaluate damages first.* It must be a very substantial case.
2. *Analyze liability carefully.* The odds for success must be in your favor.
3. *Retain an outstanding expert* and rely on his or her advice.
4. *Have an abundance of time,* patience, aggressiveness, and money.
5. *Have a large wastebasket* to hold rejected cases and those voluntarily dismissed.

WHAT TO LOOK FOR IN MEDICAL MALPRACTICE AND PRODUCTS LIABILITIES CASES

A very successful plaintiff's attorney who handles both medical malpractice and products liability cases attributed much of his success to the wastebasket in his office. Into that wastebasket went every one of the cases that he suspected he could not win—and he was very suspicious!

What are we to look for when the case first comes to the office?

Damages

If your prospective client has not sustained serious and permanent injuries, *do not accept that case*! Pitch it! These cases require so much time, effort, and money that the projected verdict or settlement must be very substantial.

Some attorneys set a monetary limit, for example, that the case must be worth a minimum of $100,000. That is a good idea. However you do it, avoid the situation where you spend hundreds of hours of time for a small fee and end up working for less than the minimum wage!

Liability

You must only accept cases in which the liability is reasonably clear. They need not be as definite as an automobile "rear-end collision" but almost. These cases are not ones in which the attorney can afford to gamble. Defense counsel love such cases—they usually can win them. The Plaintiff's attorney must be reasonably certain of success right from the start.

These Cases Must be Handled by an Attorney-Specialist

Both medicine and engineering have a jargon of their own. They employ techniques and devices with which the average attorney is unfamiliar. While an attorney can hire experts to learn as much as he or she needs to know to handle one case, it takes much more than that to work on a succession of such cases.

Someone in a law firm should be assigned exclusively to work on these cases, and that person must be trained. Ideally a small team should be organized consisting of an attorney, secretary, paralegal, or nurse assistant. By repetition, if nothing else, they will become acquainted with the language, customs, and procedures in both medical and engineering matters. Every effort should be made to send the team to seminars and other educational forums for training.

Be Prepared to Spend Money

In cases of this nature there is no question that expenses can be very high. An expert is always required and there will be numerous consultations, preparation of an initial and final report, possibly a discovery deposition, and testimony in Court. The cost will be high.

A large number of discovery depositions will have to be taken and several depositions for use at trial. Numerous documents will have to be secured, sometimes at substantial cost, and duplicates will have to be made for your expert or others. The attorney and the expert will have to review this material and discuss it. It is possible that a model should be made or that the accident be reconstructed and videotaped.

All this discovery and preparatory work adds up to money in large quantities. In the early 1990s, a legal firm can plan to spend between $15,000 and $25,000 for a medical malpractice case and possibly a little less for a products liability case. Since the client never has that kind of money, the attorney must come up with it.

Settlement Should be the Primary Goal

It is suggested that, although every case should be prepared with the expectation that it will go to trial, the primary goal of medical malpractice and products liability cases should be settlement.

The reason lies in the extremely technical and intricate nature of these cases. They are different. They are difficult for a jury to understand. In medical

malpractice cases there is a built-in bias in favor of medical doctors. "Doctor
knows best" and "Do what the doctor ordered" are ideas that are ingrained in us
from earliest childhood. That attitude poses serious problems for Plaintiff's
counsel who enter the courtroom with the scales of justice already tilted against
him or her.

Then there is the question of the amount of a settlement offer. In a properly
prepared case it will always be very high. When pondering acceptance or
rejection, the attorney must bear in mind that there is more involved that just the
case itself; the attorney is really dealing with the entire future life of a badly
injured client. The attorney might be able to reject the offer, lose the case, and
absorb the loss. Can the client? A loss can have a devastating effect on the client.
It is one thing to lose a "whiplash" case where the client is cured or substantially
improved; it is quite another thing to lose a case on behalf of an 18-year-old
paraplegic after a substantial offer is rejected. The rule of thumb? Settlement is
best.

For these reasons a fair and reasonable settlement should be the primary
goal in the handling of these cases.

DISCOVERY IN MEDICAL MALPRACTICE CASES

For the Plaintiff's attorney, two things are vital to success:

1. The deposition of the defendant-doctor, and
2. The employment of an outstanding expert.

For Defense counsel, the keys to success are in:

1. The Discovery deposition of Plaintiff's expert,
2. The employment of an outstanding expert, and
3. The preparation for deposition of the Defendant doctor, nurse, or technician.

Before you can effectively prepare for a deposition or expect a good
opinion letter from your expert, you must have facts. A Plaintiff's attorney
cannot get these facts from the client who usually knows little or nothing. The
client knows only that he or she underwent an operation and woke up paralyzed,
or that he or she went to work and a machine exploded.

The defendant has most of the facts. He, she, or it knows what happened
and why. The job of the Plaintiff's counsel is to gather all of these facts and then
use them to win the case. The three ways to get this information are traditional:

1. Interrogatories,
2. Request for Production of Documents, and
3. Depositions of Witnesses.

In a medical malpractice case, however, these traditional sources of information are handled differently from all other types of cases. For Defense Counsel, certainly Interrogatories and Depositions are most important; there really is little need for a Request for Production since Plaintiff rarely has pertinent documents.

Let us take a detailed look at the use of these various discovery tools.

Interrogatories

Interrogatories have to be used right at the start to gather basic facts constituting the background information concerning a doctor, nurse, or hospital.

Think of this for a moment. Just what do you want to know about this defendant? What is important?

Age and Marital Status. Begin with age and marital status. If your defendant doctor turns out to be 70 years old the chances are that he or she is relying on a medical education that occurred 45 years ago, and you will want to make inquiries about "continuing medical education" and knowledge of new techniques and equipment. On the other hand, a 35-year-old doctor would have been recently educated in the most advanced medical knowledge, and there is no need inquiring about "continuing medical education."

Knowledge of the facts of marriage and children may affect the way you approach a doctor during interrogation at a deposition. A single person without children may have a different attitude while treating your client than a physician who is married and has children. Mental attitudes and lifestyles are legitimate matters to be gone into during a lawsuit.

Medical Education and Teachers. There certainly have to be numerous questions about medical education and, if the defendant is a relatively young person, about the identity of professors in the subject involved in the lawsuit. That latter subject—teachers—can be very important.

How important? Let me illustrate. A young woman had undergone a cholecystectomy at a small, rural hospital and it was "botched up." She consulted another physician at a large urban hospital who advised her to consult an attorney and offered to be a witness for her. The woman retained this writer who, in due course, met with the doctor. When asked about the referral and the willingness to be a witness, the doctor explained,

> This man had been a student of mine. I am personally affronted that he would have attempted this operation and at that hospital. He lacked the expertise, experience, the personnel, and the equipment to perform this procedure at that hospital.

That was a devastating comment. It illustrates that some professors take their job very seriously and will become personally involved when a former student violates their concept of ethics and propriety.

This will not happen often, but it justifies an interrogatory or two about the identity of defendant's professors if the schooling was relatively recent.

Medical Societies and Board Certification. Another series of questions should concern Board Certification and medical societies to which the defendant belongs. Certification by a specialty board within the medical profession is eagerly sought by most specialists and is a requirement by major hospitals to become a staff member. If a doctor who claims to be a specialist is not Board Certified, then red flags are flying and sirens begin sounding for the attorney. It could be that this defendant has failed either the written or the oral examinations! It may also be that he or she is so new at the medical specialty that no attempt has been made to take the examinations due to inexperience. An attorney can do a lot with these circumstances at deposition.

Likewise, joining pertinent medical organizations is pretty much standard fare for doctors. At meetings of these organizations a doctor soaks up information concerning advances within the specialty. If a doctor does not belong to such organizations, that fact should give rise not only to the obvious question of "why not," but also to questions about whether the doctor tries to keep abreast of advances in his or her field of medicine and how this is done.

Hospital Affiliations. Questions about the hospitals at which a doctor has practiced should be routine. You should inquire about the names and addresses of the hospitals, the dates involved, and the type of staff privileges held at the hospital since there are a variety of such privileges. If your defendant is limited in some way in his or her hospital practice, the next question is clearly "why."

Textbooks. Questions must be asked about the books the doctor has in his or her personal library at the office and at home. If the doctor has performed a procedure in a certain way and yet an authoritative textbook says not to do the operation that way, the attorney is in a pretty good position. The language in these texts can really come back to haunt a defendant. An attorney can use these standard textbooks to great advantage both in depositions and the courtroom, but first the attorney must find out if the doctor owns the book, uses it, and acknowledges its authority.

Manuals, Rules, and Regulations. Questions about the existence of manuals, rules, and regulations are essential when a hospital is a defendant. A hospital is a bureaucracy and it has reams of manuals and rules. Where are they? Who has them? Who prepared them and when? Are there minutes of meetings of hospital committees and where are they kept? The answers to these questions help the attorney to know what is available and thus to decide what to include in a Request for Production and whom he or she might plan on deposing some day in the future.

This inquiry about documents—truly a kind of "paper chase"—can be very rewarding. As with the use of textbooks, one may find that the way a thing was done in the instant case was in clear violation of the manual or regulations in existence at the hospital. If this occurs, the doctor or hospital employee is in a terrible position to try to justify his or her conduct.

Incident Reports and Reports to Insurance Companies. These reports are another source of vital information. Every hospital has a system by which its employees report untoward, careless, negligent conduct by persons in the organization. These reports often contain explosive, damning information and must be secured. But do they exist and who has them? Only the use of Interrogations can give the answer.

In one case, a doctor (believed to be drunk) operated on the wrong patient over the objection of the nurses. There *was* an Incident Report, and the comments of the nurses were venomous. That case was settled solely on the basis of the Incident Report.

Reports to insurance companies fall in the same category. They usually describe a troubling incident in words that may lead to liability, contain the names of persons interviewed by a Risk Control Manager and the substance of the conversation, and often discuss the basis for the belief that a "legal matter" is involved. Naturally a Plaintiff's attorney finds this information helpful after he knows about it and secures it through Discovery.

Questions About the Medical Incident Involved in the Lawsuit. One will have to include questions relating to the incident involved in the lawsuit. A careful review of the hospital record may raise questions about data that is not included there. Maybe there are questions about:

Persons, places, and things involved with the client before hospitalization and afterwards;

Persons consulted during treatment, experience in the procedure (how many times have you done this operation?), and

Experts that might have been retained to testify in the case.

Prior Lawsuits and Claims. Many doctors and hospitals have been sued, or have had claims made against them, several times. One neurosurgeon, at last count, was successfully sued four times! And he is still practicing. (This says much about the effectiveness of peer review and medical licensure boards.) For obvious reasons it is imperative to get this information. One may find that a previous case involved the same error that exists in your case.

You have to inquire about claims in addition to lawsuits because a claim similar to yours may have been settled without suit.

For a hospital, limit your questions to suits and claims involving the particular department from which your case arose and include a time limitation. There have been so many lawsuits and claims against hospitals in the last decade that you better not use the word ''all.'' If you do—and if your opposing attorney likes practical jokes—he or she may hire a truck and ship them to you, and *insist* that you accept them!

The important thing is that the attorney must use his or her imagination and be diligent in determining what information is necessary and pertinent to the case. Interrogations have to be custom-made based on the idiosyncrasies of each individual case. A standard set of Interrogatories would be too voluminous to be included in this book, but an outline for the preparation of them would include the following:

Outline for Interrogatories

1. Personal information;
2. Medical education;
3. Names of professors;
4. Hospital affiliations;
5. Medical societies and specialty groups;
6. Books in the office and home library;
7. Experts in specialty recognized as leading authorities;
8. Specific background information about procedure, operation, or care of patient;
9. Specific questions about the procedure, operation, or incident;
10. Names of other persons involved in the operation or incident;
11. Incident reports and reports to insurance company or others; and
12. Prior lawsuits or claims.

Item 7 calls for an explanation. Your expert should be the finest doctor within the specialty that you can find. In a kyphoscoliosis case I retained Dr. Eduardo Luque of Mexico City, a world renowned expert on this subject. At a deposition of the defendant doctor, he was asked if he recognized Dr. Luque as an authority, to which he responded, "Ahh, he is the Master." Little did he know that the master was my expert! If your expert falls into this category, you must try to get Defendant to acknowledge this person's superior expertise, either in Interrogatories or at deposition.

Interrogatories are essential in providing you with basic information about a doctor, nurse, or hospital. They can tell you what data a party has and, in the case of a hospital or multidoctor corporation, who has responsibility and control over these documents. The answers can lead you on exploring trips that often are fruitful. Rarely, but sometimes, they can be dispositive of the liability side of the case. "Was this a high forceps delivery?" Answer: "Yes." If you get an answer like that in an obstetrical case, you won.

Interrogatories have to be carefully tailored to the needs of the case with the realization that, at this stage, all you are after is specific information in the possession of the defendant.

Request for Production of Documents

After the attorney has learned, through the answers to Interrogatories, what documents are out there and who has them, it is time to begin the chore of securing those materials.

Depending on local rules, this can be done either by filing an appropriate Motion or by serving a Request on opposing counsel. In the case of this author's jurisdiction one begins by Request. This can be as informal as a letter, but better practice is to prepare a formal legal document entitled "Request for Production of Documents." This is then mailed to opposing counsel with the customary reference to the procedural rule and the admonition that production is to be forthcoming within the prescribed time limit—20 days or whatever the rules set forth.

What kind of materials should be sought in a Request for Production? The answer to that is simple: everything that the attorney believes that he or she needs and that the other party may have.

Study Office Notes and Hospital Records. It is expected that the Plaintiff's attorney will have had the hospital records and the physician's office notes right from the start. These will have been secured by the use of an Authorization Form signed by the client. Both of these documents will have to be reviewed very carefully to determine whether they contain a reference to other documents.

The doctor's office notes, for example, could have a cryptic comment: 'June 8—Report to insurance company.'' That obviously opens the door to a demand for a copy of that report.

A hospital record may indicate that tissue was removed from a patient and sent to the pathology laboratory: so a pathologist's report will be part of the records. This gives rise to the question, Do I want the tissue slides?" Your expert may want to look at them.

The nurse's notes in the hospital record may reveal for a certain date, "Social Worker in to see patient." The odds are that the social worker made a report concerning this visit, and it is probably good judgment to get a copy of that report. It may be worthless on the liability side of the case but may have value on the damages side, revealing problems resulting from the injury that you may not have known about.

Review Answers to Interrogatories. After exhausting all the possible documentary material in the hospital records and the office notes, the attorney must now turn to the Answers to Interrogatories. These have to be carefully perused to see what they reveal about additional documents that are available and should be secured.

High on this list will be Incident Reports and reports to insurance companies. These vital, revealing documents are essential to Plaintiff's counsel. In some instances they can be depositive of the case. Patients do fall from x-ray tables, out of chairs, and out of bed. Doctors do fail to respond to repeated phone calls from nurses and have been known to violate hospital rules. Each of these affairs will call for an Incident Report, and the tart language sometimes used in these reports will be nearly all that a Plaintiff's attorney needs to nail down the case. It may be that a follow-up deposition will be required, but the Incident Report alone can shake up one's opponent.

Reports or letters sent to an insurance company are usually not protected by any confidentiality statute and must be secured for the same reason as an Incident report; they often contain vital and damaging admissions. Even if they do not contain material that is per se damaging, they will contain informational material that expands upon the bare-bones comments in office notes or hospital records. They often reveal that an investigation was conducted, by whom, what was done, who was interviewed, and the substance of the interview. To be honest, they are fun to read and usually contain a wealth of information.

Unfortunately the reports of Peer Review committees are frequently protected, as are reports to the hospital or physician's attorneys, unless these have been disseminated to third parties. Sometimes copies are sent to the insurance company, the Board of Directors, a state or municipal health agency, or a payor such as Blue Cross and Blue Shield who requests the information to help them decide whether coverage exists. Admittedly these are long shots, but an alert attorney must always be aware that the possibility exists and be prepared to take action if he or she thinks it has occurred.

Written Articles and Curriculum Vitae. Another type of material that should be secured consists of articles or monographs written by a doctor, his or her curriculum vitae, and hospital rules, regulations, directives, and manuals that are pertinent to the case.

We all write on subjects we know best and doctors are no exception. "How sweet it is" to find that your defendant had, in times past, written an article on the very subject that is involved in your case and that in this instance he or she violated the very precepts set forth in the article. That can happen, and the more prolific the author the more likely it is that you will strike gold. You will never know until you get the articles.

Standards of Specialty Groups. Finally, there are the standards and recommendations of various specialty organizations such as the Joint Commission on Accreditation of Hospitals (JCAH) and the American College of Obstetrics and Gynecology (ACOG), among many, many others. Each medical specialty such as orthopedics, neurology, urology, and so forth has its own "college," which provides testing and certification of applicants and which publishes guidelines, standards, and recommendations.

Many of your defendants—especially hospitals—will have these documents. As a matter of convenience, it is easier to get the material locally rather than send off to the specialty organizations for copies.

The standards and recommendations of these groups have to be studied and a determination made whether any of them apply to your case and have been violated or disregarded. Frequently—more than you would guess—you will find one or more that do apply and were ignored. This is important because the medical profession and the hospital industry take these matters very seriously. Your expert will find it quite easy to determine an "unacceptable deviation from standard norms of care" if he or she sees a violation of the standards set forth in a JCAH or ACOG bulletin or manual. Acceptable medical practice requires that these recommendations be followed.

Handling Objections of Opposing Counsel. As with any other type of Discovery proceeding, opposing counsel may balk at producing some of the requested documents. The usual objections to such things as Incident Reports and reports to insurance companies (or others) are that they contain matters of opinion, subjective judgments, or recommendations and that these are not discoverable. This can be a valid objection since discovery deals with facts rather than opinions (except the opinions of experts). From a practical point of view, the objections can be met in one of three ways:

1. You could provoke a confrontation by filing an appropriate Motion to Compel and let the court decide what portions of the document are opinion or speculation.

2. Or you can trust in the judgment of defense counsel and tell him or her to submit the document with the objectionable features "blacked out."

3. An alternative to the second approach is to meet with the other attorney, find out in detail what language he or she desires to delete, and work out an acceptable solution to the problem. Most defense attorneys are both skilled and reasonable such that, at an informal conference, the dispute can be resolved. Remember that the opinions and recommendations objected to are going to be based on the facts contained in the report and if the opinions are troublesome to the defense, a review of the facts will explain why. For that reason you and your expert can reach the same obvious conclusion, and the opinions of the others are not needed. They would be nice—as an admission of a responsible party—but one cannot have everything.

Discovery Depositions

Depositions are the most important of the discovery techniques used in a medical malpractice case. Through the skillful use of this tool you can literally win the case without a trial. A good attorney can put the opposition in such a posture that the case obviously becomes a loser—either by virtue of an admission of the Defendant, or in the case of a hospital, a crucial, responsible witness. Or you can develop testimony to such an extent that the signs all point in one direction—the Defendant's culpability. Literally a Defendant can be boxed in by discovery depositions until there is no realistic alternative except to admit liability. Naturally most defense attorneys will admit this not in a formal sense, but rather by word and gesture.

Remember that, while the deposition is most important, its foundation rests on the Interrogatories that you have served and on the documentary material that you have secured. These must be gone over in detail and, from them and the other materials in your file, questions for the depositions must be carefully prepared.

There are certain basic rules to follow in preparing for medical depositions:

1. Write out your questions.
2. Depose every person involved in the incident.
3. Keep the pressure on; be aggressive and searching.
4. Take your time.
5. Ask opinion questions.
6. Force the Defendant Doctor to admit liability or to admit facts that establish liability.

1. Write out Your Questions. No attorney can effectively depose one witness over a long period of time and about a variety of subjects, nor depose several witnesses about their roles in a case solely on the basis of memory and experience. It cannot be done. There are too many witnesses, too many questions, too many facts. *The questions must be carefully prepared and written.*

It is good to remember that you are not bound to the pace of written questions. When the attorney is making headway—"scoring with the witness" as we commonly say—keep the questions coming and forget the script. The written questions are there to help you, not to bind you. But the point is that you will have a host of material to cover with each witness and you don't know in advance just when you will strike gold and have to divert into an unexpected subject matter. That is when all your talent and experience come into play. You will have to ask questions spontaneously, and they better be good, probing, aggressive questions. It may be that you need go no further—the witness has given you all you could ask. In that event all the hard work that went into the rest of the written questions will have been wasted. That may be true but since you don't know when you will "strike gold," the questions have to be prepared so as to exhaust all the knowledge of each witness.

2. Take the Depositions of Everyone Involved. During an operation, a number of persons are gathered around the operating table. Each of them is endowed with the usual five senses and when something goes wrong they know it. The trouble is they won't tell you, not voluntarily at least.

The combination of hospital records, office notes, Incident Reports, and Answers to Interrogatories gives you a lot of information but not all—and often not enough. The missing links have to come from depositions.

When deposing doctors, nurses, and technicians, be aware of the fact that these persons regard the Plaintiff and his or her attorney as "The Enemy." They all have a tendency to close ranks and to supply little information as possible and, sometimes, to outright lie or conveniently forget.

With an awareness of this fact of life, Plaintiff's counsel must depose everyone involved in the incident at hand. Someone is going to remember an important fact and will reveal it, whether out of concern for the truth, forgetfully answering a question directly, or blurting it out in the excitement of the moment. One medical malpractice case illustrates the importance of deposing all the witnesses. In the delivery of a baby, numerous persons were involved since labor and delivery occurred over two shifts. Despite some extraordinary happenings during the delivery, no one of the first seven nurses remembered anything unusual or the preparation of any Incident Report. These depositions were particularly time-consuming and laborious since the hospital was some distance from my office and, due to circumstances, only two or three could be taken per day. It was wearying to make the journey only to have repeated disappointing results. Finally, in the eighth deposition, the nurse reprimanded counsel by saying, in effect, ''Why ask me, it's all in the Incident Report.'' The silence that followed this statement was dramatic and eloquent. Defense counsel was outraged that both he and Plaintiff's counsel had been deceived. Hospital administration came up with both an excuse (hypocritical, of course) and the Incident Report, which proved to be a devastating document. The defendant doctor and most of the other nurses were redeposed and the truth came out. The case was settled.

This sort of thing happens so often that it must be a cardinal rule to depose everyone. Some person—perhaps the anesthesiologist, a nurse, or a technician—knows the truth, remembers, and will speak about it. But the burden is on the Plaintiff's attorney to keep pounding away until the witness is found who will tell what happened.

3. Be Aggressive and Searching. A discovery deposition is really an exploration amidst a hostile environment and is no place for the shy and timid attorney. This is neither the time nor the place to worry about making friends.

The attorney must display a no-nonsense, aggressive, challenging attitude. The persons being deposed don't want to be there and don't want to be forced to give information that is going to hurt either a coemployee, their employer-hospital, or a medical doctor who may be well respected. The questioning attorney is placed in the unpopular and unfortunate position of having to force these people to do exactly the things they don't want to do.

One cannot accomplish this goal by a willing acceptance of everything the witness is saying. First of all, the attorney must have in mind every single item of a documentary nature in which this witness was involved. One must be able to say very quickly in response to an answer, ''Nurse Jones, you just said that so-and-so happened about 2:30 A.M., but your notes for that hour say differently. Which is the truth of the matter?'' The important thing is that as soon as the attorney heard the answer he or she knew that it contradicted the nurse's notes in the hospital records. The attorney must have this knowledge—and the ability to call it forth instantly—throughout a deposition.

The attorney must be prepared to contradict a witness with salient facts and to demand an explanation of the difference. One must not accept the ''I don't know'' and ''I don't remember'' answers. The attorney must go on with persistent questioning about peripheral matters until it becomes clear that the witness really does remember many things and really does know various facts, some of which may be helpful. This is what an ''aggressive and searching attitude'' means. If the witness does not know or remember Fact A, he or she may be forced to admit that they do know Facts B, C, and D which point directly to Fact A. But if one merely accepts the "I don't remember" routine, the existence of knowledge about these other facts will never be discovered.

There is never an excuse for behavior on the part of the questioning attorney that is rude, coarse, or belligerent. One can be pleasant and charming as one recites a litany of facts that fly in the face of the witnesses' answer and then demand an explanation. One can smile as one challenges a witness. Quite naturally a witness who is being forced to admit facts may describe counsel as being rude or belligerent, but that emotional reaction need not be true and should not be. Your opposing attorney is usually a pretty good guide to when one has crossed the line and should be listened to. Suffice it to say that one can be aggressive without being nasty.

4. Take Your Time. Some attorneys go into a discovery deposition expecting to be disappointed and are in a big rush to get it over with. The best advice to this attorney is, "Don't even bother taking the deposition." You waste your time and that of the witness.

Be definition a discovery deposition is an exploration, a search for facts. It has to be a careful, time-consuming matter. There is no way to avoid that. Before even beginning the deposition the attorney has to ask:

1. What facts do I need?
2. Which of these facts can this witness give me?

Then one must frame the questions and begin a thorough, diligent inquiry into the facts the witness knows. You have to lay a foundation before you come to the crucial questions, and this takes time. There are no shortcuts. The voluminous records that have to be referred to frequently only add to the time needed.

Consider the number of times a nurse may make entries in a hospital record. It is possible that she made an initial assessment, her entries appear in the nurse's notes, she drew lines on a graphic chart, her handwriting appears in a medication record, and she may be named as present during an operation. A careful attorney will want to inquire about all these things. Much of this inquiry will be in the nature of background information, but you must do it because once in awhile—and often enough to justify it—you get very helpful and unexpected answers. When this has happened a few times, the attorney realizes that he or she must be slow and careful. It pays off!

The highway signs say, "Speed kills." The age-old adage states, "Haste makes waste." Both admonitions are especially true in discovery depositions.

5. Do Ask Opinion Questions. There is always a fight about opinion questions. Many attorneys are afraid to ask them because they are afraid the answer will be negative and also because they doubt their right to ask them.

Both concepts are wrong. To begin with, you are never going to know whether the answer is positive or negative until you ask the question. Second, let opposing counsel make the objection: don't do it for him or her. Don't anticipate trouble.

The truth of the matter is that most of the persons deposed in a medical malpractice case are experts. Doctors are experts in their field of medicine; nurses are experts in matters relating to nursing care; technicians who operate equipment are experts in the use of that machinery. In addition they all have opinions and sometimes are quite willing to express them, and in a matter that can be helpful to you.

You may not be able to use this opinion in court. One cannot force a person to be an expert. But who is talking about a trial? In settlement negotiations the opinion of a nursing supervisor that the nursing care in your case was substandard can have a profound effect on a claims person's evaluation of a case at the home office. The opinion of an anesthesiologist that he or she had to literally fight for the life of the patient due to a surgeon severing numerous blood vessels and ''being where he should not have been'' can chill the enthusiasm of a defense attorney. The anesthesiologist may not qualify as a surgeon, but a candid comment can make everyone sit up and take notice.

This is why it is important to ask the opinion question. It puts on the record the attitude of one who is generally familiar with the event and the standard of care that applies to it.

Will opposing counsels object? Probably. But sometimes they do not for whatever reason: other times they carelessly let it slip by. Or, at argument, the Court may well rule that the person is an expert in fact and that at a discovery deposition the opinion may be elicited, irrespective whether that person will be called as an expert in court.

There is so much to be gained and so little to be lost that the opinion questions should be asked.

6. Questioning the Defendant Doctor. You can take two approaches when deposing the defendant doctor:

1. Box him or her in by a series of questions whose answers leave any objective expert no alternative except to declare negligent conduct.
2. Go for the jugular and force the doctor to admit to negligent conduct.

The final decision on how to proceed will be made during the deposition and after the attorney has had sufficient time to evaluate the character and attitude of the witness.

Sometimes doctors are stricken with guilt feelings after a tragic end to a medical procedure and will let this be known by word or gesture. These persons may tell defense counsel to settle the case at all costs, especially after the deposition, when he or she realizes that Plaintiff's counsel really knows how and where the negligence occurred. Other physicians are meticulous and painfully honest, and these persons will admit their error when it is pointed out to them. With this type of person one has a good chance of securing some form of admission of liability after you have demonstrated that you know what you are talking about and what went wrong.

In a way of a good illustration, the Defendant, an experienced neuro-surgeon, was performing a laminectomy at the L-5 level (the lower back). He was trying to cut out the spongy "shock absorber" that separates the bony vertebrae in our spinal column. A portion of this material had extruded and was pressing on a nerve. This is commonly referred to as a ruptured or herniated disc. These nerves, which begin at the spinal cord and proceed throughout the body, are sometimes identified by the vertebrae around and through which they pass. In this instance the doctor referred to the "L-5 nerve root." That nerve root is made up of about 15 filaments, each of which is about a millimeter thick. While endeavoring to get past the nerve root, he severed some of the filaments. The patient-plaintiff was left with a "foot drop," a serious condition in which he cannot flex the foot up and down, and thus cannot walk without a special brace. This is a common operation for a neurosurgeon, and the doctor must have performed it dozens of times.

The critical portion of the deposition is the following excerpt:

Q: All Right. Proceed now with your description of the operation.

A: As I previously stated, the Kerrison was in the process of removing some bone from the lamina when a filament of the nerve was avulsed. This bone was continued to be removed beyond that part because it still had inadequate exposure to the ruptured disc. Then when the ruptured disc and the free fragment were identified, they were removed with better exposure, and then all available disc material was removed from the interspace itself. It should be noted that no spinal fluid was seen in the wound at any time during the operation, which would indicate that the dura or the sac covering the other nerves in the spinal canal were not injured. The root, after the ruptured disc and the other disc material was removed, was noted to be relaxed. It was not tight. It was felt that there was no pressure on it at that time, and the epidural vein was then bovied. It's not my procedure to use the bovy until the nerve root is adequately removed from continuity for fear of burning a nerve itself. There was no inadvertent bleeding during this procedure, and the epidural vein was bovied at the conclusion of the removal of the disc material. That concluded the operation, and a piece of Gelfoam was placed in the laminectomy defect. It was irrigated with normal saline solution, and the wound was closed with dexon suture material to the fascia and to the subcutaneous tissue. Steri-strips were applied to the skin, a sterile dressing was applied, and the patient was returned to the recovery room in good condition.

Q: Doctor, going back to the time when you took over and were utilizing the ronguers, did you recognize that there was a danger of avulsing the nerve root?

A: There was a danger of injuring the nerve. Whether there was a danger of avulsing a nerve filament or pressing too hard against the nerve itself when you are trying to move it and stretch it, all of these things are possible during this operation.

Q: Well, in this case, did you avulse a filament?

A: Yes, sir.

Q: Did you expect that that was likely to happen at the time that you utilized the ronguers?

A: No.

Q: But, I take it, you did feel that that was the more serious portion of the operation?

A: Yes. This is the most serious part, and it's a routine operation. It is the trickiest part of the operation and the most delicate part of the operation, routinely.

Q: Using reasonable medical care, is it possible to do it without avulsing a filament of the nerve root?

A: Well, I think it is the hope of every surgeon that the nerve would not be damaged in any way and, of course, that is what usually occurs—that is, the nerve is not injured. There was nothing that was done in this particular operation that was any less careful than any other lumbar laminectomy that I have performed.

Q: And you come across nerves that are tight in other patients.

A: Certainly.

Q: And you are used to utilizing the ronguers without avulsing a filament, is that right?

A: That's correct.

Q: So that utilizing reasonable medical care, you should be able to utilize the ronguers without avulsing the filament?

A: Yes, sir, that's correct.

Those fateful words at the end won the case. Serious thought was given to moving for a Summary Judgement based *on that statement*, but there was no need to do this. The case was settled for a very substantial sum because of the doctor's statements in the deposition.

It is worthy of note that the questions were not framed in a haphazard manner. The preceding portion of the testimony constitutes about three pages in a 60-page deposition. The entire deposition was arranged into sections:

One dealt with the doctor's background and experience.

One inquired into the textbooks he used and studied from.

Another section related to his insurance and prior claims made against him.

A fourth dealt with the hospital records.

The fifth section inquired about his relations with his Resident-Assistant.

The sixth dealt with the operation itself.

A seventh section explored compliance with the doctrine of Informed Consent.

The important point is that the deposition was planned and the questions thought out in advance. Success in this case just didn't happen as a matter of luck or because the attorney happened to spontaneously think of a question. This very point is evident in a quotation from the very famous lawyer, Louis Nizer, who was asked about the role of luck in his success. He responded something to this effect:

Oh, Lady Luck visits me all right, but somehow she always appears at 2 A.M. when I'm working in my library. She never shows up when I'm out on the golf course.

Just so in this instance. The file had been reviewed, the hospital record studied in minute detail, several chapters of a text on neurosurgery had been read, some thought had been given to the questions, and an outline was prepared.

And it was all worthwhile. There was no need for a trial—thanks to a good deposition.

Other doctors are the blustering arrogant, "I can do no wrong" type of person. That attitude is perfectly all right. Since these persons know so much and are so certain of themselves, they are perfect candidates for being led through a series of questions about standards, rules, textbook recommendations, and the opinions of outstanding doctors in the specialty. Finally, they are forced into a corner and the conclusion eventually becomes apparent that they were negligent. This approach requires a lot of time and great deal of preparation. One must have ready reference to the words of a textbook, the standards of a specialty, or the regulations of the hospital. The doctor must be forced to admit that there is a right way of doing things and must be led step by step, through his or her way of doing the procedure until it becomes apparent that he or she did not do it the right way. Do not expect this witness to admit to error; this will not happen. One tries to get the witness to admit to the correctness of the standards set forth in the texts, or the specialty group, and then admit to the various acts that he or she did during the operation. As an example, read the following initial colloquy to an obstetrician:

Q: Doctor, are you acquainted with the textbook known as *Williams Obstetrics*?

A: Of course.

Q: Have you read that book, doctor?

A: Yes, I have.

Q: Do you consider that book to be authoritative on the subject of obstetrics?

A: Yes, I do.

Q: Do you apply the principles contained in that book to your own practice?

A: Of course. I'd be a fool not to.

At this point the attorney is off and running, *but* he or she had better know in detail what is in that book and how the defendant violated the principles set forth in the book.

If the attorney is knowledgeable and skilled, all the subsequent questions are going to revolve around precisely what the doctor did. At appropriate moments the attorney will point out that Williams states that things should have been done differently and demands an explanation. The answer will often be given in an unconvincing stammer.

At the conclusion of this deposition you don't need an admission of liability; the record says it all.

In the upcoming excerpt from an actual deposition, the doctor's conduct is compared to certain specific legal requirements relating to the Informed Consent Doctrine. Most states have some form of Informed Consent Doctrine, which requires that a doctor explain to patient's the nature of an operation, its risks, and alternatives to it. The more explicit the criteria required of the doctor, the better your chances of taking a successful deposition on this matter. In Pennsylvania, the doctrine was definite, requiring that a doctor advise a patient in four areas:

1. The nature of the operation;
2. The alternatives to the operation;
3. The risks, hazards, and dangers of the operation; and
4. Possible long-term ill effects from the operation.

The case involved an enlarged prostate which required an operation resulting in a permanent injury. There are several ways to remove the prostate, the most common being suprapubic, retropubic, transurethal, and perineal operations. In this case the doctor elected to do a retropubic prostatectomy. His patient was a real estate agent with no particular medical knowledge. These were some of the questions asked in the deposition of the doctor:

Q: Doctor, do you recall specifically having advised Mr. Jones of the several types of prostatectomies that can be performed?

A: Do I have a specific recollection?

Q: Yes.

A: No.

Q: Do you have a specific recollection of advising Mr. Jones that you were going to perform a retropubic prostatectomy?

A: No.

Q: Do you have a specific recollection of advising him why you were utilizing this type of procedure?

A: No.

Q: Do you have a specific recollection of advising him of any risks, hazards, or dangers of this procedure?

A: No.

Q: Do you have a specific recollection of advising him of alternatives to this type of procedure?

A: No.

Q: Or to an operation at all, alternatives to an operation?

A: No.

Q: Do you have a specific recollection of advising Mr. Jones of the possibilities of incontinence resulting from this operation?

A: No.

Q: Is incontinence a possible result of this operation?

A: Yes.

Q: All right. Now, doctor, let me ask you just a little bit and perhaps much the same questions as regards to your general procedure with your patients, since you have no specific recollection as to Mr. Jones. Do you ordinarily sit down and discuss with your patients the nature of the operation you are going to do?

A: Yes.

Q: When do you ordinarily have this discussion in terms of the date and time of the operation?

A: I have a specific plan which is that if there is any question of prostatic surgery, I will explain this to the patient as an outpatient the very first time I come to the conclusion that it is a possibility. Then when I know things I need to know about the man, I will discuss it with him the day before his surgery or the day that I know the specific method that I am going to use.

Q: How much time do you spend with the patient in this discussion in the hospital immediately before the surgery?

A: I may spend three minutes; I may spend half an hour.

Q: What determines the amount of time you spend with the patient?

A: The questions that the patient raises.

Q: If he does not ask any questions, then you spend three minutes?

A: Possibly.

Q: All right. Doctor, tell me what you tell a patient upon whom you are going to perform a retropubic prostatectomy.

A: I tell him that he will have an incision in his abdomen, that the enlargement of his prostate will be removed without entering his bladder, that he will wear a catheter through his urethra for a period of five to seven days, and that he will have a small rubber drain in his incision. He will have bottles of water irrigating his bladder for the first 24 to 48 hours, but he will be out of bed the day of the operation in most instances.

Q: Is there anything more?

A: I think that's what I tell them.

Q: I want you to search your recollection and tell me once again, can you remember anything more that you tell them? Ignoring any questions they may have, in terms of what you tell them is there anything more?

A: I don't think so.

Q: Do you habitually advise your patients upon whom you are going to do a retropubuc prostatectomy of the alternative types of procedures that you could utilize?

A: Yes.

Q: Tell me about it.

A: I tell them this when I explain the procedures that I am going to do, because I contrast it and compare it with others.

Q: You see, previously I had asked you, after you told me what you tell them, whether there was anything more, and you said no. Now it turns out that you tell them a little bit more.

A: Then I'm sorry. I must have misunderstood you.

Q: Tell me about what you tell the patient as a matter of routine.

A: I tell them that there are three common methods that we use in prostatic surgery: that we use suprapubic, retropubic and transurethral. We like to do transurethral if it is possible because we think it is a simpler operation for the patient to get over, and we hope that he can have a transurethral. I explain that the transurethral is removal of the adenoma piece by piece, without making an incision; that he will wear a catheter for three to five days following this, if this is done.

    I explain to him that the suprapubic prostatectomy is, as far as he is concerned, indistinguishable from the retropubic prostatectomy, except that he will have more pain if the suprapubic prostatectomy is done, and it will always be done in case he needs vesical drainage in addition to his prostatectomy.

Q: Do you go on and explain the retropubic prostatectomy?

A: No, not until I decide which one he is going to have, and then I tell him in detail.

Q: I want to hear the detail, doctor.

A: I gave you the detail.

Q: As to the retropubic prostatectomy?

A. Yes, I did. I described the whole thing.

Q: Now, I really want you to search your recollection. Is there anything more than what you have given Mr. Smith here and stated for the record that you tell these patients, either as outpatients or inpatients on the day before operation?

A: I tell them they are going to have to sign a permit for blood.

Q: I ask you again, search your memory. Is there anything more that you routinely tell people in the position of Mr. Jones who are about to be operated on the next day, or people like Mr. Jones whom you are sending to the hospital for an eventual possible operation?

A: I can't think of anything else that I tell them routinely.

As a result of this deposition a Motion for Summary Judgment was filed and it was granted! As the law then stood it was a simple matter for the Judge to compare the testimony of the doctor with the requirements of the Informed Consent Doctrine and to conclude that the explanation failed to comply with the established standards.

7. Timing of Defendant's Deposition. When should you take the deposition of the defendant doctor? Under ideal circumstances this person should be the last to be deposed. Careful preparation requires the attorney—and the expert—to have a chance to review all prior discovery material (interrogatories, depositions, documents), consult with regard to the errors committed by the defendant, and prepare questions. Sometimes the expert will want the attorney to ask questions that will clarify certain matters or explain things the Defendant did. Then, after detailed study of the documents and records, and after lengthy consultation with one's expert, the attorney is ready to take the deposition. The goal of such a deposition is not merely to uncover facts and opinions; it is to *win your case*. It can be done.

Occasionally you do have sufficient information to permit your own expert to conclude that negligence was present. The hospital records are silent as to vital matters, the office notes are not helpful, and your expert may be suspicious but unable to document negligence. On these rare instances, you have to depose the Defendant first. This is not a happy state of affairs. The Plaintiff's attorney is at a great disadvantage, and there is very little chance that you can take this deposition with the hope of winning the case. Nonetheless it has to be done.

In these instances your only goal is to gather all the information possible. A lengthy consultation with your expert is essential to find what facts the expert is looking for and what areas you should inquire into. After learning what you are after, the deposition can be taken to secure these facts. At this deposition the attorney need not be confrontational but must be detailed. Every effort must be made to learn everything the doctor knows about the incident.

At the conclusion of this deposition, the expert should review the testimony, and a determination should be made at that time whether negligence exists, what the theory of liability is going to be, and what is going to be needed to prove it. This is the moment to decide whether to proceed with the case or to place it carefully in the wastebasket. It is often true that, after this deposition is taken, good judgment requires that the case be dismissed or, if the client objects to this, that counsel withdraws as attorney for Plaintiff.

Incidentally the means for taking such a deposition are usually set forth in rules that provide for limited Discovery (including such a deposition) before filing a Complaint and for the purpose of deciding whether a Complaint should be filed.

The Expert and Discovery

To experts, the facts that you secure by discovery make up the essential components of their opinion. For that reason you must consult frequently with experts so as to apprise them of the facts you have already gathered and then receive their input concerning the information still needed. It is an ongoing relationship. There should be a frank and open interchange of ideas. Experts know what is needed and the attorney knows how to get it. Experts can be very helpful in guiding the attorney into unknown sources of information. There may have been testing done by a drug company or studies compiled at a university, or a prominent physician may have written an article pertinent to the case. The attorney very often doesn't even know these things exist. Now—once pointed in the right direction—the attorney can gather this additional information. It may require the issuance of a subpoena and the taking of a deposition in one case or a Freedom of Information Request to a governmental agency in another case. But with time and patience the needed information can be secured. In this way, as discovery progresses, your case gets stronger and stronger.

Another area in which experts must be used is with regard to their knowledge of hospital practices and procedures. The hospital Defendant is never going to voluntarily tell Plaintiff's counsel what it has that might be helpful, but the expert physician knows the ''in's and out's'' of hospitals and can advise counsel what the hospital ought to have. The means to get it is there: a Request to Produce or a subpoena duces-tecum and a deposition of some record custodian.

Finally, experts must be used in planning the deposition of the defendant doctor or vital nurse. Plaintiff's counsel may literally have to ''Attend classes'' with the expert to learn the intricacies and details of an operation so as to know where the defendant erred and what questions to ask to develop these facts.

After the attorney knows the way things ought to have been done, experts can help by pointing out pertinent sections of textbooks that should be incorporated in questions, statistics that are available and that can be used in questions, and tests and studies that can be the basis of questions to the doctor.

There has to be a close relationship between the expert and the attorney in the preparation for the depositions of all crucial witnesses.

Discovery and Settlement

After discovery is concluded, your case should be in prime condition to initiate settlement discussions. There should not be anything more to learn about the case. Each attorney will have watched the various deponents, listened to what they have to say, and had an opportunity to judge their credibility. All of the pertinent, relevant documents will have been secured and in the possession of both Plaintiff's and Defendant counsel.

Under these circumstances why not discuss settlement? It is the perfect time.

The primary obligation for going forward is on the Plaintiff's attorney, and this is the time to begin the preparation of a Settlement Brochure (discussed at length in Chapter 13). Settlement Brochures are a wonderful way to show a Defendant, his or her attorney, and the insurance company that you have an excellent case, that your client's financial losses are substantial and can be documented, and that your settlement demand is sensible and reasonable. It puts into the hands of those powerful, but invisible, ''home office people'' a document that clearly outlines your case as to liability, damages, and demand. Now, after discovery is finished and everything is fresh in your mind, is the time to prepare that Settlement Brochure.

Something about settlement must be reiterated: *Settlement should be the primary goal in all medical malpractice cases.* There is a widespread and powerful attitude in our country that medical doctors are nice people who know what they are doing. There are many reasons for this attitude: Doctors are taught to be nice and pleasant at all times. They hold your hand, speak in kind and comforting tones, and are always upbeat. They order medication that gives you blessed relief from pain. They keep all bad news away from the patient, never explain a test or procedure, and in the event of a poor result blame, God, fate, or bad luck. Never, never do they criticize another doctor or the hospital staff. Publicly they are endlessly praised by the media. Their income or charge for an operation or procedure is never mentioned.

As a result of this pervasive propaganda—they are let's face it—hard to beat. That is a fact of life. In the jurisdiction in which this author practices, doctors win about 65 to 70 percent of all jury trials. (This is admittedly an unfair statistic since the ''good'' cases are usually settled, but the enormous prejudice in favor of doctors still has to be taken into account.) This bias is the most important reason to make settlement the primary goal of these cases.

A second reason is that the Plaintiff is usually a very seriously injured person—frequently an infant or young child—with a permanent disability. The attorney has to remember that he or she is dealing with the entire future life of that person. It is one thing for a disabled client to look forward to being able to move into his or her own home someday—especially equipped to suit his or her needs—and with trained personnel for assistance. It is quite another to move into a public, hospital-like facility for the rest of one's life. That is what an attorney has to think of when pondering the problem of settlement versus trial.

Finally, the insurance companies will pay very substantial sums in settlement. If they see a potential million-dollar verdict, they will settle that case for $800,000. If Plaintiff's counsel has a reputation for good judgment in evaluation of cases and is known to be willing and able to try a case, every insurance company will want to try to settle. The motive is to save money on a potential verdict and to save the fees and expenses involved in a trial. It just makes good business sense.

Suggestion: Suppose you get a substantial offer that will pay you a good fee and will provide for your client's future needs, but you are inclined to reject it. Stop for a moment and consult with a close friend. Get out of your office and talk it over with someone you trust. It may be that liability is not as clear as you think or that in the excitement and jubilation of having done well in discovery, your demand is excessive. In that event, a fresh point of view from an experienced friend will help bring you back to earth.

Doctors are hypersensitive persons who shun public embarrassment like the plague; insurance companies are business corporations who pay when they have to. Both of them will fight if you force them into a corner and try to keep pounding. In that fight you are the one who goes to trial with the odds against you. Possibly you can afford to lose the case. The question is can your client? Think about that.

DISCOVERY IN PRODUCTS LIABILITIES CASES

In a medical malpractice case, a plaintiff's attorney is usually suing a medical doctor who was the actual "doer"—that is, he or she did the operation. Even if a hospital is involved, it is relatively a small, self-contained, local unit in which everything is done within the walls of one building or complex. The attorney can zero in quickly on the specific department and even on the very persons who did the dirty deed. Perhaps it was this nurse who gave the injection or that technician who performed the CAT scan. It is possible in these cases to actually find someone to blame.

None of that is true in a products case. Instead, one deals with a big corporation with many departments, offices, and plants scattered all over the country and with dozens of people involved in the design, testing, and manufacture of a product.

Building an airplane is far different from performing an appendectomy. If the surgeon cuts an artery, the attorney can demand an explanation from *a person*. If a wing falls off an airplane, to whom do you go to find out why? It could be the design, which involved many engineers. It could be faulty testing, and it could be poor quality control during manufacture. Which is it? Who knows?

That is the problem in a products liability case. Sure, that good old Restatement of Torts Section 402A solves lots of problems. But you really hate to rely on presumptions, especially when the defense is prepared to bring in multiple experts who swear their product performed as advertised and that Plaintiff's own miscues caused the problem.

Sooner or later these cases always come down to the eternal questions:

What went wrong?

Why did it happen?

Who was at fault?

The jury expects an answer: Plaintiff's attorney better provide a good one. So it's back to Discovery to get the information. And what a job it is—with people, places, and things in great number and scattered all over the country.

As with the medical malpractice case, the direction, counsel, and advice of an expert is necessary and invaluable. Only an experienced engineer, architect, scientist, or toxicologist can guide you through the maze of divisions, departments, laboratories, and manufacturing sites to tell you what documentation is out there and who is likely to have it.

And documentation is what you are after.

In a products case documentation is everything. No one person can answer all your questions. The work is so spread around that many people are involved in each step of a design or manufacturing process. They keep in touch and inform each other by means of documents, whether those documents are blueprints, test results, or letters.

Request for Production of Documents

This is the primary discovery tool in a products liability case. Persons in a corporation report to each other with regard to their work by some kind of writing, and it is this writing that you must secure.

Make Your Request or Demand as Broad as Possible. When requesting documents most attorneys err in making their demand too sweeping or too narrow. If the case involves a defect in the steering mechanism of an automobile, do you really want "all blueprints and drawings relating to the 1987 Ford Thunderbird automobile?" Do you really want to have thousands of drawings suddenly dumped on your desk? Be sensible.

On the other hand one cannot restrict the Request to, for example, only the mechanical aspects of the steering mechanism. What about the hydraulic and electrical systems? The drawings relating to those systems must be secured.

Likewise the idea for a new drug, car, or household product may have been conceived years before work began to develop it. If your case involves a new drug that caused harm, and if you suspect inadequate testing and a cover-up of test results in the period 1989–1990, your request for "all letters or memos relating to the drug" can bring you a veritable flood of papers that will fill every nook and cranny of your office. You don't want this material even if the Defendant was willing to give it to you.

Common sense has to be practiced. Limit your request in terms of subject matter, time, and type of document. Your expert can help you on this. But, after having done so go after every single document that is included in that category of paperwork. If you're after test results get every test that was ever conducted on Drug A during the time period involved.

Expect Evasion from the Defendant. It is unfortunate to have to make this statement, but most corporations and businesses will scrutinize your demand or request with a view to complying by giving you as little documentation as possible and hiding documentation that hurts. Often this will require you to turn to the Courts with a Motion to Compel Compliance.

Most of the time documents are interrelated so that a careful reading of the papers you do receive will lead you to conclude that there are others you have not received. Incriminating evidence is hard to hide. A bad test result will be referred to in letters, memos, design changes, or complaints from one department or another. A bureaucracy just simply cannot "sanitize" every paper it sends to you, and a careful reading of the papers you get will lead you to the papers that were not sent.

It is a kind of game that will go on forever. Who, having a smoking gun in hand, won't try to hide it? That is pretty normal behavior. Expect it. Be prepared for it. Plan in advance to have to go to Court with an appropriate Motion to Compel the production of other documents that defendant has not given you.

Go After Tests and Test Results with a Vengeance. When a product does not work the way it was expected to and causes injury, the problem is usually one of faulty design or manufacture. Testing and quality control are an essential part of both aspects of the manufacturing process. You must get those reports.

It is normal to go after the tests but memos, letters, and reports must have been written about those tests analyzing and criticizing them. Can anyone forget the memos and letters about the Pinto gas tank which reflected the view that, while test results indicated the likelihood of explosion, cost factors dictated that it was cheaper to pay the occasional verdict than to make the gas tank safer! Undoubtedly the testing showed the problem but it was the later memo or report that demonstrated the callous negligent conduct—i.e., sending out to the marketplace a product known to be defective.

Your expert can certainly analyze the test results and decide whether the product is defective. But it is *so* helpful to get all the paperwork about those tests from the Defendant which may reveal that it definitely knew that the product would not work as advertised.

Finally, you cannot ignore the fact that some testing may be done by an independent laboratory. Do not be put off by assertions (or your suspicions) that the Defendant did limited or minimal testing of a product. If that is true, you may justifiably suspect that more extensive testing was farmed out to an independent laboratory. Those results will be in Defendant's files but your Request has to be broad enough to encompass those records.

Get All Blueprints, Specifications, Drawings, and Design Changes. This material represents the basic information about all products. No manufacturer can exist without drawings and specs. It is the most easily procured because everybody knows it exists and no Defendant will fuss about submitting it. Quite naturally your expert has to have it as it represents foundation material for his or her study of the product.

Design change specifications and blueprints are a little bit different. A Defendant may not want you to have them because they were not implemented, or were implemented for miscellaneous reasons (cost, cosmetic improvement, etc.), or because they reveal a significant flaw in the original product. You may have to fight for these documents and you are in the position of having no alternative but to do so. You must have them.

Letters, Reports, Memos. These documents are also essential, but they are not the factual foundation materials like specs and drawings. This material is informative and important because many times it contains admissions of failure. Like an Incident Report in a medical malpractice case, a letter, memo, or report can contain the very information you are seeking regarding careless or negligent conduct.

Lawsuits and Complaints. It may be that your case is only the latest in a long list of complaints about a product. When corporations operate in all or many of the fifty states, there is no way you are going to know about a lawsuit filed against the Defendant (raising issues similar to yours) one year ago in some far distant state. Likewise, the marketing or sales department could have a dozen letters of complaint from exasperated customers that the product just doesn't work and is defective. All of these documents are available to you in a Request for Production and demand for them must be made. [Incidentally, the American Trial Lawyers Association (ATLA) maintains an extensive library of lawsuits and other materials on a host of products and should be consulted.]

Occasionally one will find a lawsuit that involves the identical defect that exists in your case, along with one or more letters of complaint from a customer about such a defect. These gems can be used to devastating effect against Defendant. They alone can be the basis for settlement of a case, and your work is essentially done when they are produced—at least as to the liability side of the case.

Interrogatories

Little new need be said about the use of Interrogatories. As in other kinds of cases their use represents the essential first step and the answers provide information:

1. What is out there that I need?
2. Where is it?
3. Who is the custodian?

In this matter, particularly, you have to rely on your expert since simply too many documents might be pertinent, and you have to limit requests for information to a certain extent.

In addition an attorney is generally ignorant of the kinds and types of documents that a Defendant may have and the "jargon" and parochial language used to describe them. Every occupation and profession has a language of its own, and an attorney has to turn to a member of the particular industry to learn how to identify and ask for particular information.

With the help of your expert you will be able to prepare a set of Interrogatories that will lead to the identity of the numerous documents that you need— and in language that is understandable by the Defendant and its employees.

Depositions in a Products Case

There are so many people involved in the design, testing, manufacture and sale of a product that trying to decide whom to depose becomes a major problem. Duties and responsibilities are spread out among many people.

A secondary problem is that, the higher one goes within the corporate hierarchy, the less personal knowledge an individual has. For example, forget about deposing the president of a corporation; he or she doesn't know anything! If ever a person dealt with generalities, summaries, and statistics it is the top person within a corporation. Senior executives are usually of no help.

Knowledgeable Persons Occupy the Lower Rungs of Power. The persons who really know a product occupy significant positions of authority but they are in the class of middle and lower managers. Even a small laboratory has a director or chief. The development of every new product is placed in the hands of a Project Manager. The production or manufacture of a product is usually under the general supervision of one person. So, for deposition purposes one has to find that person who is in charge of a group of:

Design engineers,

Laboratory and testing,

Production of the product, and/or

Marketing and sales.

The identity of these people is nearly always revealed in the documentation you have secured. As you and your expert go through the papers, you will find the same names popping up over and over again. Reports and memos will be directed to Joe Jones or Mary Smith. Design changes will be approved by a person. Transcripts of meetings will contain references to the personnel in charge of different aspects of the work. In this way you will be able to begin a list of possible persons to be deposed and then to narrow it to the precise individual that you want to examine.

Taking the Deposition. In addition to the ordinary rules relative to depositions set forth elsewhere there are a few specific admonitions that apply to products liability cases.

1. Engineers and Scientists Are Very Precise, Exacting Persons. And exasperating! They refuse to deal in generalities and will evade a question unless you ask it in exactly the right way. All of the documents you have received and reviewed refer to a very specific object, such as a ladder bearing Model #7234A. There is no point to your phrasing questions about "ladders" since the deponent will demur on the ground that the company makes one hundred different ladders. Nor is it helpful to refer to Model 7234 since you will be told very quickly that there are two adaptations of that model, and which are you referring to?

Attorneys are not used to dealing with this sort of precision and it requires a determined change in attitude and language. This may require a bit of practice on your part but it is important if the deposition is to be successful.

2. Go into Detail with Regard to the Matter Under Discussion. This requires that you know your subject. Let's say you are deposing the head of the laboratory. You should know the details of the test results, and the purpose of the deposition should be that faults were detected in the testing process and that knowledge of these faults was conveyed to higher authorities within the company.

You have to go into detail regarding these faults or problems. What kind of testing was done? When were these faults uncovered? What are the nature and cause of the problems? To whom was this information given? What correction, if any, was made? One answer should lead to additional questions until you have finally exhausted the knowledge of this witness and presumably will have scored some points with him or her.

3. Explore the Application of Government Rules and Industry Standards. Generally speaking industry standards represent guidelines and government regulations are requirements. Let's put it this way: it is embarrassing not to comply with industry standards, but it is sinful to fail to comply with government regulations.

However, if you find a violation of either, you are well on your way to proving negligence. While it is true that compliance with industry standards does not mean there has been no negligence—industry standards are not rules of law—failure to apply industry standards nonetheless does point to negligence. A particular company has a hard time justifying its violations of standards accepted by the whole industry.

Government regulations are a different matter; their violation can be negligence per se. They weren't devised so as to be accepted or rejected according to the whims of the management of a particular company; they are to be accepted and adopted by all.

And there are so many of them! Just consider for a moment the BOCA Codes which have been adopted by most cities and municipalities to control and guide the building industry. The quantity of precise regulations is mind boggling. Yet each and every one of those rules must be complied with by architects, construction engineers, and builders. These standards and regulations are a gold mine for attorneys. One frequently finds violations.

For that reason the attorney, at a deposition, must go into this matter in great detail to learn whether a violation exists and, if so, how and why it occurred.

AFTER DISCOVERY

After depositions reevaluate your case: the bubble may have burst.

It is never too late to reject a case.

Very often an attorney will accept a case based on an intuitive belief that a legitimate cause of action exists. Usually the client knows very little that is helpful. One confers with an expert and secures a cautious, "It sounds like a case. You better look into that a little further." Then you go ahead either with a Complaint or, under your own Rules, invoke some discovery before filing a Complaint.

You have served your Interrogatories to learn what documents exist and where they are, and your Request (Motion) for Production has delivered the documents into your hands. You and the expert have reviewed them and it still looks like there is a case but it's not clear. This happens often.

Then depositions are taken. Suddenly you find that the defendant did everything right and has a good explanation for everything that happened. You confer with your expert again, and he or she now confronts you with the fact that no negligent conduct can be proved.

At this point plaintiff's counsel faces one of the toughest decisions that he or she will ever face—to go on with the case or get rid of it.

Do not proceed with a case that you are not likely to win.

As we said at the beginning of this chapter, these cases are time-consuming, expensive, and treacherous. At the beginning—and even well into the case—you don't know what happened or whether negligence is present. That is why Discovery exists. Now, after extensive discovery you and your expert are satisfied that there is no legitimate case in this instance. That is the signal to quit. To use a cliche, "Don't beat a dead horse." Quit. Get out as gracefully as possible.

Does this lead to the possibility of a legal malpractice action against you? Yes. It is a realistic possibility? No. If it is either consolation or encouragement, this author has been in that position several times and has never been sued.

A Defendant is usually so pleased to get out of the lawsuit that the thought of starting a new one against Plaintiff's counsel or Plaintiff is the furthest thing in their mind. Secondly, the courts applaud the candor of counsel and look with dismay (or anger) at an attempt to penalize counsel with a lawsuit when he or she has been honest enough to stop a case when clearly the evidence is not there. Thirdly, any case against counsel, or Plaintiff, is a very poor one when all they have done is to utilize Discovery techniques to uncover the facts and then dismissed the case when the facts were found to be inadequate. In my jurisdiction such suits are usually subject to dismissal as a matter of law.

An alternative to dismissal is the possibility of settlement for a small amount. This is often difficult to achieve if the consent of Defendant doctor, hospital, or corporation is required. Very often the willingness to settle depends on defense counsel and your relations with him or her. If you have been decent and fair in the past, your conduct may bear fruit in this case. If not, "What goes around comes around."

However you choose to walk away from the case, the attorney has no right to continue with a case when logic and reason point to the fact that it likely cannot be won. Note the word "likely." Life is a gamble to some extent and all kinds of strange things happen. People live whom doctors have declared doomed to die. People "total" their cars and walk away unscathed. Airplanes crash to earth and a baby is thrown clear and lives. The impossible happens.

But no sensible person lives their lives expecting it to happen.

For that reason when you and your expert have carefully sifted through the documents and studied the depositions and have concluded that there is no reasonable basis for believing that the case can be won, then stop. Withdraw from the case, dismiss it, or settle it for whatever you can get—but don't go on. The road ahead leads to a quagmire.

Clients will generally agree with your analysis and conclusion. Once in a while they will desire to consult with another counsel and that is perfectly alright. Rarely they will leave in anger and possibly find some other attorney to take the case. That has happened to this writer a few times and the other attorney has never been successful. You can be confident that if both you and a good expert conclude there is no case, no one else is going to be able to do any better.

CONCLUSION

Both medical malpractice and products liability cases are a joy to work on. Each of them is very interesting and they lead the attorney into wonderful new worlds of exciting ideas, different language, and accomplished men and women with whom one would never mingle under ordinary circumstances. It is pure fun to trade thoughts with a neurosurgeon and to listen to a nuclear physicist. And at the end one can have the thrill of victory and a substantial fee to go with it.

These cases take great effort, an enormous amount of time, and are expensive, but they are worth it. If handled carefully and diligently they can be the jewels of great worth among the files in your office.

10

Paper Chase: Governmental, Industry, and Professional Society Standards That Help You Win Your Case

We lawyers are among the luckiest people in the world for many reasons. One is the fact that there are thousands of persons and scores of agencies and institutions in these United States who stand ready, able, and even eager to help us win our cases. Universities are conducting research on the very problems that exist in our lawsuits, and the construction industry is busy setting detailed standards for its members and those standards guide us in determining the existence of negligent or careless conduct. The Federal Transportation Safety Board conducts investigations into the cause of airplane crashes and train derailments, and these are available to us. We could not even approach the scope and extent of their work with our own investigators. The National Oceanic and Atmospheric Administration has photographs of every square inch of our country, and the U.S. Corps of Engineers can provide us with every imaginable detail concerning our navigable rivers.

Best of all, most of this information is either free or can be secured at negligible cost. Bureaucracy—it's wonderful.

Some might inquire, "What this has to do with Discovery?" The answer is everything. Until you gather the available information from these governmental agencies and private institutions, you will never know what questions to ask in Interrogatories, what documents a Defendant may have in its files, or how to conduct a probing deposition.

WE ARE OVERWHELMED WITH GOODIES

Like a child in a candy shop, we have too many selections to choose from and that in itself tends to inhibit some lawyers from moving ahead with the business of collecting this important information. If we want a photograph of a tiny section of the shoreline of the Ohio River we could go to the Corps of engineers, the NOAA, a neighboring municipality, a local photography shop, the state Department of Highways if a state road is nearby or a barge company.

If we want data concerning the glue or cement used in hip replacements we could go to the Food and Drug Administration, the American Board of Orthopedic Surgery, the medical school at a university, a State Department of Health, or a manufacturer.

Having this kind of choice many attorneys, do nothing! Or they make an attempt to secure the information and, failing once or twice, just give up. This is incredible but true. I have seen it happen time after time. The information is somewhere out there but locating it requires time, patience, persistence, and footwork. Many attorneys, overwhelmed with the choices, uncertain where to begin and anticipating a time-consuming paper chase, simply give up. Rather than make the effort to go mining for gold they prefer to sit in their comfortable offices and "hope" or "wish" their way to a good result. These attorneys deserve what they get—usually nothing. This is no way to win a case.

USE YOUR PARALEGAL TO GET THIS DATA

This is the time and occasion to put your good paralegal to work. That person is the one who can make the numerous telephone calls, fill out the forms, and roam through the corridors of a university or a government building looking for exactly the right office and person who can direct him or her to the desired information. This work is enormously time-consuming and can be frustrating as one hears over and over again, "Sorry, You have the wrong office."

In addition one must be something of a Sherlock Holmes in tracking down the right office and finding the knowledgeable person to speak with. Suppose your case involves the mechanical equipment used in a hip replacement and you are looking for university research concerning that equipment. It makes sense to turn to the medical school for starters but after a fruitless search one could well end up talking with a professor in the bioengineering department of the School of Engineering! He is the one who did the research you seek.

This kind of work—checking details, going door to door, spending long hours at a library, using the phone—is ideally suited to your paralegal. The major function of the attorney is to give the paralegal clear directions as to what is sought, plenty of time to do the work, and the financial and moral support to see the job through. The end result can justify the effort.

WHO CAN GET YOU STARTED?

How do you begin to look for the things you want? The very thought of the words "bureaucracy" or "institution" makes us shiver—with just cause. Just say the words "Mayo clinic," "Harvard University," "The Pentagon," and you immediately conjure up the vision of a maze of buildings and corridors, a beehive of busy humans, and places where nobody knows anyone else or where anything is. That horrible vision is almost true. There is no Great Receptionist at the front gates of these institutions who can immediately tell you, "Oh yes. You want a 1985 study of the effects of delay in the second stage of labor. Go see Dr. Robert Brown in Room 289, the Smith Building. That's the next building over."

This will never happen.

Someone has to guide you to determine what information is available, who prepared it and where it is.

Among the people you can call on for help are:

1. An expert,
2. Your state or federal legislator,
3. A librarian,
4. An industry directory, and
5. An industry journal.

Start with an Expert in the Field

Independent experts are available in every field of endeavor. If your case involves a collapsing building due to subsidence, find a soils engineer and a geologist; if it involves two colliding airplanes, begin with an air traffic controller and a pilot; and if it is about the disastrous effect of a drug, go to a toxologist and an internist.

These are the persons who can tell you about research studies, articles in journals, the standards of their specialties, and the identity of individuals who have done work on the problem involved in your case. They are the ones who can point you in the right direction.

It isn't necessary that you retain one of these persons as an expert; all you want to do is to meet with him or her and to "pick their brain." However, if you do not have a paralegal to follow through with the detailed leg work necessary to secure the data you want, a retired person in one of these specialities is an excellent choice. Such a person is willing to work for much less than the normal fee of an active practitioner, and they can usually collect the desired information quickly.

Use Your Legislator

You may be surprised to know that your elected representatives in government are dying to help you. They look upon "constituent service" as a necessary and appropriate part of their legislative duties.

Best of all they have the staff who know their way around the intricacies of governmental agencies, personnel, and buildings. These people are more than willing to help you.

You have to use this help because there are too many departments and bureaus for you to attempt to learn which among them has the material that you want. That effort could take many days—even a couple of weeks—if you tried to do it yourself. The staff of your legislator can cut through that bureaucratic mystery quickly and help you to find the "who" and the "where."

Your legislators are there to serve you; why not start using their service?

Get Help from a Friendly Librarian

Librarians are among the nicest people in the world and are trained to help you to track down anything in print. It is my experience that they are always willing to help you find that treatise, directory, journal, or research paper that you so desperately need and can't find.

Fortunately most large libraries today are computerized, which facilitates your search for a particular book or document. There may be a fee for a computer search, but it is always minimal and it quickly comes up with the answer to your question about whether a certain item is available and where it is located.

If the search has to be lengthy for some good reason, retain the librarian to do it for you after their regular day's work is done. These people—like experts—know their way around and can conduct a detailed search much more quickly than you can.

Consult an Industry or Governmental Directory

There are directories that apply to all industries and to both state and federal governments. Certainly everyone is familiar with Standard and Poors and Moody's directories relating to corporations and insurance companies. There are directories for different types of businesses (forestry, oil, transportation, etc.), varieties of professional societies, and biographies of important people, such as, *Who's Who in American Law.*

These directories are invaluable in providing leads to where you can gather the information you want. Since the federal government is so big and contains such a gold mine of useful information attorneys should turn to them often for help.

One directory that can assist in knowing which organization to go to and whom to call is the *Federal Regulatory Directory* published by Congressional Quarterly, Inc. This book should be in the office of every lawyer. It costs $85 and is published by:

Congressional Quarterly, Inc.
1414 22nd St. N.W.
Washington, DC 20037
(202-887-8500)

It may be ordered by writing to:

Congressional Quarterly Customer Service
300 Raritan Center Parkway
P.O. Box 7816
Edison, NJ 08818
(1-800-543-7793)

It is a jewel—short, compact, and filled with vital information. It contains a breakdown of all major federal regulatory agencies and departmental agencies. Among the most useful ones for personal injury and negligence attorneys are:

Consumer Product Safety Commission
Environmental Protection Agency
Federal Trade Commission
Food and Drug Administration
Occupational Safety and Health Administration
National Transportation Safety Board
National Oceanic and Atmospheric Administration
Army Corps of Engineers
United States Geological Survey
Federal Aviation Administration

For each of these the book summarizes

Background of the establishment of the agency;

Pertinent legislation relating to its work;

Responsibilities of the agency;

Authority to perform its function;

Organization;

Who's who in major positions with names, addresses, and telephone numbers;

Regional offices; and

Information sources including Freedom of Information Requests.

With this book and a telephone, you are off and running in your effort to secure the information you want. This is a wonderfully helpful guide to the principal U.S. government agencies and departments.

Director of Medical Specialists

Since medical malpractice cases are—or should be—so much the work of trial counsel, another directory that must be a part of every lawyer's library is a directory of medical specialists.

This invaluable directory lists detailed biographical data for every board certified physician in the United States.

Two companies publish such a directory. These are:

Marquis Who's Who Directory of Medical Specialists
Macmillan Directory Division
3002 Glenview Rd.
Wilmette, IL 60091
(708-441-2387)

The price of this directory is $295.00.

A second such directory is published by the American Board of Medical Specialties. This set of books (priced at $250) is known as the *ABMS Compendum of Certified Medical Specialists*. You may order it by writing to the Board at:

One Rotary Center
Suite 805
Evanston, IL 60201
(708-491-9091)

Each of these directories contains information you must have about a Defendant, an expert, or a nonparty treating physician. It contains all pertinent facts relative to his or her educational background, hospital appointments, and teaching positions. Part of a page from the Directory of Medical Specialists is included as Figure 10.1.

HUTCHINS Laura Fulper Cert M 80 (Hem) 84 (MedOnc) 87. Institutional Care & Medical Teaching. b 52 Trenton NJ. MD Ark 77. Categorical Med Intern 77-78 Res in Int Med 78-80 Fell 80-83 (both at Ark). 32 Crownpoint Rd 72207 4301 W Markham St 72205 (501) 661-5222

HUTCHINS Steven Wayne Cert M 81 (Cv) 85. b 52. 32 Crown Point Rd 72207

JACKSON James Presley Cert M 75. 10001 Lile Dr 72205

JOHNSON Jerri Lichtenstein Cert M 88. b 59.

JONES Eugene Madison Cert M 78 (Cv) 83. 1821 N Spruce St 72207

JONES Roy Steven Cert M 86. Direct Patient Care & Group Practice. b 56 El Dorado AR. MD Ark 83. Mod Intern 83-84 Res in Med 84-86 (both at LaShreve) Fell in Ge (NC) 86-88 Staff (NC Meml Hosp Chapel Hill) 86— Prac Ge (Little Rock Diag Clin AR) 88—.

JORDAN Randy Allan Cert M 82. Direct Patient Care. b 53 Great Falls MT. MD Ark 79. Intern 79-80 Res in Med 80-82 (both at LaShreve) Fell in Cardiol (Ark) 82-85. U of Ark Med Towers 72201

KAHN Alfred Jr Cert M 50. Retired or Inactive. b 16 Little Rock. MD Harvard 40. Intern (Michael Reese Hosp Chgo) 41-42 Grad·Asst Path 40 House Officer 45-46 (both at Peter Bent Brigham Hosp Boston) Asst Res 46-47 Fell in Ge 47-48 (both at Barnes Hosp StL) Att Staff (Univ Hosp) Past Chief Div Int Med Past Chief Staff now Att Staff (all at St Vincent's Hosp) Past Chief Div Int Med (Ark Bapt Hosp) (all Little Rock) Pres (Kahn Med Corp) 55— Med Dir (Union Life Ins Co) 64-76 Asst in Med (Wash) 46-48 Staff Mem 48-52. Asst Clin Prof Med 52-55 Assoc Clin Prof Med 56-83 (all at Ark) Ed (Jour Ark Med Sci) 56-86 Mem & Past Chm (Found Fund for Ark for Med Sci). Capt MC AUS 42-45 (1st Armored Div-60th Sta Hosp-10th Field Hosp). AMA - SMA - ALIMDA - ACP(F). Box 7585 72217

KANE James Jenkins Jr Cert M 73 (Cv) 77. VA Hosp 300 E Roosevelt Rd 72206

KENNEDY Eleanor Ennis Cert M 82 (Cv) 85. b 53. U of Ar Med Sci 4301 W Markham Slot 532 72205

KEPPEN Michael D Cert M 81 (Hem) 84. 2512 Arkansas Valley Dr 72212

KIZZIAR Jim Charles Cert M 74. 10001 Lile Dr 72205

KOVALESKI Thomas Matthew Cert M 80 (Rheum) 82. 1 Longlea Dr 72212

KUMPURIS Dennis Dean Cert M 77. 417 N University 72202-3192

LAVENDER Robert Charles Cert M 83 (GM) 88-95. b 54. Univ Arkansas Medical Schl 4301 W Markham Slot 641 72205

LEONARD Donald Gerald Cert M 73 (Rheum) 78. b 43 Houston Texas. MD Bowman 70. Straight Med Inte n 70-71 Jr Asst Res in Int Med 71-72 Sr Asst Res in Int Med 72-73 (all at Ala Hosp & Clins) Fell in Rheum (Mayo Clin) 75-77 Clin Asst Prof Med (Ark). Maj MC USAF 73-75. SMA - ACP - AMA - ARA. Ark Rheum-Int Med Assos Profl Assn 1 St Vincent Circle 72205

LEWIS Robert B Cert M 71 (Rheum) 78. b 40 Dumas Ark. MD Ark 66. Rot Intern (US Naval Hosp Phila) 66-67 Res in Int Med (US Naval Hosp Chelsea Mass) 67-70 Staff Int (US Naval Hosp Newport RI) Fell in Rheumatol (Mich Med Center) 73-75. Comdr MC USN 66—. VA Hosp 300 E Roosevelt Rd 72206

LEWIS William Sexton Cert M 64. b 31 Strong Ark. MD Ark 56. Intern Int Med 56 57 Res Int Med 57-60 (both at Ark) Instr Cardiol 60-61 Asst Clin Prof Int Med 63— (all at Ark). Capt MC USA 61-62. AOA. 700 Med Towers 72205

LIPPMAN Stephen Samuel Cert M 83 (Endocrin) 87. Medical Research. b 50 Los Angeles. MD 78 PhD in Molecular Biol 82 (Both at CalifLA). Res (Los Angeles Co Med Ctr-SoCal) 79-81 Res (NIH-NHLBI Bethesda MD) 81-82 Fell in Endocrin 82-84 Med Staff Fell (both at NIH) 84-87. Asst Prof Div Endocrin & Metabol (Ark) 87—. APHA - EndocrinS. Univ of Arkansas Med Sci Slot 587 UAMS 4301 W Markham St 72205-7199

LIPSMEYER Eleanor Ann Cert M 71 (Rheum) 74 Al 74. Recert M 80. Medical Teaching & Institutional Care. b 36 Little Rock AR. MD Ark 62. Straight Med Intern 62-63 Res in Int Med 63-66 Staff 69— (all at Ark Med Center) NIH Fell in AI & Immunology (Yale) 66-68 Staff (Yale-New Haven Hosp) 66-69 Instr (Yale) 68-69 Asst Prof Med 69-74 Assoc Prof Med 74— (both at Ark). ARA - AAAI - AFCR - Alpha Omega Alpha - Sigma Xi. 4301 W Markham St 72205 (501) 661-5585

LOVE Tommie Lee Jr Cert M 81. 9218 Rutgers Dr 72204

LYNCH Patrick Michael Cert M 86. 1001 N Mellon 72207

MALLOY Mark Jefferson Cert M 88. b 52. 5304 Crestwood 72207

MALOTT Jerry Dean Cert M 76. b 44 Jackson Co Ark. MD Ark 73. Intern 73-74 Res 74-76 (both at Ark) Active Staff (Bapt Med Center) 77— (St Vincent Infirmary) 78— (both Little Rock Ark). Med Towers 9601 Lile Dr Suite 670 72205 (501) 224-2424

MONSON Roberta Ann Mills Cert M 72 (ID) 86. Recert M 80. Direct Patient Care. b 42 Niagara Falls NY. MD Harvard 67. Intern 67-68 Res in Med 69-71 (both at Cleve Met Gen Hosp-Case-West Res) Res in R (U Hosps of Cleve) 68-69 Chief Res in Med 71-72 Stetler Research Fell 72-74 Chief Outpatient Ser 74-76 Assoc Med Staff (Ed) (all at VA Hosp Madison Wis) Dir Continuing Med Ed 85— Chm Inves Rev Bd & Pharmacy Comm 87— (both at St Vincent's Hosp). Instr Med 72-74 Asst Prof Med 74-76 (both at Wis) Asst Prof Med 76-80 Asst Dean for Clin Affairs 77-79 Assoc Prof Med 80— (all at Ark). ACP(F). 5 St Vincent's Circle Blandford Physician Center 72205 (501) 663-2333.

MONSON Thomas Phillip Cert M 74 (ID) 76. Medical Teaching. b 41 Mpls. MD Minn 67. Intern 67-68 Res in Med 68-69 & 70-71 Res in Infectious Dis 69-70 (all at Cleve Met Gen Hosp) Fell in Infectious Dis (Wis Hosp) 71-73 Acting Chief Infectious Dis (VA MC Little Rock) Assoc Prof Med (Ark). 4300 W 7th St 72205 (501) 660-2080

MOORE Robert Booth Cert M 70. b 36 Little Rock Ark. MD Harvard 63. Intern (Ore Hosps & Clins) 63-64 Res 66-69 Fell in Hematol & Oncology 69-70 (both at Ark Med Center) Assoc Staff (St Vincent Infirmary) 70— (Ark Bapt Med Center) 70— (all Little Rock) Clin Instr Med (Ark) 70—. Capt MC USA 64 - 66. 5918 Lee Ave 72205

MORELAND Nancy Kathryn Cert M 82. 6508 Brentwood 72207

MORRISON Debra Jo Cert M 86 (Ge) 87. b 56. 1410 N Hughes 72207-6113

MORRISON Jimmy Joe Cert M 88. b 60. 1508 Old Forge 72207

MORSE James Carey Cert M 77. 2705 Echo Valley Dr 72207

MORTON William Jack Cert M 73 (Ge) 75. Direct Patient Care. b 45 Sherman TX. MD SW 70. Straight Med Intern 70-71 Res in Med 71-73 Fell in Ge 73-75 (all at Barnes Hosp StL) Active Staff (Bapt Med Ctr) 77— Cons Staff (St Vincent Infirm) 77— (all Little Rock). AMA - ASGE - ACG(F) - ACP(F) - Alpha Omega Alpha. 10001 Lile Dr 72205 (501) 227-8000

MURPHY Bruce Edward Cert M 84. Group Practice. b 52 El Dorado AR. MD Ark. 1814 Shumate Dr 72212

MURPHY Eileen Norma Cert M 82. 605 N Monroe St 72205

MURPHY Jeanne Ann Cert M 86. 1814 Shumate Dr 72212

MURPHY Marvin L Cert M 63 (Cv) 77. Recert M 74. Medical Teaching & Medical Research. b 30 Woodston Kan. MD Kan 56. Gen Rot Intern (Indpls Gen Hosp) 56-57 Res Int Med (Kan Med Center) 57-59 (Ark Med Center) 61-62 Att Phys (Consol VA Hosp Little Rock) 63-69 Chief Cardiol Sect (VA Hosp Little Rock) 69— Dir Div Cardiol (VA Hosp, Ark MC) 77-80 Instr Med 63-65 Asst Prof Med 65-69 Assoc Prof Med 69-74 Prof Med 74— (all at Ark). 4300 W 7th St 72205 (501) 660-2032 · ·

MURPHY Robert Alderman Cert M 86. 2803 Flakewood Rd 72207

MURPHY Tena Elizabeth Cert M 87. b 53. MD Ark 83. Flexible Intern 83-84 Res in Int Med 84-86 Fell in Cardiol 86-88 (all at Ark). Dept of Cardiology 4300 West Markham 72207

NGO Lam Cert M 87. 2nd year fellow. b 55 Vietnam. MD Kaohsiung Med Coll (Vietnam) 82 MPH Johns Hopkins Univ 84. Res (Cook Co Hosp Chgo) 84-87 Fell (Ark) 87—. 1502 Green Mountain Dr Apt 172O 72211

NICKS Sally Agner Cert M 86 (Rheum) 88. b 58. 14 Turtle Creek Cir 72211

O'BRIEN Mary Elizabeth Cert M 83 (GM) 88-95. Direct Patient Care. b 54 Pitts. MD Mass 80. Intern 80-81 Res 81-83 Chief Res in Int Med 83-84 (all at Worcester Meml Hosp Mass) Staff (Bapt MC) (St Vincent's Infirmary) (both Little Rock) Staff in Int Med (Little Rock Diag Clin). ACP - AMA. 10001 Lile Dr 72205 (501) 227-8000

PAL Primepares Gono Cert M 87. b 59. 5215 Park Village Dr 72209

PETERS Phillip Joseph Cert M 76 (Endocrin) 79. Direct Patient Care & Medical Teaching. b 45 Columbus OH. MD WVa 71. Straight Med Inter 71-72 Res in Med 74-76 Chief Res in Med 75-76 Fell in Endocrin & Metabolism 76-78 (all at WVa Hosps) Instr Med 77-78 Asst Prof Med 78-79 (both at WVa) Clin Asst Prof Endocrin (Ark) 79—. Capt MC USAF 72-74. ACP(F) - EndocrinS - ASIM - AMA - ADiabA. 10001 Lile Dr 72205

PEVAHOUSE Joe Beeler Cert M 85. 2411 N Filmore 72207

PILCHER Michael Todd Cert M 79. 7916 Harmon Dr 72207

POWER Robert C Cert M 72 (Ge) 75. b 35 Lockesburg Ark. MD Ark 60. Straight Med Intern (U Hosp-Ark) 60-61 Res in Int Med 64-67 Fell in Ge 69-71 (both at Brooke Gen Hosp Ft Sam Houston Texas) Chief Dept Med (Womack Army Hosp Ft Bragg NC) 72-73 Instr Dept Med (Tex) (Fort San Antonio) 70-71. Lt Col MC USA 61-73. AMA - ACP - ASGE - ACG(F). 409 N University Ave 72205 (501) 664-6980

PRICE Ben Olyn Cert M 62. b 31 Monticello Ark. MD Ark 55. Intern (Phila Gen Hosp 55-56 Res in Med 56-59 Fell Cardiol 59-60 (U Ark) Active Staff (St Vincent Infirmary) Courtesy Staff (Ark Bapt Med Center) (VA Hosp) Cons Cardiol & Med (Consolidated VA Hosps) (all Little Rock). Asst Clin Prof Med (Ark). Lt Comdr MC USNR 60-62. AMA - AHA - ACC(F) - ACP(F). PO Box 4728 72214-4728. (501) 664-9535

Figure 10.1

If one of these persons was somehow involved in a case of yours, you would want to study this medical biographical data very carefully. There are many things that you might want to look into. Take Dr. Stephen S. Lippman, for example. He was involved in medical research. That is a fact you would want to note. He probably has written articles and published the results of his research. If so, on what subject? You might want to get those articles. Look at Dr. Ben O. Price. He is on the Active Staff at St. Vincent Infirmary but only the courtesy staff at Arkansas Baptist Medical Center. Why? Jot that down. If he were involved in my case, I would want to find out. Dr. Lam Ngo was born in Vietnam, but is now practicing in Arkansas. That is interesting. We might want to go into the details of that migration. We do know about American education: four years each of high school, college, and medical school. Is that also true of Vietnam?

As you can see, these little sketches provide information but also begin to raise all kinds of questions concerning the career and practice of the physician.

As a point of beginning, a directory such as this is necessary and valuable. You must have it.

Medical Specialty Societies

While we are on the subject of medical malpractice, it is appropriate to bring up at this time the subject of the medical specialty societies.

These medical societies—there are 23 of them—publish reams of material that are of great help to the attorney. Most importantly they establish standards accepted as axioms by the medical profession. In the courtroom, when the expert for a party is testifying, he or she is always asked whether the conduct of the Defendant comported with "acceptable standards of medical care" or some similar words. If a Defendant doctor failed to comply with the standards established by his or her own medical specialty, the answer to that question is nearly always "no."

That is why it is so necessary for counsel to get the brochures, guidelines, and studies published by these specialty societies. Literally, they can make or break a case.

Figure 10.2 sets forth the names and addresses of all of the 23 specialty societies. Note that there are 24 specialties because the American Board of Psychiatry and Neurology certifies in both Psychiatry and Neurology.

ALL INDUSTRIES HAVE STANDARDS

Today you would have to search for an industry or business that does not have published standards or guidelines for those who engage in that line of work. It is almost impossible to find one.

American Board of Allergy and Immunology,
Inc (A Conjoint Board of the American
Board of Internal Medicine and the American
Board of Pediatrics)
University City Science Center
3624 Market Street
Philadelphia, PA 19104
Telephone: (215) 349-9466
Executive Secretary:
Herbert C. Mansmann, Jr., M.D.

The American Board of Anesthesiology, Inc.
100 Constitution Plaza
Hartford, CT 06103
Telephone: (203) 522-9857
Secretary-Treasurer:
Robert K. Stoelting, M.D.

The American Board of Colon and Rectal
Surgery, Inc.
8750 Telegraph Road, Suite 410
Taylor, MI 48180
Telephone: (313) 295-1740
Secretary-Treasurer/Executive Director:
Hurand Abcarian, M.D.

The American Board of Dermatology, Inc.
Henry Ford Hospital
Detroit, MI 48202
Telephone: (313) 871-8739
Executive Director:
Clarence S. Livingood, M.D.

The American Board of Emergency Medicine
A Conjoint Board (Modified)
200 Woodland Pass, Suite D
East Lansing, MI 48823
Telephone: (517) 332-4800
Executive Director:
Benson S. Munger, Ph.D.

American Board of Family Practice, Inc.
2228 Young Drive
Lexington, KY 40505
Telephone: (606) 269-5626
Executive Director and Secretary:
Nicholas J. Pisacano, M.D.

American Board of Internal Medicine, Inc.
3624 Market Street
Philadelphia, PA 19104
Telephone: (215) 243-1500
President:
John A. Benson, Jr., M.D.

The American Board of Neurological Surgery
Smith Tower Suite 2139
6550 Fannin Street
Houston, TX 77030-2701
Telephone: (919) 966-3047
Secretary-Treasurer:
Julian T. Hoff, M.D.

The American Board of Nuclear Medicine,
Inc. (A Conjoint Board of the American
Boards of Internal Medicine, Pathology, and
Radiology, and sponsored by the Society of
Nuclear Medicine)
900 Veteran Avenue, Room 12-200
Los Angeles, CA 90024-1786
Telephone: (213) 825-6787
President:
Joseph F. Ross, M.D.

The American Board of Obstetrics and
Gynecology, Inc.
4225 Roosevelt Way, N.E.
Suite 305
Seattle, WA 98105
Telephone: (206) 547-4884
Executive Director:
James A. Merrill, M.D.

American Board of Ophthalmology, Inc.
111 Presidential Boulevard, Suite 241
Bala Cynwyd, PA 19004
Telephone: (215) 664-1175
Executive Director:
William H. Spencer, M.D.

American Board of Orthopaedic Surgery, Inc.
737 North Michigan Avenue, Suite 1150
Chicago, IL 60611
Telephone: (312) 664-9444
Executive Director:
Donald B. Kettelkamp, M.D.

American Board of Otolaryngology, Inc.
5615 Kirby Drive, Suite 936
Houston, TX 77005
Telephone: (713) 528-6200
Executive Vice President:
Bobby R. Alford, M.D.

The American Board of Pathology, Inc.
Lincoln Center
5401 W. Kennedy Boulevard, P.O. Box 25915
Tampa, FL 33622
Telephone: (813) 286-2444
Executive Director:
Murray R. Abell, M.D., Ph.D.

The American Board of Pediatrics, Inc.
111 Silver Cedar Court
Chapel Hill, NC 27514-1651
Telephone: (919) 929-0461
Executive Secretary:
Robert C. Brownlee, M.D.

American Board of Physical Medicine and
Rehabilitation, Inc.
Norwest Center, Suite 674
21 First Street, SW
Rochester, MN 55902
Telephone: (507) 282-1776
Executive Director:
Gordon M. Martin, M.D.

The American Board of Plastic Surgery, Inc
1617 John F. Kennedy Boulevard, Suite 860
Philadelphia, PA 19103-1847
Telephone: (215) 568-4000
Secretary-Treasurer:
Elvin G. Zook, M.D.

The American Board of Preventive
Medicine, Inc.
Department of Community Medicine
Wright State University School of Medicine
P.O. Box 927
Dayton, OH 45401
Telephone: (513) 278-6915
Secretary-Treasurer:
Stanley R. Mohler, M.D.

American Board of Psychiatry and
Neurology, Inc.
500 Lake Cook Road, Suite 335
Deerfield, IL 60015
Telephone: (708) 945-7900
Executive Secretary:
Stephen C. Scheiber, M.D.

The American Board of Radiology, Inc.
300 Park, Suite 400
Birmingham, MI 48009
Telephone: (313) 645-0600
Secretary/Executive Director:
Kenneth L. Krabbenhoft, M.D.

The American Board of Surgery, Inc.
1617 John F. Kennedy Boulevard, Suite 860
Philadelphia, PA 19103-1847
Telephone: (215) 568-4000
Executive Director:
Ward O. Griffen, Jr., M.D.

The American Board of Thoracic Surgery, Inc.
One Rotary Center
Evanston, IL 60201
Telephone: (708) 475-1520
Executive Secretary-Treasurer:
James V. Maloney, Jr., M.D.

The American Board of Urology, Inc.
31700 Telegraph Road, Suite 150
Birmingham, MI 48010
Telephone: (313) 646-9720
Executive Secretary:
Alan D. Perlmutter, M.D.

Figure 10.2. Directory of Medical Specialists 1989–1990

Suppose you have a case involving a young boy who dove into a private swimming pool and broke his neck when he struck the bottom where it slopes upward from the deep end to the shallow end. Are you aware that the swimming pool industry has standards that apply to the construction of such private swimming pools and that those standards may have been violated in your case? Just take a look at the standards of the National Swimming Pool Institute. But while you're at it, also check with the American Red Cross, the Consumer Product Safety Commission, the Federal Trade Commission, and talk with a local architect. You may well have a beautiful case based on the recommended design specifications of the trade organization and investigations of a federal or state agency. After you have collected enough documentary material to establish a violation, be sure to include it in your Settlement Brochure. There it will do wonders toward persuading insurance representatives that you have a clear case of liability. Written material of this nature makes an impression—much more than all of your "huffing and puffing" about how good your case is.

One can find the equivalent for just about everything—ladders, window glass, steel beams, as well as matters involving birth, disc surgery, and human body parts transplant. Do you think that every organ removed from a deceased person is usable for transplantation? Wrong. There are rules and regulations—standards—involving even this medical procedure.

These standards are everywhere.

For example, cases that you handle may involve some aspect of construction.

Example 1: A woman shopper in a grocery store is detained at the exit and chatting with a neighbor. As she turns to leave, her hand pushes on the glass in the door which shatters and badly lacerates her hand. The glass is not safety glass. Does a standard apply here?

Example 2: A business visitor elects to walk down the steps in an office building to get to the next lower floor. He suddenly stumbles and falls down the balance of the steps and is badly injured. Your investigator discovers that the distance between the step at which he stumbled and the lower step is only 5 and three quarter inches. Is there a standard that applies?

Example 3: A small fire occurs in a department store. The smell of smoke causes shoppers to race to the exit at which there is a revolving door. That door moves slowly and does not collapse inward with the pressure of the excited shoppers. Since the door is only 8 feet from the bottom of an escalator a frightened crowd gathers. Your client is knocked to the ground, trampled, and injured. What standards, if any, relate to that door?

The answer to each of these questions is that standards do exist within the building industry and they are very specific and precise. In each of these examples existing standards were violated.

As an illustration of the specificity of industry standards, consider those set forth in the codes of the Building Officials and Code Administrators (BOCA), which are today officially adopted as ordinances in many cities and towns across the nation. Thus violation of the code can be negligence per se. This code is found in another book that should be in the library of every litigation and personal injury attorney. It is:

The BOCA National Building Code
Building Officials & Code Administrators International, Inc.
4051 W. Flossmoor Rd.
Country Club Hills, IL 60477-5795
(312) 799-2300

This book is issued every three years and costs $46.

A sample page involving revolving doors is shown in Figure 10.3. Notice the tremendous details. The doors shall collapse "when a force of not more than 180 pounds (880N) is applied within 3 inches (76MM) of the outer edge of a wing." In addition it speaks of "an aggregate width of not less than 36 inches (914mm)," and that the doors "shall not be located within 10 feet (3048mm) of the front or top of stairs or escalators."

An attorney simply cannot ask for anything more definite than that. It is a simple matter to make these measurements and if there is a failure of compliance negligence exists. If, by chance, the code has not been adopted in a given area any architect or builder can testify as an expert that this code is accepted within the construction industry and that its violation in the instant case constitutes negligence.

The BOCA organization has other codes which can be very helpful in particular cases. As mentioned earlier these codes are so important because they have been adopted as city, borough, and township ordinances. Thus if a Defendant builder violates them, you will have a case of clear negligence.

The other codes include:

National Mechanical Code,

National Plumbing Code,

National Fire Prevention Code,

National Existing Structures Code,

National Private Sewage Disposal Code, and

National Energy Conservation Code.

812.5 Security grilles: Horizontal sliding or vertical security grilles which are a part of a required means of egress shall be openable from the inside without the use of a key or special knowledge or effort when the space is occupied. The grilles shall remain secured in the full open position during the period of occupancy by the general public. Grilles shall not be brought to the closed position when there are more than ten persons occupying spaces served by a single exit or 50 persons occupying spaces served by more than one exit. When two or more exits are required, not more than one-half of the exits shall be equipped with horizontal sliding or vertical grilles.

812.6 Level of exit discharge doors: Where glazed, doors at the level of exit discharge shall be glazed with approved safety glazing. Approved doors having one or more unframed edges shall be constructed of safety glazing not less than ½ inch thick.

SECTION 813.0 REVOLVING DOORS

813.1 General: All revolving doors shall comply with Sections 813.2 through 813.5. Revolving doors to be considered a component of a means of egress shall comply with Sections 813.2 through 813.6.

813.2 Collapse: Each revolving door shall be capable of collapsing into a book-fold position with parallel egress paths having an aggregate width of not less than 36 inches (914 mm). The revolving door shall collapse when a force of not more than 180 pounds (880 N) is applied within 3 inches (76 mm) of the outer edge of a wing.

> **Exception:** The maximum collapsing force shall not apply if the force required to collapse the door is reduced to not more than 130 pounds (635 N) when:
> 1. There is a power failure or power is removed to the device holding the wings in position.
> 2. There is an actuation of the automatic sprinkler system when such system is provided.
> 3. There is an actuation of a smoke detection system which is installed to provide coverage in all areas within the building which are within 75 feet (22860 mm) of the revolving doors.
> 4. There is the actuation of a manual control switch which reduces the holding force to not more than the 130-pound (635 N) force level. Such switch shall be in an approved location and shall be clearly identified

813.3 Dispersal area: A revolving door shall not be located within 10 feet (3048 mm) of the foot or top of stairs or escalators. A dispersal area shall be provided between the stairs or escalators and the revolving doors.

813.4 Speed control: The revolutions per minute for a revolving door shall not exceed the speeds indicated in Table 813.4.

Figure 10.3

As you can plainly see, the problem attorneys have is not in applying these standards once we have them, but in locating and securing them. Thus the thrust of the earlier part of this chapter. They're out there all right, your job is to find them

Study Industry Journals

All hail the *New England Journal of Medicine*, along with the journals on obstetrics, architecture, steel, and chemicals. In these magazines you are sure to find articles on the very subject involved in your case. Here you will find reports on the most advanced studies and research. Are these too modern for your case? After all the standard of care relates to knowledge that existed at the time of the accident. Well, read on. That latest study nearly always will have a referral back to earlier ones that will take you to the state of knowledge existing at your accident date.

Fortunately, many of these journals are indexed and in the computers of major libraries. It is not hard to find an article on a very specific subject that is five or six years old. Once again this is where a good librarian can be of invaluable service to you.

Take that Dr. Lippman who at one time was involved in medical research. The odds are that he is published in some journal perhaps in *Internal Medicine* or *Molecular Biology*. It's not hard to find out once you have a place to begin—a name, specialty, school, time period. The articles he has written could be very important to your case.

The journals are lively, current, and they contain news about all kinds of research that is going on. But read them very selectively. They are so interesting that if you are not careful you will be seduced and led astray with some fascinating article that has nothing to do with your case. Look out for this temptation! You have work to do, and you have to get in and out of these journals quickly if you want to get anything accomplished.

USE JOURNALS TO LOCATE EXPERTS

Your expert should be one of the leading authorities in the subject involved in your case. The men and women who are really expert, who do a lot of research, and who pioneer advanced techniques usually write about their accomplishments. Knowledge gained must be shared.

As a result, journals are a prime source for locating the expert that you want and need. Peruse these magazines to find a person who has written on the very subject in which you are interested. Then contact that person by phone or mail. I guarantee you that if you will contact five of the leading authorities in any field—assuming they have no personal or business connection with the case or those involved—three of them will agree to review your case or to meet with you. In addition, if they see clear negligence in the case, two out of the three will agree to be expert witnesses for you. The leading authorities in any field of work are frequently shocked and personally affronted by careless, slip-shod conduct by a person who is clearly incompetent and who is involved in your case.

Defense counsel—if his or her insurance company will allow it—can do the same thing. These outstanding professionals are equally shocked by unjust and improper allegations about one of their own.

But you must ask! Too many attorneys are frightened at the thought of contacting the professionally recognized authorities to review a case or be a witness. They talk themselves out of it by hypothesizing that the person is too important, busy, disinterested, unreachable.

The opposite is true. These persons are interested in their profession, they are accessible and they will come to court or give a deposition in a proper case.

Don't be shy. Go to the top for your expert and locate him or her from books they have written or journals to which they have contributed articles.

HOW DO I USE CODES, STANDARDS, REGULATIONS AND RESEARCH STUDIES?

Where do I go from here? You must keep in mind certain legal principles as you gather such diverse documents as codes, regulations, and the results of research. Each of them fits into your case preparation but in a different way. Let's take a look at them.

1. Government Rules and Regulations

Governments, from the federal to the municipal level, have a right to make rules that all must comply with. If a state Motor Vehicle Code states that the speed limit in a school zone is 25 miles per hour, then that's it and there can't be any argument. A Defendant driver going 30 miles per hour is deemed negligent as a matter of law. That same principle applies to BOCA standard in municipalities that have adopted it and to a regulation of the Federal Environmental Protection Agency.

For this reason the attorney has to search carefully to determine whether such a violation exists in his or her case. The end result—a Summary Judgment or a quick and easy settlement—justifies the time and effort involved in locating the regulation and seeing how it fits into the facts of your case.

Certainly the substantive law, legislation, and Rules of Evidence differ from state to state, and it could well be that the courts in your state draw a distinction between a statute and the rules of an agency. Your courts may have ruled that a statutory violation is negligence per se, while the deviation from a rule of the State Department of Health may only be evidence of negligence or will simply raise a rebuttable presumption of negligence.

That is something that each attorney must determine individually, but if you can find either negligence per se or a presumption sufficient to take the case to the jury, you're well on your way to success.

2. Industry Standards

Generally, industry standards are considered to be significant guides to good conduct and are not legally binding in the sense that a court could grant a summary judgment for a violation.

When an attorney relies on a violation of a standard, he or she still has to produce expert testimony that that deviation constitutes negligent conduct.

This is not to put down standards violations in any way. They are very powerful weapons to help you win your case. If the American Board of Obstetrics & Gynecology recommends that a certain procedure be done at prenatal examinations (let us say, a sonar scan to determine the size, position, and weight of the baby) and the Defendant obstetrician has not complied with this "suggestion," then he or she is in serious trouble. Which would you rather be—the cross-examining attorney or the witness on the stand? The witness is desperately thinking, "How do I get out of this one?" It's tough. In the meantime the judge is thinking—or saying, "If it's good enough for the College of Obstetrics, why isn't it good enough for you?" That Defendant is not in a happy position.

Long before trial, however, the violation of a standard has a really powerful effect—and that is with regard to settlement. Insurance companies are always pondering how strong a case Plaintiff may have as they consider whether to settle a case, and if so for how much. If Plaintiff's counsel is able to put into a Settlement Brochure, a copy of the standard that has been violated together with a letter from an impressive expert that this constitutes negligence (a significant deviation from accepted standards of care) that can have an overpowering influence both with defense counsel and the home office. Such a case is nearly always a settleable one.

For these reasons industry standards have to be located, studied, and put to use. They go a long way in helping you win your case.

One final word about industry standards. While proof of their violation can go a long way to establish negligence, the converse is not true: that is, if there is no violation, there is no negligence. Not at all! The law says that industry can go ahead and establish such standards as it deems best for its members. Presumably that is for the private benefit of the industry. But the industry is not permitted to tell society that its standards are the law. Courts and legislatures tell industry what conduct constitutes negligence and they often have a different view of the matter than industry or medical groups. So you may have a very good case despite the fact that the conduct of your Defendant complies with industry standards.

3. Studies, Test Results, and Statistics

All these documents constitute evidence which, cumulatively, leads to a winning case. As far as your Case in Chief is concerned, they are exactly like the pieces of a puzzle; each is minor but essential, and if you don't have one piece the picture will not be complete.

For purposes of cross-examination they are useful and can be devastating. If an opposing expert chooses to rely on studies that you can prove—through a journal article or research findings—is outdated or no longer accepted, you can put that witness on the defensive. If you are effective at this tactic, you could get the witness to change his or her mind.

You must have these things. Even though they do not rise to the importance of codes and standards, they are essential for the proper preparation and presentation of your case.

THE FREEDOM OF INFORMATION ACT

This is the basic tool in dealing with federal departments and agencies. (Many states now have a similar statute which authorizes release of information from state agencies.)

This Act became law in 1966, and the full text is set forth in 5 U.S.C.A. 552. There are certain exceptions (nine in all) to your right to get information but they are really immaterial insofar as the kind of information you are after is concerned.

Some agencies will have forms that you can use when requesting information but all you really need is a simple letter:

To: (Appropriate Agency)

Re: Freedom of Information Request
    Drug: Asperol
    Manufacturer: ABC Corporation

Dear _____:

Pursuant to the Freedom of Information Act (5 U.S.C. 552) please send me the following:

1. All test results in the possession of your agency, conducted either by this agency or ABC Corporation.
2. Complaints about this drug received from any person or organization.
3. Results of investigation conducted as a result of those complaints;
4. Any letters, reports, analysis, studies or investigation by ABC Corporation concerning those complaints.

Please advise me of the charges for this information.

Sincerely,

It doesn't have to be any longer or more formal than this. The longest part of your letter will be the identification of the documents you want. After you have received the initial response, you can look them over and then order such additional material as you may need.

The response time in general seems to be about 60 to 90 days. Much depends on the agency (some get more requests than others) and on the time period involved. As you might expect, it may take longer to get old material than current data. The variety and volume of material requested also affects response time.

Also bear in mind that, while the persons in these agencies are willing to be helpful, they are not exactly standing around with nothing to do and waiting for your request to arrive.

The Freedom of Information Act has really worked a wonderful change in opening up to you the vast investigative, testing, and regulatory resources of the government.

The material available to you is bountiful and useful—make certain that you get your full share of it.

HAVE THESE BOOKS IN YOUR LIBRARY

1. *Federal Regulatory Directory,*
2. *Directory of Medical Specialists, and*
3. *The BOCA National Building Code.*

Just remember:

1. Federal and state agencies establish rules, make studies, and conduct investigations. All of this material is available to you.
2. Consult with an expert about rules and standards—who's done what and where it can be found.
3. Use your paralegal; this kind of work is squarely within his or her job classification.
4. Get your expert for use at trial from the authors of textbooks and journal articles.
5. Use your legislator for help in getting around federal and state agencies.
6. All industries have their own societies who conduct research and issue reports. They also establish standards, and violations of those standards is a "no-no."
7. Look to librarians for help. They know where the books and documents can be found.

Do not be overwhelmed by the mystique of governmental agencies, professional societies or universities; they have what you want. Now go get it!

11

Winning the Hopeless Case with Discovery

There are hopeless cases. On the other hand, there are seemingly hopeless cases that can be won. Telling one from the other and detailing the ways to win such a case is the subject of this chapter. This chapter is also written for the purpose of preserving your emotional sanity while enhancing your financial security.

Just look at the following extracts from rejection letters of other attorneys. These letters were brought to me by my clients at the initial interview.

The first case involved a young man who was run over by a train and his attorney wrote:

> In summary my investigation has determined:
>
> 1. A train of that size traveling at the speed registered could not have stopped in the distance available. This is based on my visit to the scene of the accident which disclosed that the sight distance basically runs from just east of the crossing to the point of impact.
>
> 2. I can find no legal duty or negligence on the part of the railroad in failing to stop the train under the circumstances.
>
> 3. I cannot establish that stopping the train prior to the entire train passing over you would have prevented the injuries.
>
> I therefore have concluded that I am not willing to accept this case and it would be my opinion there is no case against the railroad.

This attorney was wrong on all counts.

Another case involved a middle-aged man who, on a hot summer afternoon, suddenly lost control of his car while driving on the highway, went into a spin and crashed his car. His attorney stated:

> Regretfully, I cannot represent you due to facts revealed in your accident report without the retaining of experts to examine the roadway and your vehicle. I do not feel that the liability is such that we could front the cost for experts.

That attorney should have risked the money.

Finally, the third case involved a young man riding a motorcycle who came around a curve in the road, found a school bus in front of him, swerved to his left, struck the right front of the school bus, and then crashed. His original attorney rejected the case, saying:

> To confirm our personal conversation I must respectfully deny you further representation in this matter as I do not feel that a liability case exists on your behalf in light of the comparative negligence standard in existence in the Commonwealth of Pennsylvania.

This attorney missed the point: proving Defendant's liability was the problem, not Plaintiff's suggested comparative negligence.

Each of these cases was brought to a successful conclusion through the use of extensive discovery.

What happened here? I am not a miracle worker, nor are the other attorneys incompetent. What happened might well be happening to you at this moment. The attorneys took in these cases and then:

1. Relied solely on an investigation which turned up nothing;
2. Trusted in their personal life experiences in analyzing the facts;
3. Failed to file a lawsuit so as to invoke Discovery Procedures;
4. Demonstrated neither curiosity nor imagination.

This conduct is normal, everyday practice by too many lawyers. Because of this attitude clients are deprived of a rightful recovery and the attorneys lose a substantial fee.

It doesn't have to be that way.

Many attorneys make two common errors in the handling of this type of case:

1. They get excited at the beginning, take the case, and then, as problems mount one after another, lose their enthusiasm and give up. These attorneys basically lack intellectual stamina combined with little curiosity and imagination.

2. They continue to hang onto a case after doing all of the right things when logic, reason, and common sense dictate that the case should be rejected.

And some cases must be rejected! You reach a point when you must say to yourself that enough is enough. Forget about hanging onto the case in the hope of a settlement. It isn't going to happen. If there is some embarrassment in getting rid of a case after having worked on it for six months, so be it. Better that than dragging it on and on—expending more time, energy, and money—until finally you are nonsuited or, having gone through a foolish trial, end up with a defense verdict.

This type of conduct does not represent extremes. This happens routinely in too many law offices. If it is happening in your firm, stop it now.

If a case is truly hopeless get rid of it. Just make sure that it is "truly hopeless." Very often it is not.

Let us take a look at the facts of these cases and see what was done to win them.

The first was really a bad situation. A young man, married with a child, was a neer-do-well and a drug addict. He went to visit friends who lived in a rural area in a house adjacent to some railroad tracks. There was another house next door. A few hundred yards away a road crossed the tracks and there were three houses along the road.

The Plaintiff drank liquor and smoked pot with his friends. Shortly before noon he decided to go hunting, took a rifle, and was last seen crossing the railroad tracks heading for the woods beyond.

Around 7 P.M. a train came along with seven diesel units pulling 120 cars. A brakeman on the front unit saw a "pile of rags" lying between the rails and notified the engineer who slowed down and eventually stopped but did not apply the emergency brakes. The entire train passed over the body before it stopped.

The Plaintiff was found with a severed leg and head injuries. It was clear from the tears on his clothing, objects dropped from his pockets, and the condition of the dirt between the rails that he had been dragged some distance.

The client suffered amnesia and remembered nothing from the time he left his friend's house to go hunting.

Persons in the several houses nearby saw and heard nothing prior to the accident, except that the train whistle sounded as the train approached the road crossing and later the squealing of the brakes.

Investigation by the railroad and the state police showed that the train crew acted properly once they saw the body between the rails.

Tough situation. Hopeless? Yes, on the basis of the information then at hand.

The second case involves a middle-aged man, married, with children, who at about 2 P.M. on a hot afternoon was driving down a two-lane, asphalt highway. Suddenly his car began to bounce a little, then it went into an uncontrollable skid, and went over an embankment. He sustained fractures of many of the bones in his body and a serious head injury. There were no witnesses. The state police blamed excessive speed and inattention as the cause of the accident.

Where do you go with this one?

The third case involves a young, single man who was riding a motorcycle on a two-lane asphalt road. The road had many curves, hills, and dips. A school bus, loaded with children, approached from the opposite direction coming up-hill toward a curve to the left. Just before the bus got to the curve, the motorcycle came around it, then swerved to its left in front of the bus, struck the right front of the bus, and catapulted the driver into a bank and trees. The motorcycle driver lost an eye and suffered brain damage. He stated that the school bus was in the middle of that narrow road, that an embankment blocked his ability to go to the right of the bus, and that his only recourse was to swerve to the left. The bus driver, a very pleasant, experienced lady insisted she was in the extreme right lane and that the motorcyclist lost control on the curve and swerved in front of her. The state police agreed.

That case had an inauspicious beginning.

In each of these cases the initial attorneys did all of the usual and proper things. A police report was ordered, together with a weather report. Photographs were taken, and an investigator was sent to the scene to make measurements, to interview people in the neighborhood, and to report back his personal ideas. In the railroad case the railroad even provided statements of the crew members.

Everything was negative. At this point the original attorneys rejected these cases.

Too soon—much too soon.

The one thing these cases had going for them was the nature of the injuries. Each of these Plaintiffs was very badly hurt. This leads to a fundamental point:

Evaluate the injuries and damages first!

It was obvious that if anything was to be done in these cases a lawsuit would have to be filed and discovery undertaken.

Before you file that lawsuit, you *must* be certain that the eventual recovery justifies what is clearly going to be a considerable expenditure of time, effort, and money. Ninety-nine percent of the time these clients have no money, so that whatever sum is going to be spent will be that of the attorney. In addition the time that will be involved in working up these cases will be in the order of hundreds of hours. Effort will be expended in going repeatedly to the scene of the accident, taking depositions, meeting with experts, conferring with your paralegal and investigator, and mulling the case over and over again in your mind trying to figure out what happened and how you're going to prove it.

Don't even begin this effort unless the injuries are severe, the past and future medical expenses and wage losses are high, and the potential recovery is substantial. If it is otherwise—if the case involves a whiplash, or a few minor fractures, a laceration or a mild traumatic neurosis—then drop it. Simply put, you cannot work for nothing. Your spouse and/or children will object and if they don't your partners will.

These cases must be of sufficient value to justify the work.

FILE YOUR LAWSUIT AND GET STARTED

You cannot do anything until you file a lawsuit. If the facts are sufficient that you can make some reasonable allegations of negligence, begin with a Complaint. If you cannot do that, utilize whatever procedure exists in your jurisdiction to begin a lawsuit for discovery purposes only. In my jurisdiction we begin by filing what is known as a Praecipe and follow up with Discovery for the Purpose of Preparing a Complaint.

You must have the discovery. The essential problem with these cases in the beginning is that there are insufficient facts upon which to form a judgment whether liability exists. After you have conducted a routine investigation, the only way to get additional facts is through the use of discovery techniques and you can't start discovery until the lawsuit is filed.

NEXT, CONSULT WITH AN EXPERT

One's own experience in life is not good enough to pass judgment on these cases or on others like them. Thinking otherwise was the first error made by the original attorneys handling these cases.

In the railroad case the first thought was to locate a retired engineer or brakeman and to consult with him. Then, since the actual layout of the railroad tracks and matters of topography were involved, it seemed wise to consult a civil engineer who knows about such things.

The school bus case and the skidding accident both involved highways; so in each instance a civil engineer who was a specialist in highway construction had to be retained. Beyond this an accident reconstruction expert was hired to help out on the school bus case, and eventually a chemist who knew a great deal about road asphalt was brought into the skidding case.

From the various experts new ideas—theories, really—began to arise concerning what might have happened and why. Each of these ideas was based on certain assumed facts. The question that cried out for an answer in each case was whether the "assumed" facts could possibly be supported. The only way to find out was by invoking discovery.

USE DISCOVERY UNDER THE GUIDANCE OF YOUR EXPERT

You may have driven a car for many years but that does not mean that you are an expert on highways. What do you really know about grading, subsurface construction, drainage, or the composition of asphalt? Not much I suspect. So why should you even try to analyze the cause of that skidding accident case without consulting with a highway engineer?

You may have ridden on trains and been stopped at a grade crossing while a frieght train rumbled past, but does either riding on a train or looking at one make you an expert regarding their movement and operation? Of course not. If you have a case involving the operation of a train, you must go to experienced people in the railroad business to learn the details about how things are done.

The experts have the knowledge. They can come up with ideas about the way things ought to have been done and what might have gone wrong in your case. You can present them with a paucity of facts, and they can tell you what is missing and where to go to look for more information.

You must rely on these people to guide you in your discovery.

It is very important that you not waste time and energy in a pointless, aimless scatter-gun type of discovery that leads nowhere. You have to have some general idea of where you are headed—a direction so that your discovery has a purpose.

This direction—perhaps we could call it a Theory of Liability—can only come from an expert. Use this person to the fullest to give meaning and sense to your work.

AN ANALYSIS OF THE RAILROAD CASE

Truthfully this case had nothing going for it at the beginning. The Plaintiff suffered total amnesia, the investigation done by the previous attorney was complete but useless, the state police report raised more questions than it answered, and the attached statements of the crew members predictably indicated that they did no wrong.

There was not even enough information to draft a complaint. Accordingly the only recourse was to utilize local rules, to initiate the lawsuit by filing a simple Praecipe to get the lawsuit started, and to begin discovery.

Depositions of the train crew, the investigating claims agent, and the state trooper were a place to start.

Subpoenas were served which included a demand that documents be produced. Under the guidance of our railroad engineer expert these included:

1. Investigation file;
2. Photographs and drawings;
3. Book of Operating Rules;
4. Time table;
5. Train profile; and
6. Speed tapes from the engine.

Later our two experts, the civil engineer, and the railroad engineer would have us filing a Request for Production of such esoteric matters as the *Association of American Railroads Manual of Standards and Recommended Practices*, particularly as it related to Brake Shoe Force Tests, Train Handling Rules–CDT-30, Safety Rules DF-32, and FRA RR Freight Car Safety Standards.

Now you don't know what those documents are; neither did I. I never heard of them. But the experts knew about them and they wanted them. Bowing to this superior knowledge the documents were requested, the railroad had them, and, after two trips to Court on Motions to Compel, the documents were secured. It was significant to me that the railroad fought not only the production of these documents, but later the answering of certain Interrogatories.

The depositions of the engineer and head brakeman went into detail concerning the movements of the train up to the accident scene and everything that occurred from the time the plaintiff was observed lying between the rails, unconscious, until the time the train stopped and plaintiff was removed by ambulance.

Of note were the facts that these crewmen clearly saw the Plaintiff but thought he was a "pile of rags," did not throw the train into emergency, and permitted the entire train to pass over him as it gently slowed down and stopped. It travelled about a mile before it stopped.

The crewmen to the rear—the conductor and rear brakeman riding in the caboose—and the state trooper testified to their observations that the Plaintiff had been snagged by some part of the train, dragged along the ground for many feet and diagonally toward a rail, and the position of his severed limb.

Now facts were being accumulated at a rapid pace. Documents were studied and both experts began to come up with very specific ideas of negligent conduct.

They suggested Interrogatories among which were such questions as:

1. Set forth the normal stopping distance of a train such as that involved in this accident, under the conditions then existing, with the brakes in full emergency, from a speed of 26 mph.
2. From the time an engineer applies the brakes on a train such as was here involved, how long does it take before the brake shoes are fully loaded against the wheels?
3. What is the deceleration rate for this train under emergency braking conditions?
4. What is the range of normal braking for a train such as the one involved in this case in "feet/second^2"?

And so on. Perhaps the most important Interrogatories were the series that asked—as to every engine and car in this long train—the distance above the rail of the lowest portion of each car.

I had no idea that the railroad had this information but the answers came back:

> Car No. 11–C048459–Hopper Car–Bottom of car body: 8¼″ ATR (above the rail). Lowest part of car (brake rigging); 2¾″ ATR and located 24″ and 32½″ inside rail.
>
> Car No. 26–SCL22259, Box car–Bottom of car body: 27½″ ATR. Lowest part of car (brake rigging): 10″ ATR and located at center of car.

Our civil engineer was able to take this information and plot the distance above the rail of the lowest part of each car in that train. From this graph, and given the depth of Plaintiff's body, he was able to locate four cars that were low enough that they could have snagged and dragged Plaintiff over to the rail where the amputation occurred.

With all of the braking information that was secured, it was possible to prove that, properly handled, the train could have been stopped before any of these four cars reached the plaintiff.

So the case was brought to a successful conclusion and was settled. The client was jubilant and the fee justified the efforts of the attorney. It was a happy ending. The first attorney didn't share in the joy.

What was the difference? The answer, simply put, was that the original lawyer didn't try. He relied too much upon a superficial investigation into the matter, his own life experiences (which proved to be inadequate for the exercise of good judgment), and a lack of imagination. Perhaps he was busy at the time and didn't want to go that extra mile in which event he should not have accepted the case.

But the very important lesson is that discovery won that case. The facts were out there all the time, but they couldn't be secured without the Depositions, Interrogatories, and Requests for Production.

Equally important is the realization that I would never have known what to ask for or the significance of the information secured except for the knowledge and advice of the experts. These persons were of invaluable assistance, and to them and the Rules of Discovery goes all the credit for a successful result.

There is one more word to be said, and that concerns the settlement.

ABOUT SETTLEMENT

This case was not settled for 100 percent of its value. Sixty percent? Yes. Maybe seventy percent but not one hundred percent.

It is true that in Pennsylvania we have a variation on what used to be called the Last Clear Chance Rule. Perhaps your jurisdiction applies this legal principle. It says in essence that when a Plaintiff has placed his or herself in a position of peril and Defendant knows or should know Plaintiff is in that position and Defendant has an opportunity to avoid the accident and does not do so, then Defendant may be found to be negligent.

That rule surely applied to this situation. That would be enough to take the case to the jury.

But certain realities intruded.

The Plaintiff, despite his being a pleasant person and badly injured, had been a drug addict and a drunk. Evidence concerning this could not be excluded; in fact Plaintiff was drinking heavily and smoking pot immediately before he started his eventful journey. Secondly, it was not the fault of the railroad that he somehow lay unconscious between the railroad tracks. In addition, there was the possibility, for what it was worth, that he awakened as the train passed over him, and rolled in such manner that his leg extended over the rail. Perhaps the fact that he was snagged by a particular car and dragged had nothing to do with his leg being amputated.

Perhaps.

There were other problems. A poor work history and marital discord were additional headaches. The existence of those problems and the recognition of the seriousness of them is what should lead to a settlement.

In evaluating a case, an attorney must consider not only the probability of establishing liability on a Defendant but also how a jury might consider the attending circumstances and how they will view the lifestyle of the client. These are factors to be considered along with the purely legal ramifications of the case. It did here. In other cases the unreasonable stubbornness of either counsel would bring this case to trial and most likely would result in either a very high verdict for plaintiff or a defense verdict. One party or the other would regret the decision. That didn't happen here.

The Plaintiff and his family in this case were in no position to accept a defense verdict. To say that they were in desperate straits would be to put things mildly. They needed this settlement and wanted it so the case was closed.

But I have seen clients—as have you—who are desperate, but who suddenly, when their attorney tells them that they will get to a jury, see a pot of gold at the end of the rainbow and want to "go for broke."

I abhor this attitude and strongly suggest that you have a duty to do everything in your power to dissuade such a client from going forward to trial. In this instance you are the expert on valuation, you know the risks involved, and you are the only one who can calculate the likelihood of success and the harm of failure. You cannot permit a client to proceed to trial when you know there is a good chance of losing and when you are aware of the client's necessitous circumstances. You must exercise your powers of persuasion, appeal to the good sense of the client's family and friends, and if necessary, convince the client to seek another opinion from a competent trial counsel.

If you succumb to your client's views, try such a case, and lose it, you will find that in *nearly every such case* the client will turn on you and find some way to blame you for the loss. This leads to nasty recriminations.

Spare yourself the pain and do yourself a favor; work up a good and proper settlement and close your file. Good judgment and your client's well being require it.

A LOOK AT THE OTHER CASES

The other two cases were also "winnable" through the proficient use of discovery and the careful advice of experts.

The Skidding Accident Case

In the "skidding accident" case, the highway engineer was curious about the "steady succession of bumps" the Plaintiff described, as well as the sudden spinning of the vehicle on that hot afternoon. The chemist was also intrigued by the spinning. Was there a grading or a drainage problem here? Was there some abnormality in the asphalt mix used to pave this roadway? The answers turned out to be "yes." These gentlemen were right on both counts. But that answer did not come out of the clear blue sky.

Each of these experts worked with counsel in designing Interrogatories that would seek out specific facts about this particular section of the highway, which has been built by the state and maintained by it. While all of the answers to the interrogatories were helpful, the group that was most interesting were those that said, "Yes, we have received complaints about this section of the road" and, "Yes, we know of problems in the roadway"—along with those answers which included the formula for the asphalt mix.

It turns out that this section of the road was simply a bad scene anyway you looked at it. A lot of things were wrong.

So far so good. Now the documentation was needed. Once again the experts provided the crucial information, in the proper engineering and highway department language, as to what was probably available. A Request for Production was filed. In due course the written materials were supplied and among them was a letter from the state legislator for this district complaining bitterly about this portion of the highway, referring to complaints of his constituents, and raising cain because he had been promised action and none has been forthcoming.

Can you ask for much more than that!

It didn't stop there.

After a review of the documents, it was decided to depose the state highway engineer who was in charge of the road where the accident happened. He admitted to everything (not that he could have done otewise), but he added important details about trying to fix the road at one time (after the state congressman's first complaint), not doing that job correctly (the asphalt mix was bad), knowing that accidents were occurring there, and then not doing anything further. Why? Because his department spent its money according to certain priorities, and this road was way down on the list of priorities. There was simply no money available to fix this known hazardous condition.

It is understandable that any state may not have enough money to do everything that has to be done. But decades ago the Courts in my state had addressed this problem by holding that, if the state lacks funds to repair a highway, then shut it down! Put up warnings and have police there to supervise traffic. Do something! Just don't let the innocently ignorant public use the roadway on the assumption that it is a perfectly safe highway.

The district engineer gulped and acknowledged that he couldn't agree more except that the solutions were out of his hands and higher authority had failed to take action. So another case was "won."

Look again at the method used in this case.

1. The identification and retention of experts.
2. Conferences with the experts to devise a theory of liability.

3. Preparation of Interrogatories with the help of the experts.

4. Review of the answers to Interrogatories with the thought in mind "Where do we go from here?"

5. Request for Production of documents prepared with the help of the experts. They knew what ought to be "out there" and the proper names of the documents.

6. Deposition of responsible persons taken after all of the pertinent facts were known and the documents secured.

It is discovery that won the case. Not magic or pious hopes. The knowledge and advice of the experts were essential but in the beginning even they were guessing. They were saying, "Look into this," "Maybe that was all wrong— ask about it," and "See if so and so actually happened." Experts are idea men; the attorney has to test the validity of the ideas by accumulating facts through discovery. But it should not be hit or miss, scatter-gun shot discovery. You must have a general idea of what you are after, in what direction you are headed: then you devote your energy and talents to securing the unique and particular facts that are helpful.

The School Bus Case

This case followed the same path as the other two cases.

The school bus was on its regular route. Interrogatory: what is that route? It probably had a schedule. Interrogatory: it did. The civil engineer could make accurate measurements of the highway but he will need the precise measurements of the bus. The bus company probably has a manual from the manufacturer giving those dimensions. Request for Production: it did. What about the driver's experience and accident record? Easy. Interrogatories and Request to Produce personnel file: she had a spotless record, by the way. Did the bus company perform an investigation or have pictures of the bus at the accident scene? Interrogatory: yes and yes. Well, let's look at them. Request for Production: they didn't help.

The Civil Engineer and the Accident Reconstruction expert decided that since this bus operated on a schedule they would go to the scene and watch this driver in action. Arriving at about the time of the accident, they watched as the bus came down a hill and stopped to discharge a child at a nearby farmhouse. Then the bus pulled back into the road. Ahead, the road made a 45° right turn and started up hill. The driver made the turn but drifted to her left, and coming up hill continued to straddle the yellow medial line until she was near the top of the hill and approaching the left curve where the accident happened. Only at this point did she get back into the right lane and then proceed into the left-hand curve.

They saw what they wanted to see. To verify this photographs were taken.

Now this evidence is inadmissible. After all, just because the driver behaved this way on some occasions after the accident doesn't say she did so on the day of the accident.

But it put minds to work.

After the accident the bus was found with its right front against a hillside (only a few feet from the road) and its right rear wheel was inches off the road. That much showed in the photographs, was set forth in the police report, and admitted in the deposition of the driver. The bus was angled to its right.

But where was the left rear of that bus? Strange to say no one had inquired about that. There were no photographs of the back of the bus.

The state police report contained the comment of Trooper Jones that he stayed behind the bus directing traffic around it. A neighborhood woman who lived in the farmhouse at the bottom of the hill had given a statement that she walked up to the accident scene from her house to render assistance to Plaintiff. In fact she had gone back home to get a blanket to cover Plaintiff until the ambulance came. She must have walked past the rear of the bus not once but twice.

It was time for discovery depositions.

Depositions were taken—carefully and planned: "When are we going to to ask the crucial question?" "How shall we phrase those questions?" Both witnesses testified that the left rear wheel of the bus was about eighteen inches to the left of the medial line. Since that wheel was several feet forward of the rear of the bus that part of the bus was even further to the left of the yellow line.

That was all that was needed. Both the engineer and the accident reconstruction man went to work with the tools of their trades and concluded in strongly worded opinion letters that the bus was straddling the center line when plaintiff came around the curve, that he had nowhere to go (it was a very wide bus and a very narrow road), and that he could only cut to his left and try to cross in front of the bus to get away.

For a variety of reasons this case had to be tried and resulted in a very substantial verdict. It was the highest verdict ever achieved in this rural county.

Be that as it may, discovery won the case. What started out as nothing ended up in a very big something.

A WORD ABOUT THOSE PHOTOGRAPHS

The photos taken by the two experts were useless as evidence. Nonetheless they were worthwhile in lending credence to the theory of liability and were of great help in settlement discussions even though those negotiations came to naught.

When a claim representative has visual proof that your theory of the case is credible, it is very difficult for him or her to discount your claim.

Much the same situation exists in a medical malpractice case where the defendant doctor has already been sued successfully in other cases. Granted that the operations may have been of different kinds and the evidence inadmissable, still the fact of the prior successful claims lends credence to your argument that this medical doctor really doesn't know what he or she is doing.

This sort of thing lends force to your position and should be utilized to the fullest in a Settlement Brochure and in negotiations.

Let's put it this way: if the other side has this kind of material about your client, would you be worried? Just a little bit?

HOPELESS CASES CAN BE WON—WITH DISCOVERY

The preceding cases are designed to encourage you to take a good long look at seemingly hopeless cases and to ponder just what you might do with the case by using discovery techniques. The mere fact that the information before you is sparse and fragmentary does not mean that no case exists. All it means is that you don't have enough data to decide whether a legitimate claim exists. That is not the time to give up on the case. Rather it is the point at which you begin consulting with people more knowledgeable than yourself about what might have happened. These experts can tell you about possibilities and probabilities. You will hear from them, "Maybe this happened" or "Why don't you try this idea." Then they will go on and tell you where you might find the information that will turn an assumption into a fact and an idea into a workable theory.

But after all the consultations and the good suggestions of the experts, the invocation of discovery is up to you. You have the hard work of deciding which techniques to use, how to phrase the questions, when to use Interrogatories and when to take depositions, whom to depose and what documents to demand. It's hard work. It takes diligence and imagination. Gradually, bit by bit, you begin to accumulate the pieces to the puzzle and they all fit together.

There is a great deal of satisfaction in winning the hopeless case. There is a sense of accomplishment against odds, a feeling of professional fulfillment, and the bank account gets an injection—perhaps just in a moment of need.

Discovery is the key to success. Use it wisely and well.

12

Settlement—Achieving the Goal

The *only* purpose in indulging in the various discovery procedures that have been discussed in this book is either to get your case in such condition that you can try it well, or to settle it on terms favorable to yourself. That is the pay-off. To be frank, the end result I much encourage is settlement, and good, thorough discovery should make every case "settleable." By the time you conclude discovery you should have a pretty clear idea of the nature of your case. If it is exceptionally strong, or weak, it is a prime candidate for settlement; if it falls within that broad middle range of cases about which you can say "I have a shot at winning it" (but with serious reservations), then discovery will have enabled you to know precisely where your strengths and weaknesses lie. These are the troublesome cases and they comprise the bulk of those that go to trial. They should—and can—be settled, but it does take (1) some *hard work* and (2) *lengthy bargaining*.

THE TRIALS AND TRIBULATIONS OF SETTLEMENT

No case is settled with one telephone call or one casual conversation. Would that they were! It takes time, energy and effort to bring about a settlement, and that is the principal reason why more cases are not settled in the hiatus between completion of discovery and trial. It's hard work, associated with an uncertain conclusion. Given that combination, it's not surprising that many lawyers prefer to postpone making hard decisions and instead wait until the day of trial when pressure forces hasty conferences, snap judgments, and a settlement for good or ill, quickly arrived at. This is all right—except for the fact that most of the time the case could have been settled six or more months earlier for the same figure, and many settlements made in this manner are poor ones. Someone gets burned.

It doesn't have to be that way. Granted that the settlement process can be laborious and frustrating. The careful efforts of both Plaintiff and Defense counsel can result in a conclusion long before trial—and one that is fair and reasonable.

Unfortunately the burden, in settlement negotiations, is relatively one-sided—the Plaintiff's attorney usually has the task of initiating the subject and keeping it moving. He or she is the one who wants some money, and the Defendant (whether individul, business corporation or insurance company) finds it painful to pay and tends to drag its feet to avoid doing so. Thus the Plaintiff's attorney finds himself or herself in the position of being the person who:

1. Has to initiate the negotiations;
2. Must make the telephone calls and the seemingly endless follow-up calls;
3. Has to collect the tax returns, profit and loss statements, or bills and medical reports, and send them to the defendant;
4. Must keep pressuring the local claims people to put pressure on that faceless, anonymous individual in the home office whose decision is holding up the settlement;
5. Has to try to satisfy that person with more documentation—wage records, photographs, death certificates and other papers; and
6. Must keep his or her client informed with what he or she is trying to accomplish.

This work cannot be done quickly because there are so many people involved. To begin with, one deals with opposing counsel who then confers with the client who then may consult with various specialists—accountants, experts in the field of work involved, committees of different kinds, and decision-making officers of a corporation. When a decision is made it comes back down through the chain to the Plaintiff's attorney and then to his client. If an offer is rejected and a new demand is made it goes back to the Defense attorney and he or she starts through the whole process again. Along the way, of course, someone asks for more data so that the process is short-circuited until the demand is satisfied and straightened out. This can happen several times.

Thus the delay.

Granted that the settlement process takes time and is hard work, the result justifies the effort. Anytime you can close a case, months before trial, with a settlement that satisfies you and your client, you can be assured that the effort was worthwhile.

SETTLEMENT VIS-À-VIS TRIAL

I am a Trial Lawyer. You are a Trial lawyer. Yet if the truth be known, neither of us tries, to verdict, six cases a year. If you are a defense attorney you might get above that figure since defense attorneys usually try more cases than Plaintiff's lawyers. The reason for that is simple enough: the defense business is usually concentrated in a relatively small number of law firms while the Plaintiff's Bar is composed of a large number of individuals or small-member firms, all of whom have a few cases filed in Court at any one time.

If you doubt my statistics go to your Court Administrator and find the number of jury verdicts last year; you will be shocked at their small number. Even if you include Non-Jury cases, the total, in comparison with the number of cases filed, will be around 10 to 15 percent or less.

I took the opportunity to check this recently in my own Court. Allegheny County, Pennsylvania, with 1,336,449 people, ranks as the nineteenth most populous county in the United States and, as you would expect, has its fair share of litigation. Yet in reviewing the 1990 Annual Report for the Court of Common Pleas I learned that only 261 cases were tried to verdict! How many cases were settled at some stage in the judicial process? 2,522 cases. Of the total number of jury trial cases handled by our Civil Division, 2,052 cases, only 13 percent went to verdict. Obviously 87 percent settled. That is a matter for sober reflection. Since so many cases do settle, why not settle them promptly after you have completed discovery and when both you and opposing counsel know practically all that you are ever going to know about the case? It should be done and it can be done. The burden rests on you to initiate settlement discussions, to keep them moving, and to reach a satisfactory conclusion.

Let's face reality—settlement is the life blood of our judicial system. And it's an absolute necessity for the monetary success of many lawyers—especially the Plaintiff's lawyers who work on a contingent fee basis. When you think about trying every case, just remember two things:

1. It's a long wait between trials, and while you're waiting there is no money coming in; and

2. You have to lose some cases, and on those cases your fee is zero, which doesn't pay the rent or put food on the table.

On the defense side one might suggest that insurance companies and industrial corporations begin to complain as your hourly charges reach mountainous heights, and the complaints become an uproar if the conclusion is a high verdict which they have to pay. It's also quite embarrassing if the case wasn't worth much to begin with and your fee bill turns out to be higher than the verdict!

So it behooves all of us to take a long look at settlement as the proper basis for concluding a case—and all the results of your discovery should be utilized toward accomplishing a good settlement.

AFTER DISCOVERY, THE PRINCIPAL HANGUP TO SETTLEMENT IS YOU

Despite their years of training and experience and their professionalism, many lawyers still find it difficult to "look the facts in the face" and act on what they see. How very often I have heard a Plaintiff's attorney say, "It's not much of a case but I'm going to try it and see what happens." What "happens" 95 times out of a hundred is that he tries the case and loses it. Such persons are mesmerized with the gambling instinct, and view a trial much like the roll of the dice. They forget that nearly all gamblers are poor men. On the defense side one bears the flippant remark, "I don't have a very good case but Plaintiff wants too much money and maybe I can bring it in at a lower figure." This quite ignores the fact that if Plaintiff does have a good case, he or she is quite justified in making a demand somewhat higher than ordinary and a reasonable jury will probably agree with him or her. Yet the attorney just can't bring himself or herself to acknowledge that the demand is justified by the facts and ought to be paid.

It's hard to put a name on this attitude. Perhaps it's a combination of pride (arrogance), a little greed on Plaintiff's part, or a miserly, stingy attitude built into the defense attorney. Certainly stubbornness and vanity have a lot to do with it. Occasionally stupidity plays a role. Whatever the reason, the attitude and its end result are not professionalism. The very concept of "lawyering" demands a high degree of objectivity, honesty, good judgment and self-control. Venality and a whimsical attitude truly belong at a race track and not in a lawyer's office.

When you have carefully exhausted your discovery techniques and have all the facts available, it is time to say to yourself, "If I analyze this case carefully and properly there has to be a settlement here." Most of the time you'll be right.

WHEN SHOULD YOU BEGIN SETTLEMENT NEGOTIATIONS?

There are two aspects to every case—the liability side and damages. When you have established your case on the liability side as firmly as you can, it is time to begin to prepare for settlement negotiations. That is the major hurdle in nearly every case. When you have the answer to the question "Can we win?" then the issue of "How much do we pay?" almost naturally falls into place. Certainly one must inquire at great length into the question of losses or injury, but that is done to verify the claims and to narrow the range of potential payment. But the principal decision affecting settlement is the one involving the "Can we win?" question.

I caution you at once that it is a mistake to answer that crucial question with a simplistic "yes" or "no" answer. A quick overview of your file might lead to the impression, "I have a pretty good case here," and that may be true, but a detailed analysis is necessary before you can say "how good" is "pretty good." There are several facts to consider:

1. Can Plaintiff get past a nonsuit?
2. How many witnesses can each side produce on the liability question?
3. How strong are these witnesses?
4. Can their testimony be buttressed by documentary evidence?
5. Do you have damaging admissions that can be presented in Court?
6. Is the Law definite and clear on the subject matter of this lawsuit, or is it in a state of flux?
7. Is the attorney—your opponent—skilled and careful or is he, or she, inexperienced, reckless, or lazy?
8. How have cases like this fared, in your court, in the past?
9. If this case is assigned to a Judge, or you have an idea which Judge may handle it, what do you expect his, or her position to be?

When one speaks of appraising a case for settlement, all these factors have to be considered and then you can answer the question, "How good is my case?" And you might find yourself answering—I can win this case...

- Unless Judge Smith hears it;
- If witness Jones holds up;
- Provided Sam Brown tries it and not a better lawyer in that firm;

- If the Appellate Court doesn't change the law on the case pending before them;
- If the other side does not bring in those witnesses who have moved to Florida.
- And so on—and on—and on.

You know, as I do, that all cases have problems, so let's not delude ourselves that we are positively going to try this particular case. Now that discovery is concluded, analyze your case carefully and make every effort to settle it *now*! This is no horse race, so put your gambling instincts aside and take a long careful look at the facts and your degree of proof.

SIX KEYS TO EFFECTIVE SETTLEMENTS

1. Settlements are not merely desirable; they are necessary to your financial well-being.
2. Begin to form your idea about settlement when the liability problem becomes clear.
3. Carefully consider *all* the elements that lead to success or failure—the facts, law, quality of witnesses, supporting evidence and the important "outside" factors.
4. Study your file seriously and in detail.
5. Put away the gambler instinct and be objective, disciplined and honest in your analysis.
6. Avoid delay; when Discovery is finished proceed at once to work on settlement.

Now let's go to work on achieving a settlement:

START WITH A CLIENT CONFERENCE

If cases were left with the lawyers, I daresay that 99$^{99}/_{100}$ percent would be settled. Unfortunately, lawsuits belong to the litigants, not to the lawyers. And clients often taken an entirely different view of people, events and amounts than do their attorneys.

In this respect Defense attorneys are usually in a much better position than the Plaintiff's lawyer. Most defendants in this day and age are insurance companies and commercial businesses. The persons involved are often well educated and always experienced. A Claim Supervisor or Manager has been doing claim work for years. He knows the law, can appreciate the "weight of the evidence," is familiar with the "going rate" and possible exposure in a given type of case, and is constantly making value judgments. He has probably dealt with the same defense firm for years and has worked out a good relationship and modus operandi. He or she will respond easily to your reasoned and sensible analysis of the case.

The business executive is in much the same position. He, too, is called upon, almost daily, to analyze facts and figures and to make judgments in an impartial and objective manner. It's second nature to him. If the litigant is a corporation, it has a law department or a firm that provides legal advice and direction, and these people have no other purpose than to evaluate the facts, know the law, and, applying the one to the other, exercise a judgement as to the best course to follow. As a result they will listen attentively to your proposal and will be inclined to follow your advice.

The Plaintiff's attorney, on the other hand, has no such good fortune. While it is true that our Courts entertain many lawsuits between corporations, most of the plaintiff-litigants are individuals. The vast majority of these people are woefully ignorant of law, do not spend their days amassing and anlyzing facts, and habitually do not make judgmental decisions. To make things worse, the ordinary plaintiff is the person who has been injured or, in an Assumpsit matter, suffered a grievous financial loss, so that there is a great deal of raw emotion involved in his or her every thought concerning the lawsuit.

Whichever type your client may be, the first step in effecting a settlement is to secure the consent and advice of the client.

1. Educate the Client

One thing is certain in every case—the client has turned the case over to you, with trust and confidence in your abilities, and by that act has signified his or her willingness to be guided by your good judgment. So begin your efforts by working with the client. In doing so there are a few things you must prepare for:

2. Know Your Case Well

You can't do a selling job if you don't know what you're talking about. You must have gone through your file thoroughly—beginning with the pleadings, extracting pertinent Answers to Interrogatories, flagging certain pages in the depositions, noting the answers to particular Requests for Admissions, and jotting down the impressions of your investigator after his interviews with witnesses. If you think it necessary prepare a little memo on the applicable law, especially if there has been a recent change or it is in a confused and uncertain state.

3. Have an Opinion and Express it

Your job is to give advice. The client retained you as an expert and you are expected to express a strong, definite opinion concerning the proper course of action. A busy executive does not want to hear your analysis of the care followed by a plaintive query, "What do you want me to do, sir?" He'll tell you soon enough what he wants to do after you have told him what you think he ought to do and why.

In like manner your individual lay client doesn't know any more about analyzing a lawsuit than he does about flying a plane or performing an operation. That's why he hired you. He or she wants you to decide what is the best thing to do. Sometimes they don't like what they hear, but they understand that you know more about the subject than they do.

I find it aggravating to sit with another attorney, from time to time, while he explains the case in a vague, general manner, then offhandedly says, "Well, it's up to you—whatever you want to do." How in the world can he expect the client to make a sensible decision when the client lacks knowledge, experience and expertise? I have found that this is a common fault among attorneys who are not active in litigation matters. They lack confidence in their ability to justify their opinion and prefer not to express one at all! This is wrong and should be absolutely avoided.

> HAVE A DEFINITE OPINION, EXPRESS IT WITH
> VIGOR, AND BE PREPARED TO JUSTIFY IT!

4. Talk About a Range of Settlement, Not a Particular Figure

When you discuss settlement, the bottom line is money. Defendants ask, "How much shall we pay?" Plaintiffs ask, "What can we get"?

Under no circumstances should you permit yourself to be boxed in by agreeing on a specific sum. It's a mistake to say, "This case should be settled for $12,500," or any other precise figure. To begin with, at this stage you don't know if you can get that figure, and, second, the amount itself becomes a fixation in the mind of the client. If you do this as a Plaintiff's attorney and the final offer is $11,750 the client may well reject it on the ground that "you told us it was worth $12,500." If you're a Defense attorney and by hard bargaining you drive the Plaintiff down to $13,500, you may find yourself the butt of some snide comments from the home office about your evaluation. As I mentioned before, the experience of the Claim Supervisor, together with your explanation, may well result in your getting the extra $1,000, but the Plaintiff's attorney—dealing with an emotional and inexperienced client—will hear that wail of "You told me $12,500" for the duration of the case.

From a practical point of view it's better to talk to your client in terms of a settlement range. If you can convince a client that the case should be settled if you can negotiate a figure "between $15,000 and $20,000," you're in a much better position. It gives you some needed flexibility and the client does not become unalterably attached to a specific sum of money.

5. Get the Client Committed—In Writing

Once you have discussed the case with your client and have batted around various monetary values, come to some final conclusion about a settlement range. Don't let the client leave the office with the matter just hanging in the air. You should beware of phrases like "See what you can do," "Talk to the other side and get back to me," "Get a firm offer (or demand) and I'll let you know." Those comments are anathema. Why? Because they're meaningless. When you finally negotiate with the other side that person wants you to have (1) a reasonable degree of authority, and (2) a figure, or figures, in mind that can be the basis for firm negotiation. Otherwise your adversary is dealing with ephemera—nonsense talk. Why waste the time?

As to the suggestion that the agreement with the client be in writing, this, for defense attorneys, will be a matter of routine correspondence.

With Plaintiff's attorneys it's a different matter. Many Plaintiff's attorneys do not do this and I know that it is a constant source of irritation, confusion, and ill-feelings. The common cause is simply slipshod office administration combined with a pious hope that it's not necessary. It's also a mistake. Given the ability of many clients to "disremember" what was discussed at your conference regarding evaluation, and considering the natural desire of most clients to have second thoughts and want "more" and then to claim confusion and misunderstanding when you remind them of the agreed-upon settlement range— granted all of that, do yourself a favor and GET IT IN WRITING. All it takes is a simple memo that you can prepare in a few moments:

MEMO OF AGREEMENT REGARDING SETTLEMENT

October 10, 1991.

I, James Jones, do hereby acknowledge that I have discussed my case against Smith Company with my attorney on this date. We have reviewed all aspects of the case, its merits and problems have been explained to me, and my attorney has given me his evaluation of the case. I agree that if the defendant makes any offer in the range of $15,000.00 to $20,000.00, I will accept it and I authorize my attorney to negotiate on that basis.

_____

James Jones, Plaintiff

Witness:

_____
_____

It's always advisable to have someone witness the Agreement, even if it is the wife, a friend, or your secretary. It's amazing how a person who wants to forget a commitment will finally acknowledge that he made it if prodded by a child, spouse, friend, or third party.

You should run off twenty or so of these forms and keep them in your form file for the occasions when you need them. This practice is extremely beneficial, because there is nothing more embarrassing than to negotiate a settlement and then have to go back to your opposing attorney and tell him or her that the deal is off and that you need more money, or that you can't pay the amount you agreed on. This creates antagonism, gives the appearance that you don't know what you're doing, and damages your credibility. Protect yourself; have the memo signed—and nearly always your client will abide by it.

REMEMBER THESE RULES

1. Educate your client.
2. Know your case thoroughly.
3. Have a definite opinion and express it.
4. Discuss a range and not a precise amount.
5. Get your client committed in writing.

NEGOTIATE THE SETTLEMENT

Dealing with the client is just plain hard work; negotiating the settlement is fun. All parties have an understanding of the law, the facts, and some of the intangibles that go into settlement negotiations. (Is so-and-so a good witness? Are we a target defendant? Is the law about to be changed? In what county or district will the case have to be tried?) In short, everyone knows the rules of the game.

This is the time to pull together your data, polish up your powers of persuasion, and make your discovery pay off.

The first thing to do is to gather every salient fact, restricting yourself to crucial, significant matters. (Settlement negotiations are not like trying a case in court where you have to be prepared to prove every fact.) All the other side is really interested in is whether you can genuinely prove the gravaman of your case. So stick to that. Pull out the admissions in the depositions, the peripheral support in the Answers to Interrogatories, the significant documents, and the damning Answers to Requests for Admissions.

Now call your opponent and set up a meeting. (Do not negotiate on the telephone unless you really know the opposing attorney very well, have dealt with him for a long time, and the two of you understand each other thoroughly. Otherwise the conversation becomes just another telephone call with little significance and poor results.) When you arrive be prepared to overwhelm him or her with the solid case you have developed. Unless you have deceived yourself the time will come when he or she has to acknowledge that you have a winner. But before this happens there will be much justifying and shifting ground. That is why you must have anticipated some counter-argument and prepared the data to meet it. It's impressive as can be when your opponent tries to shift the blame in some manner and you can produce a document that shows that "it just ain't so," or he tries to claim that his client misunderstood a portion of a contract and you can point to the deposition of a partner which shows that he understood very well indeed. It's this kind of thing that leads to good settlements. As long as your opposing attorney can rely on "imaginative talk" and bluff, you're not going to get anywhere. When you can meet his or her arguments with facts and documents, sooner or later it becomes obvious that you are in a pretty good condition.

Even Questionable Cases Can Be Settled

If, after you review the product of all of your discovery, you realize that yours is not the greatest case in the world, even then do not hesitate to approach opposing counsel about settlement. Most cases are in this category—in which each side has something to say about the event at issue but neither is in an especially strong position.

Thanks to discovery you can now see the flaws in your case very clearly. If you will evaluate the case with those flaws in mind you have a good chance of settling it. Above all—don't succumb to the temptation to hold it for trial when you know in advance that it's a weak case. That leads to a terrible waste of time, money and effort. Aging is good for wine, not for weak cases.

Instead, once again, go to opposing counsel prepared to point out—vigorously—the many problems that he or she has, while acknowledging your own. I find that humor, candor, and a realistic appraisal of the case will work wonders. When the case is laid out for both you and your opponent to see clearly, with the gaps and missing links shining like the stars at night, then, most surely, a common agreement and understanding can be reached. Neither attorney wants to try a case when the proofs, as to each of them, remind one of Swiss cheese, and the only argument is whose slice has the biggest holes!

ARRIVE AT THE SETTLEMENT RANGE

There is no working area in the law that is more difficult than this—how to arrive at the proper figure for settlement. Pulling figures out of the clear blue sky doesn't work; they are always unrealistic. There is not—yet—any computer to solve the problem. At least, in most Assumpsit cases, the facts themselves set the outer limits of recovery, but that's not true of Trespass cases, with the sole exception perhaps of a Wrongful Death case where the death was instantaneous. How does one evaluate a Sexual Harassment case or a claim for damages for a violation of Civil Rights? In any case in which intangibles are involved—pain, loss of opportunity, embarrassment, compensation for disability, loss of future income—you must rely on judgment born of experience. There are no positive, definite standards. You are not helpless, however. There are a few guidelines:

1. Verdicts Set the Standards for Settlements

As a general rule no one is going to pay more in a settlement than the highest verdict that has been obtained in your area in a similar case. That is one place to start your search. Court personnel freely trade gossip about verdicts, and a good friend on the staff can help you immeasurably in locating the verdicts in cases similar to yours. Look them over, compare the special damages (medical bills, lost wages and the like), the nature of the injury, the liability, and if they are reasonably close to your own case use them as a guide.

2. Settlements Recently Made By Fellow Lawyers Are a Reasonable Guide

More than once I have had an unusual type of case only to find, on making inquiry, that other lawyers had a case that was close in point and settled it for so-and-so a figure. That helps—provided that lawyer is as good as you are, that the two cases are really comparable, and that there was not some special, novel, factor that brought about his settlement. I call to mind a recent case, widely reported on the television and in newspapers, in which a young steel worker was trapped on a girder of a bridge that was being demolished. TV cameras focused on him as he screamed and writhed in pain while his fellow workers worked with terrible slowness to free him for fear the whole structure would collapse, killing them all. Finally an orthopedic surgeon had to be summoned who, right on the girder, in full view of all, and administering a minimal amount of anesthetic, had to cut off the leg. That case eventually settled for an enormous sum, but it hardly stands for a standard by which to measure the value of all "leg off" cases. It's that kind of thing you have to beware of when talking with your friend.

Likewise, in an assumpsit case, you can hardly use for comparison a similar case in which the defendant corportion burned records to avoid discovery, bribed employees to lie, and sent a key officer-witness to Europe to avoid the taking of his deposition or appearance at trial. Settlement in such a case should be at the rate of 100 percent of value and it cannot be used as a standard.

But your brethren at the Bar have been through most of the cases that may be new to you and dutiful inquiry will enable you to turn up enough cases to provide an emerging pattern to help you.

If you are a defense attorney, the problem of evaluation is a little easier since your insurance company or corporate client will have both statistics and a company policy to assist you. You aren't left to grope your way quite as much as Plaintiff's attorney is required to do. Quite likely an opinion letter will have been written and a reserve established so that you already have guidelines to assist you in settlement. Thereafter it is a matter of evaluating the changes developed during the discovery process and then arriving at a more up-to-date settlement range. But still novel and unusual cases will come along from time to time, and you too will be thrust in the position of searching for a verdict in a comparable case or "sounding out" your contemporaries about their settlements, if any, in similar situations.

3. Utilize the Various Books and Guides Found in Every Law Library

There are many books on the subject of settlement that should be perused if you have an especially troublesome problem. In addition, there is one set of handbooks that I have found to be especially helpful in giving general guidelines. That series is

Personal Injury Valuation Handbooks
by Jury Verdict Research, Inc.
Caxton Building
Cleveland, Ohio 44115

This series of handbooks divides its review into sections dealing with verdicts for all kinds of specific injuries and also analyzes verdicts from the point of view of different liability situations. For example, on the injury side the handbook will take a "below-knee amputation," and give you a Midpoint Range, Probability Range, Verdict Range and Average Value, followed by references to specific cases. On the liability side they will cite "Medical Malpractice—Fracture Treatment," and in a brief discussion give the total number of cases reviewed, the percent that were Plaintiff's verdicts, and again, a reference to some specific case examples. It's a good series and I recommend that you look at it for help in evaluating your case.

Unfortunately, however, there is no book or manual that can give you specific help to answer the twin questions: "What is my case worth?" and "What shall I offer (or demand)?" You can only review the verdicts, consult with your acqaintances and friends, study your case and make adjustments in the figures you learn of, as needed, and then, based on your own experience, arrive at a settlement range that you deem fair and reasonable.

WORK WITH OPPOSING COUNSEL

Please notice the use of the word "with" in the title above. It's a common mistake to treat opposing counsel almost like an enemy—as if he or she was *personally* paying the money (or receiving it) and *deliberately* obstructing your honorable efforts to secure a just settlement of the case. While this may be a slight exaggeration of the true state of affairs, it is correct that many attorneys enter into settlement negotiations with a chip on their shoulder, daring the other side to knock it off. All these lawyers get is a fight—not a settlement.

Instead, actively strive to work with your adversary. He or she can help you by pointing out the problems he or she has in dealing with the client, or areas in which you will need additional proof, or doubts that have been expressed about the integrity of your principal witness, or the state of the law. Once you recognize these matters as problems, you can arrange to have on hand the manner of resolving them quickly. Yet you would never have known of these obstacles if opposing counsel was offended by your attitude and kept still. And don't forget that very often your adversary has a good deal of discretion given him by his client. He can use that discretion in a friendly or a hostile manner, to help you or hurt you. Why invite trouble? Go out of your way to work *with* the attorney on the other side and you can accomplish wonders. It's still true that honey gets more bees than vinegar.

There are several specific areas in which Defense attorneys usually need some help:

1. Documentation of a Plaintiff's Claims

The Defendants always need proof—preferably of a documentary nature—of various aspects of a Plaintiff's claim, but principally in the area of damages.

Thus, if a Plaintiff claims that he or she was working at a second job, received payment in cash, and is demanding this loss as part of his or her damages, you will have to do more than rely on Plaintiff's bare assertion of that fact. The Defendant, legitimately, will want to see income tax returns and/or a statement from the employer regarding hours worked and payments made.

As another example, while medical and hospital bills are easily and routinely procured, payments for household services—a legitimate claim—are usually not made on the basis of a written contract and are often paid in cash. Here too, a statement will be needed that the work was done and the payments made.

Large corporations frequently get into violent disputes—especially when working on a "cost plus fixed fee" basis—as to the legitimacy of the claims "cost," or if on a "time and materials" contract, as to the amount of time that was necessary and the true cost of the materials. While representing a steel fabricating company in a claim against a major construction company I had to be amused as the respective teams of accountants, engineers and managers took off their coats, sat at a long table, and went at it one day—and the whole fight was over the bills for time and materials from the fabricator: whether the "time" was inflated, and whether the costs for material from the sub-contractors were correct. If my client had not had detailed statements, financial records and affidavits, the case would never have settled—but we did and it did.

Your opponent wants proof, not mere verbal assertion of fact, regarding damages. Your job is to see to it that he, or she, gets what is needed.

2. The Current State of the Law in Novel Cases

If plaintiff is proceeding on the basis of some esoteric, novel, or even slightly unusual theory of law it is only reasonable, when defense counsel expresses doubts, to provide him or her with a memo explaining why the theory is justified. To illustrate, the City of Pittsburgh owns a very steep hillside covered with trees and underbrush—and rocks. A major road runs along this hillside, and on the day in question as a taxicab proceeded up the hill a large rock rolled down, came through the windshield, and injured the passenger. The City took the position that this incident was a natural event over which it had no control and for which it was not responsible, even though it had happened before. Essentially the position was that the rocks could not be controlled and that the only alternative was to shut down the road, which it felt the law did not require.

This was certainly not a routine case and defense counsel was impressed with the logic of his position and felt no need for legal research. Since he wouldn't do it, I had to. Lo and behold—I found that there is authority that if a municipality cannot control natural forces that endanger a road it has the duty to close the road rather than subject its citizens to known dangers while using it. A short brief to that effect was sufficient to convince both the defense attorney and the city fathers, and the case was settled.

There are a lot of things like that which can be resolved if you will do the research, write a Brief or memo, and use it to convince the other side that liability exists. I recall a case in which two automobiles collided head-on at night on an isolated country road, killing both drivers. The only witness was a passenger who died soon after, but not before giving a brief statement to the driver of a car who arrived at the scene sometime later. The issue was whether the statement constituted a Dying Declaration exception to the Hearsay Rule. The burden was clearly on Plaintiff's counsel to satisfy the Defendant that it did, and a good brief on the subject accomplished that purpose.

In another case you might be confronted with the issue of whether an agent was within or without the scope of his authority when he performed some unusual act. If you will do the research to satisfy the Defendant that the person was acting within his delegated authority, the case may settle; if you won't do the work, now, it will not be settled. At the same time remember that the issue will remain to haunt you and will still be there at trial time. Then you will most certainly have to brief it for the Court. Why wait? If that is a central issue in the lawsuit let the Defendant know, early in the case, that you have a solid position and settle the case!

Don't permit yourself to be either too proud or too lazy to do a little research and brief writing for the opposition. It's in your best interest to do so.

3. Letting Your Opponent Have Your Items of Proof as to Liability

When some attorneys have an item of evidence that represents a key to the liability side of the case, they tend to clutch it to their chests as though they had just lifted the Hope diamond from the Smithsonian and you literally have to pry it from them, if you get it at all. Their fear is that if the opposition knows of it they (the opposition) will connive to destroy its effectiveness or utility. That attitude is absurd. To begin with, under current discovery rules the evidence can be uncovered one way or another, and second, most lawyers aren't in the "conniving" business. If the evidence is as damning as one thinks it is, the other side will want to settle—not lie or evade. However, they have to see it before they can acknowledge that it is damning; and if you don't show it to them they can never make a judgment in the matter. That's why it is so silly and self-defeating to "hide" evidence. Give it to your opponent so that he or she can see for himself or herself that your case is strong; the next topic for conversation will be the subject of settlement.

One sad but hilarious example of the benefits of this approach involved a case where a young child received a bicycle for a birthday present. While riding it that day the brakes failed, and the child was struck by a car and injured. The father was a mechanical engineer who assured me that the brakes were poorly designed and inoperative, but he adamantly refused to permit the Defendant's experts to see the bike. That was THE EXHIBIT, THE PROOF, and no one could see it. In due course of time I persuaded him that he was wrong and arranged a time for an inspection, and on the day appointed the defense attorney and the expert showed up and examined the bike in Plaintiff's garage. The expert pronounced the brakes sound over my client's howling objections. The defense attorney—a husky man—asked my permission to ride the bike and I assented. He circled the garage once and flew down the steep driveway—directly into the path of an oncoming car. He just barely shot past it as we all raced to the street. Ashen-faced, he pushed the bike back to us and, glaring at his expert, said to me: "Let's settle this case. The goddamned brakes don't work!"

So much for keeping evidence from the other side.

Seriously, if you have evidence that clinches the case, let your opponent have it. If it is as sound and relevant as you think it is the other attorney will appreciate the poor position he or she is in and will want to settle the case.

4. Evaluating a Difficult Case

This is one more area in which your assistance might be helpful to the other side. It is possible that you have the kind of case in which the normal guidelines and standards are inapplicable. If you have scouted around and learned of settlements or verdicts by other attorneys—perhaps in neighboring jurisdictions—don't keep them under your hat. Share the information with defense counsel so that he or she knows that there is exposure and that your demand was not wholly a product of whimsy and imagination.

If you have friends in the Legislature and have based your case on a bill that is about to become Law, or has just been passed, you might as well tell the defense attorney instead of having him or her floundering around wondering about the basis of your claim. They have as much trouble keeping up with the changes in the law as you do, and any help you can give in that regard will be appreciated.

Finally, if there is some significant aspect to either side of a case that lifts it out of the normal situation, that should be specifically called to the attention of Defense counsel so that he or she can take it into consideration. For example, you may have a case involving a serious injury to a young child who is being attended to by its mother, and predictably, this will continue. Now if the mother should develop a tumor which both limits her life expectancy and requires serious medical treatment for her, then the claim for damages on behalf of the child can change abruptly and significantly.

There can be other events such as this which suddenly appear and significantly change the ordinary appraisal of a case. When they do occur be certain that the other side is informed so that they can understand your evaluation of the case.

5. Giving the Other Attorney the Documentary Information He Needs

I have often heard attorneys express their strong feelings that they will not turn over to their opposing counsel various documents that he or she wants. Usually they refer to experts' reports, letters from attending physicians, income tax returns, statistical analysis and other important data. This always seemed strange to me; if the other attorney is to be kept in the dark about vital information pertaining to the case, how will he or she ever be in a position to evaluate it for settlement purposes? The answer is obvious—he or she can't do it. To refuse to divulge pertinent information is simply to cut off your nose to spite your face. It's ridiculous. If parties are seriously interested in settling a case and a Plaintiff's attorney has experts' reports that clearly point to liability on the part of the defendant, he should run—not walk—to get them into the hands of the defense attorney. That is exactly the kind of information your opponent must have to evaluate the case himself and to discuss it intelligently with his client. It's in your best interest to show your adversary counsel that you do have a strong case. You do that best by overwhelming him or her with factual data. So, let your emphasis be, not on withholding significant data, but on divulging it—promptly. The more your opponent knows, the more realistic he or she will be in settlement negotiations.

KNOW YOUR OPPONENT—WHAT KIND OF PERSON IS HE OR SHE?

It is trite, but necessary, to mention that everyone has a distinct personality and a particular way of doing things. Since, to effect a settlement, you have to reach an agreement with the other lawyer, go out of your way to learn what kind of person he or she is and how that person conducts his or her business. If that lawyer is a "detail person," give him or her a detailed analysis of the case; if he or she is proud of being a scholar, prepare a little brief; if longwinded talk is their forte, be prepared to spend an afternoon with them. You're trying to convince the other attorney and you must adjust to his or her foibles. There are other things you have to bear in mind:

1. Does this lawyer speak with authority? If you reach an agreement with him or her, can he or she produce?
2. Is this a person who will reach an understanding with you and then come back later with a tale of woe asking that you increase (or lower) the agreed-upon figure?
3. Will this attorney take the time to go through the facts and the proofs with you?
4. Will this attorney be honest in appraising the facts with you? Or is he or she one of those persons who won't even acknowledge the identity of the Plaintiff and Defendant?
5. Does this lawyer know the case well enough to debate its virtues and vices with you?

These are some of the things you have to learn before you meet to discuss settlement. Each type of personality, each varied attitude, can be handled if you just know about it in advance and take the time to figure out how to resolve it.

PREPARE A SMALL BROCHURE OR SYNOPSIS OF YOUR CASE

This is most important for Plaintiff's attorneys. Very often pertinent facts are scattered in a dozen different places in a file. If you consider that most defense attorneys have dozens of files and are quite busy, you will realize that it is both difficult and time-consuming for them to search for and summarize these facts. It helps your cause to do it for them. In addition, when you present them with a little summary of the case it gives them something concrete to pass on to their insurance company or corporate client as a basis for justifying their recommendation for settlement.

Your summary can be detailed if you think it will help—going into your theory of liability and referring to specific evidence you have for each element of your cause of action. Usually, though, you can leave that matter to verbal discussion with the defense attorney. Most often your summary can be directed to biographical details and proofs relating to losses and damages. The following represents just such a summary prepared in a death case for settlement discussion. Attached to it, as exhibits, were letters from the employers verifying the wage record, copies of funeral bills and other last expenses, and copies of the hospital and medical bills.

This was a medical malpractice case in which the decedent died because a nurse in the Intensive Care Unit had, allegedly, prematurely withdrawn an endotracheal tube after surgery. The man involved was a retiree who, although on a pension, had secured another job which provided him with a little activity and income. The liability side of the case was the subject of several conferences but the damages aspects were pretty well covered by this summary.

SUMMARY
JOHN P. JONES

BIRTHDATE: 2-13-12
DATE OF BIRTH: 6-1-80
AGE: 68

LIFE EXPECTANCY: 13.4 years

RETIRED J&L—11-2-71—See Exhibit 1.
PENSION—$388.67—Subject to Increases of a Non-Predeterminal nature
1979—$4,664.04 Total Pension Paid

II. *WORKED FOR COMMONWEALTH OF PA.*—See Exhibit 2. Began—
10-29-71
Position—Administration Assistant I—Inheritance Tax Office $1,332.00/mo.

EARNINGS

1976-$13,101.23	1979-$16,862.55
1977-$13,429.37	1980-$ 7,392.60

No Compulsory Retirement

III. ESTIMATED RECOVERY-
Work: $17,000.00 × 7 years $119,000.00
Pension: $ 4,700.00 × 13.4 years.................................... 62,980.00

TOTAL $181,980.00

IV. FUNERAL, BURIAL AND OTHER LAST EXPENSES—See Exhibit 3.

TOTAL $7,182.07

V. MEDICAL EXPENSES—See Exhibit 4.

TOTAL $8,868.17

TOTAL LOSS OF EARNINGS OF MR. JONES $181,980.00
TOTAL EXPENSES .... $ 16,050.24
LOSS OF CONSORTIUM OF MRS. JONES
For 13.4 years...???

This made a nice package for the benefit of both defense counsel and the claims persons at the insurance company. Since the case was settled for a fair sum, this little summary obviously did some good. At least there was no argument about these various elements of damage.

MAKE A SENSIBLE, REALISTIC OFFER OR DEMAND

There are few things more irritating than to have a case that truly has a value of, let us say, $50,000 and to receive an offer of $7,500, unless it's one that has a value of $2,500.00 and the demand is $100,000. Ridiculous offers and demands are the cause of death of more settlement negotiations than any other reason. You've seen this sort of thing happen. The case plods along to a trial date, and lo and behold—the one settles for $47,500 and the other for $2,000. Chat some day with a trial judge and he will tell you, wearily, story after story like this. Most of the time the problem lies with inexperience on the part of counsel, but once in awhile it is caused by the deliberate policy of some insurance company or the intransigence of a stubborn client.

Insofar as it is within your power don't play this game. Certainly it is expected that Plaintiff's attorneys will start high and then come down just as defense attorneys start low and come up. But there are sensible parameters to this bargaining called for by the facts of the case. I knew a wonderful Federal Judge who always had fun with Plaintiff's attorneys during his inevitable settlement conferences by asking:

"What is your demand?" [Then]

"What do you really want?" [Then]

"Now, what will you take?"

It was good-natured fun until one got clearly out of line, then hell broke loose. He was even-handed—many a defense attorney made hurried calls to his client, from Chambers, with an Order from the Judge as to what the offer was going to be! This Judge had a settlement rate of about 95 percent and they were fair, equitable settlements.

So appraise your case realistically, allow a little room for bargaining, and give a demand or an offer that can lead to settlement and accomplish the purpose of the meeting.

KEEP AFTER THE OTHER ATTORNEY

It's rare to be able to settle a case in one meeting. Afterward each side will want to think about the negotiations, look again at the evidence and confer with their respective clients. At the same time remember the old adage, "Out of sight, out of mind.'' It's too easy to dictate a letter after the conference, set the file aside, and forget about it. That won't do. It's a little like making fudge: somebody has to go to the stove and stir it from time to time or it turns bad. You have to do that with settlements. If there has been no word from the other attorney in two or three weeks you will have to call and inquire as to what is happening. Frequently you will learn that he forgot to send a letter or someone was out of town the last time he called and he just forgot to try again. This may go on several times— that's normal—but if you will just be persistent it will pay off. There may be one last go-round of bargaining and then the case is settled. It's hard work, but it's worth it.

DON'T TRY TO DO THE IMPOSSIBLE; SOME CASES CAN NOT BE SETTLED

There is an old cliché that ''politics is the art of the possible.'' It's a good saying and it implies that, from time to time, certain things simply can't be done. That is certainly true of settlements. Try as you might there are some cases that can't be settled. Don't fight it. With your discovery completed, the case is in the best possible posture for a trial, so simply set it aside until it is called.

There are several reasons for a failure in settlement negotiations. The principal one is an unrealistic demand or offer on the part of the attorneys. If the culpable party adamantly refuses to reconsider his or her position the settlement talks collapse. A second common explanation is an unreasonable attitude on the part of the client. As I mentioned before, emotions are a part of every lawsuit and sometimes they blind the client to reality. The client simply refuses to believe a certain witness is valueless or that the law prohibits him or her from using certain evidence. When you're faced with this kind of intransigence there is nothing else to do but to try the case and, as it unfolds in Court, hope that your client will accept the fact that things are not as he or she wants or believes them to be. Unfortunately, by that time any hope of a reasonably good settlement will be gone.

In addition to these reasons for failure to negotiate a fair settlement, one must know that some insurance companies and corporations have an established policy of not negotiating in good faith, of waiting to the bitter end before offering a fair amount in settlement. Plaintiff's attorneys will talk of being ''nickled and dimed to death'' as the multiple offers are made in small, increasing increments. From this comes the saying that ''the best settlements are made on the court-house steps.'' By experience, and friendly talks with the other lawyers, you will learn which companies these are and you will have to react accordingly. Fortunately that approach has pretty much gone out of style due to criticism from scholars and the public, pressure from the Bench, changes in the Rules of Procedure, and, probably, sound business practices.

Finally we have the Plaintiff's attorney who will not give up his or her gambling "go for broke" attitude until the day of trial when he or she suddenly realizes he or she is bluffing no one—or the defense attorney who hangs on to the bitter end because he is being paid an hourly fee and the longer he hangs onto a case the more money he makes. The reputation of these people is known in your community, and when you come up against them all you can do is accept them for what they are and forget about settlement.

GUIDELINES FOR NEGOTIATING
A GOOD SETTLEMENT

1. Determine a reasonable settlement range.

    a. Check verdicts in similar cases.

    b. Make inquiry about settlements from your friends.

    c. Check books and manuals in the library.

2. Make a realistic offer or demand.

3. Work with—not against—opposing counsel.

4. Know the kind of person you are dealing with.

5. Give the other attorney the data he needs.

6. Prepare a brochure or synopsis of the case—especially relating to damages and losses.

7. Bargain on a face-to-face basis; avoid telephone conferences.

8. Keep after the other attorney; don't let the negotiations get cold.

13

The Preparation of a Settlement Brochure

There is no better way to bring your substantial cases to settlement than to prepare a Settlement Brochure. In addition, the greatest favor you can do for a client in the instance of a high recovery is to arrange a detailed, well planned structured settlement. These statements represent axioms in the practice of law today. There is no sensible alternative.

Most attorneys quail at the thought of the work that goes into the preparation of a Settlement Brochure, and there is no question that it is hard work. But when one is dealing with a case having a potential value of $250,000 to upwards of a $1,000,000 or more, you must convince the numerous decision makers on the other side of these three ideas:

1. You can't win;
2. You ought to settle now; and
3. My demand is reasonable and can be justified.

It takes some nerve to make these statements, and the attorney who stakes out this position better have something to support this bold stand. That "something" is a Settlement Brochure.

RECENT DEVELOPMENTS IN PERSONAL INJURY LAW

Let's take a moment to look at the changes in the Law as it relates to personal injury and other claims over the past several years.

To begin with, the million-dollar verdict has arrived and it's here to stay. That fact is doubly important since verdicts establish the value of settlements.

In the present era, it is obvious that the value of damage awards is steadily increasing. This applies to every kind of case—personal injury claims, lawsuits for libel and defamation, complaints about civil rights violations including racial, age, and sex discrimination, and those occasional cases in which punitive damages are sought and awarded. A glance at the morning newspaper announcing the latest million or multimillion dollar verdict, or riffling through the pages of a weekly news magazine where the wails of business persons, medical doctors, and special interest representatives are recorded, firmly establishes that we live in an age of The Big Award.

Every lawyer knows that the number of multimillion dollar verdicts is a minute potion of the total number of cases tried. That 1 percent (or less) of total verdicts makes the headlines in the newspaper while the 99 percent are ignored.

However, many attorneys mistakenly believe that these high awards have no significance in his or her daily practice. But there is a fall-out effect here. The case that was worth $50,000 at the beginning of your career may well be worth $200,000 today because of those high verdicts. And that case you are so proud of settling for $150,000 ten years ago could probably bring in $500,000 today for the same reason. A series of high verdicts in Chicago and Los Angeles does have an effect on jurors in Cleveland. In addition, the basis for those high verdicts—astronomical medical expenses, higher earnings of employed persons, increased emphasis on quality of life—exists today in Cleveland as well as they do in Chicago and Los Angeles. The overall result is the very substantial verdict, which reflects itself in higher settlements everywhere.

Marching hand in hand with these high awards is a proliferation in both the numbers and variety of cases that attorneys work on today. Defamation and libel actions were not filed very often in the 1960's, medical malpractice cases were a rarity, and most civil rights and discrimination cases didn't even exist as legal claims. Today that are a common and a significant part of litigation. The metropolitan area of my community is the nineteenth largest in the United States; at one time, there might have been 25 or 30 medical malpractice actions filed, but today there are 1500 such cases! And since negligent doctors can produce terrible injuries, the verdicts and settlements are very high in comparison with those in days gone by.

The net result of this increase in the amount and variety of litigation, combined with the willingness of jurors to return high verdicts, is that every attorney—those in a rural community as well as those in a big city—is now likely to get new, complicated cases that have a potential for a very high settlement or verdict. Unfortunately, many attorneys do not know how to handle these cases well. The liability side of the case can be complicated, esoteric, and demanding; it may require knowledge and skills previously unheard of or unknown. The damages side can suddenly involve economists, actuaries, and medical cost specialists whom most attorneys have not had occasion to use in previous (and smaller) types of cases. These are serious problems.

In the midst of all of these changes, the one consistently immovable object has been the attitude of the corporation, insurance company, or individual defendant who is asked to pay—or approve payment of—large sums of money. These persons and groups are still all from Missouri, the Show Me state, and they will not pay you large sums of money until you prove to them that they have no other choice. With these persons talk is cheap. With these people you don't talk and reason; you *show them*. Let's face reality. One of two things can happen: You can prove your case in court after waiting two or three years, and after incurring frightful expenses for experts and trial preparation. Or you can effect a good settlement of your case in a reasonable period of time by convincing the other side that they cannot win and that your demand is justified. This latter is a goal definitely to be desired.

And the best tool for doing so is a good Settlement Brochure. A carefully prepared Settlement Brochure is your best means of attaining this goal. It is a direct, positive, and challenging method of convincing a skeptical defense attorney, claims manager, or obstinate defendant that (1) they cannot win the case and (2) that the case is worthy of the demand that you have made.

A spin-off effect of the work that goes into the preparation of such a brochure is that, when it is completed, your case will be beautifully prepared for trial if that becomes necessary. Your Theory of Liability will be clearly thought out and expressed; critical witnesses will have been deposed; the opinion letters of expert witnesses are now in the file; necessary photographs have been taken; pertinent statistics and treatises secured; medical (and other) bills assembled; and vital computations of future losses and expenses have now been made. A good Settlement Brochure helps the Plaintiff's attorney in two ways: (1) in settling the case if possible or (2) in preparing the case if a trail is necessary. Either way, you can't lose!

WHY A SETTLEMENT BROCHURE IS A MUST

1. High verdicts and settlements are possible in your cases.
2. The volume and variety of all types of cases are increasing.
3. Defendants and their insurance companies will not pay substantial amounts until convinced that they have to.
4. A Settlement Brochure can clearly announce to them:
   a. You can't win, and
   b. My demand is justified.
5. Preparing a Settlement Brochure forces you to prepare for trial.

WHAT IS A SETTLEMENT BROCHURE?

A Settlement Brochure is a binder containing all pertinent information about your case, designed to convince the reader that your case is sound and that your demand is just. It takes hard, detailed work to prepare one, but the reward is great: a good settlement in a reasonable time rather than an expensive, chancy trial after a number of years.

It Is Essential in Major Cases

No one is going to pay you $500,000 because of your good looks, sparkling personality, or the fact that you graduated at the top of your law school class. When you make a demand of a large sum of money, your Honorable Defense Counsel will listen to your Theory of Liability, your claim for damages, and how you think you will prove all of these things. Then counsel will discount all you have said by 90 percent as so much "hot air." As one of my colleagues was prone to say, "He is good at puffing smoke but it all gets blown away by the harsh winds of proof." Talk is cheap. If you want a defense attorney and an insurance company to pay attention to your demand for $500,000 or $1,000,000 you have to (1) catch and hold their attention with something they can read, hold, take home from the office and (2) give them written details and solid proof of your claim. That "something" is a settlement brochure. With one in the hands of the defense attorney and another with the case manager at the home office, they can review—and groan—together at what you are prepared to prove and they can justify a recommendation to pay your demand. Without it you are just "puffing smoke"; with it you are taken seriously and paid rapt attention. Do not try to negotiate a big settlement without a brochure; it won't work.

THE ARGUMENT FOR DISCLOSURE

Many Plaintiff's attorneys instinctively balk at providing defense counsel or an insurance company with documentation of their claims. Part of the reason is the embarrassing fact that they don't have it; another part is the old-fashioned idea, "I'm not going to give away my case." When one sensibly inquires, "Why not?" there is never a good reason. Clearly one "gives away" one's case at a trial. In many jurisdictions it is required in a Pretrial Statement, at a Pretrial Conference, a Status Hearing, or at Conciliation or Settlement Conferences. When a Judge, at a pretrial Conference, demands a medical expert's report or an itemized list of special damages, you better have it and produce it. Why not do the same six months or a year earlier for a claim manager to produce a settlement? The entire premise of, "I'm not going to give away my case" is simply ridiculous. Sooner or later you *are* going to give away your case—usually in bits and pieces during depositions, in Answers to Interrogatories, or Requests for Production, and surely in a Pretrial Statement. The real truth of the matter is that midway through the litigation the average Plaintiff's attorney is not prepared, hasn't thought through his or her case carefully, and doesn't have documents and reports that he or she ought to have. That is too bad because a case in such a posture can't be settled.

If you have the information, put it into a brochure and give it to the whole world! Be confident of your proof of liability and dare the defense attorney to find fault with it. Give claim managers your medical reports and estimates of future medical costs and claim for lost wages; how else can they evaluate your case?

"Give and you shall receive." It's as true here as elsewhere in life. If the other side lacks the information they need to appraise your case, there can never be serious and productive settlement negotiations.

Convincing Those Mysterious, Unknowables in the Home Office

Sitting at a desk far, far away from you is a miserly grinch who works in a strange and mysterious place called The Home Office. This grinch holds the key to a fortune, but rarely unlocks the vault. By devious methods that person will know a good deal about you, but in turn you know nothing about him or her.

Now, somehow you have to get through to and galvanize that stranger into the undesirable and unusual activity of opening the vault and delivering a portion of the fortune to you. A phone call won't do it. Neither will a personal meeting where you regale the grinch with flattery, logic, reason, bombast, or threats. It won't work; the grinch has no ears.

It does have eyes and it can read . . . and think . . . and contemplate . . . and discuss. Your key to catching the attention and holding the interest of those "unknowables" is a Settlement Brochure. They can't ignore it. Their jobs require that they read it. With your voluminous and detailed brochure before them, they are in a position to analyze, debate, and decide. You have given them the opportunity and need to make a decision. If you have done your job well, the word will get down to the defense attorney and the local claims people, "Negotiate and settle this case."

Make Copies for Everyone and Distribute Them Yourself

Your counterpart in the Defense Bar is a very busy person—under pressure, harassed, with more cases to worry about than you have, and with secretaries, paralegals, and junior partners to supervise. It's hard enough to get these attorneys to read your brochure; it's almost too much to ask that they make the requisite number of copies and see to their distribution to necessary persons. Don't rely on defense attorneys; do it yourself. More than once this writer has gone to the office of opposing counsel and found the copies of his brochure lying in a chair or in a corner of the room, gathering dust, weeks after it was sent. This is bad news. You must get these copies disseminated to all of the decision makers. It is my suggestion that you make numerous copies and send them to:

1. The lead defense attorney;
2. His or her assistant or paralegal;
3. Other defense attorneys who may be involved in the case;
4. Local claims personnel, especially the claims manager; and
5. At least two copies to the home office of the insurance company.

In this manner you can be assured that the people who ought to read your brochure at least have the opportunity to do so.

A Brochure Must Be Bound, Neat, Clean, and Orderly

The advertising cliché is that, ''The packaging is the product.'' You are doing a selling job with this brochure and everyone is impressed with appearances.

Cover. Let's start with the cover. If your law firm has a logo or a very attractive letterhead, put that on the cover. If nothing else, get a colored piece of poster board and have a skilled person letter the case name and your name on the cover. Just make sure it is attactive and eye catching.

Next is neatness. Be certain that every page is $8\frac{1}{2} \times 11$. If a certain photograph or set of statistics is larger than that, either trim it or fold it over. See to it that smudge marks are erased. Make certain that in the duplicating process certain pages don't come out either so light or so dark that one must strain to read them. If cassettes or videotapes accompany the brochure, put them in the back (inside jackets or envelopes to keep them secure). Are these suggestions nothing but common sense about details? Yes, but the truth is that many lawyers sometimes get indifferent and this is not the time to prepare a shoddy product. If you want a ''top of the line'' settlement, then submit a brochure that is of equal quality.

Finally the brochure must be bound for appearance sake and to keep the pages permanently in place. You don't have a binding machine in your office? Unbelievable. Go buy one now! They cost next to nothing, are easy to operate, and have a thousand uses. You can use one to bind bulky medical records, to keep engineering drawings together, or to package accountants' work papers backed up by your clients' documents. A binder is an invaluable little machine in an office and is a necessity for tying together the pages of your brochure.

The Contents of the Brochure

Your brochure should be arranged in a sensible, logical, and orderly manner, but you must keep in mind that it is a sales document and the prime rule is this:

Get their attention fast and hold it!

And what is the best way to do this? Photographs! Strong stirring photographs. Let us suppose that your case involves third degree burns to a child. Let the very first page be a large photograph of that child as a beautiful, healthy, smiling young person. Every family has these pictures. Then let the second page be an equally large picture of that child showing hideous burns, ugly scars, and/or bandages. Beyond a particle of doubt, you will get attention instantly! The powerful, dramatic effect of such a juxtaposition of photographs is such that the reader's eyes and emotions are immediately and shockingly drawn deeper into the brochure seeking an answer to the question that comes instantly to mind. "My God, what happened here and why?"

Now your readers are hooked. They are going to literally devour that brochure at least for the next few pages. Your next job is to keep them reading.

The following method of organizing your brochure is suggested:

1. *Photographs*
   a. Of client before accident;
   b. Of client after accident showing injuries;
   c. Of client at home and at present;
   d. Of prostheses;
   e. Of accident scene, damaged vehicles, property.
2. *History of the case in one page*
3. *Discussion of liability*
   a. Police report or portions of hospital records;
   b. Statements of witnesses or excerpts from depositions;
   c. Selections from Answers to Interrogatories, Requests for Production, Requests for Admissions;

   d. Accident Reconstruction Experts Report or Medical Experts Report;

   e. Brief memo on applicable law.

4. *Medical information*

   a. Hospital records, physical therapy records;

   b. Medical reports regarding treatment (with diagnosis, nature of treatment, prognosis, and causation);

   c. Medical reports about future medical care in detail.

5. *Itemized breakdown of medical expenses*

   a. Past;

   b. Current;

   c. Future.

6. *Discussion letter from medical cost expert re: future expenses*

7. *School records if dealing with child or young adult*

   a. Report cards or transcripts of grades;

   b. Letter from teacher, professor, or principal.

8. *Wage records*

   a. Payroll records;

   b. Letters of commendations from supervisor or other person;

   c. Records of promotion and pay increases.

9. *Report from economist about past lost wages and projection of future lost earnings*

10. *Report from employment specialist*

    a. Regarding present and future job opportunities;

    b. Regarding increases in pay scale, bonuses, and promotions.

11. *Specialty matters*

    a. Cost of new house;

    b. Cost of renovations of old house;

    c. Cost of car or van;

    d. Tuition and special training;

    e. Companions, tutors.

12. *Summary page*

    a. Medical expenses, past and future;

    b. Earnings loss, past and future;

    c. Special expense;

    d. Compensation for pain, suffering, and inconvenience.

13. *Demand page*
   a. State demand clearly;
   b. Justify the demand.
      1. Verdicts in your court
      2. Settlements in your area
      3. Referral to "Modern Jury Verdicts" or similar volumes.

These items constitute the structure of your brochure. By the very nature of things there have to be variations. One client may have won awards from a country club for his or her golfing prowess, another may have participated in a Triatholon or Marathon, and a third may have won a piano competition. There may be other proofs of the quality of their lifestyle. If the client is now injured and unable to participate in these activities, these accomplishments should be included in the brochure to lend credence to a portion of your claim.

With the outline, let us proceed into a little more detailed discussion of each of these items.

1. Photographs of Your Client. A photograph is still worth a thousand words. In selecting photos you should pay attention to quality and number. Use only those that are really effective and only as many as are sensibly appropriate. These are the photographs you need:

Photographs of the Client Before the Accident. Every family has plenty of these and you must select only the good ones. Choose the very best of the client only (no friends or relatives) and taken as close in time to the accident as possible. Try to locate the negatives and take these to a professional photographer for development and possible enlargement. Many times the negative will be missing, but a good photographer can make a picture from a positive.

Among the kind of pictures that you will be looking for are baby pictures, graduation pictures, wedding photos, prom night shots, or sports team photos. You may get tired looking through the family album, but that dust among those pages is gold dust!

Photographs of the Client's Injuries. These may be difficult to find. Remember that many plastic surgeons do take "before and after" photographs. Some hospitals have photographers as employees, and it would be wise to inquire about this and find out whether photographs of your client were taken. Aside from this, you must once again go to family, friends, and relatives. Finally, once you secure the case and find that there is scarring present, an amputation, or some obvious dislocation, immediately send the client to a professional photographer for detailed, high-class pictures of these injuries.

Pictures of the Client at Home. Many seriously injured clients are recuperating at home for long periods of time. If you were to enter their living room or bedroom (and you sure better view these places), you will see a veritable gymnasium of medical appliances and devices. Above the bed will be chains and a bar; crutches lean against a chair; nearby is an I.V. stand on wheels with an I.V. bag and the plastic tubing. You may see a portable aluminum commode glistening at the far end of the room and a squat wheel chair may be waiting, expectantly, in the middle of the floor. What a mess! What a glorious opportunity for your photographer. Take pictures of everything—individually, in groups, long shots, and close-ups. They will give visual proof of your doleful narrative about the impaired quality of your client.

Prostheses. These should be "shot" separately and views taken from the front, side, and, if there is anything to show, from the back. Such objects as artificial arms and legs, knee braces, orthopedic shoes, "halo traction" devices, finger supports or braces are all prime targets for photographers. After they have been filmed individually, be sure to take additional pictures of your client wearing them.

The Accident Scene and Damaged Vehicles or Property. It almost goes without saying that one must have photographs of an accident scene. There ought to be several shots from different angles to illustrate whatever point you intend to make concerning the accident.

The same is true of vehicles, machinery, sports equipment, and other objects that were involved in the accident. Take one picture to identify the entire object, then zero in with some close-ups of significant details on the equipment.

Cautions: (1) You can overdo photographs. Do you remember how bored you became while going through your client's family album? That same thing can happen to your brochure. Use good judgment. If one photograph tells the story, don't use two. Rarely will you ever utilize more than two or three photographs of a person, scene, or object. (2) Disperse these photographs

---

TAKE PHOTOGRAPHS OF:

1. The client before the injury.
2. The client after injury showing burns, lacerations, bandages, and general hospital condition.
3. The client at the present time.
4. Medical or rehabilitation equipment in client's home.
5. Prostheses.
6. The scene of accident.
7. Machinery, vehicles, or equipment involved in accident.

throughout the brochure. In addition to telling their own story, they serve a purpose in breaking up the monotony of narrative, reports, and figures.

2. History of the Case. Not every person who receives your brochure is going to be intimately acquainted with the details of your case. You should start with the supposition that the reader does not know all of the pertinent facts. In one page, summarize all the important material so that the reader has a clear overview of your client, the facts of the accident, the injuries to your client, and a few words about losses. This can be done in four succinct paragraphs:

The first paragraph discusses the accident or incident which gives rise to the claim.

The second paragraph details the injuries received by your client and includes such things as periods of hospitalization and the types of surgery performed.

The third paragraph goes into detail with regard to financial matters— expenses incurred, wages lost, and anticipated future expenses.

The final paragraph is a general discussion of the client setting forth his or her age, life expectancy, accomplishments, educational level, current physical condition, the degree of impairment caused by the injuries received in the accident, and some mention of necessary changes in lifestyle.

This page cannot be detailed, but should be sufficient to give the reader an idea of what has occurred, the things that exist presently, and what the future holds for your client. The material should be written in your most lively and interesting manner, and should encourage the reader to move on to the more detailed material in succeeding pages.

3. Discussion of Liability. This must be the strongest section in the brochure.

Every attorney knows that the major obstacle to settlement is the issue of liability. A Defendant legitimately asks, "Why am I obligated to pay this Plaintiff anything?" This section of the brochure is designed to answer that question. If you can overcome this hurdle, you are well on your way to a good settlement.

You should begin with a long, detailed narrative statement, fully supported by reference to extracts from the record which cannot be disputed, and which are damning to the Defendant's position, experts' reports, photographs, excerpts from treatises, and any other documentary material you may have that clearly points to the liability of the Defendant.

The most important quality of your narrative statement must be accuracy! This is no time to play games with words, to exaggerate, or to distort the record. You are trying to convince a skeptical person. The surest way to turn off your reader is to assert as facts things the reader knows are not true or can easily check and thus learn that your assertions are untrue. Once you have done this, all of your efforts will have been in vain. Never more true is the adage, ''He who lies in little things will lie in big things.'' For this reason you must go out of your way to be as accurate and precise as you can in making assertions and in referencing them to the record or to other documentary material contained in the brochure.

Because the liability section is so very important, and the narrative statement is such a vital part of this section, Figure 13.1 contains an illustrative narrative statement.

Excerpts from the pleadings, especially discovery materials, are absolutely vital. If you have a deposition of a Defendant doctor or truck driver, as a result of which you have a clear, positive admission of certain crucial facts, then these must be excerpted and included in this brochure. You will have the inclination to want to include long paragraphs, maybe even pages, but fight the temptation. This is a brochure, not a thesis. You have room only to put in a few excerpts. If it is necessary to describe some preliminary matter, you can do that in one or two sentences leading to the excerpt. Quite obviously what you are trying to do is to demonstrate that, on the basis of the defendant's own testimony, liability exists in this case.

Just as you excerpt portions of the testimony of a Defendant, you must do the same thing with depositions from witnesses or statements from witnesses. Once again, you don't have to attach the entire statement unless it is convenient to do so. A one- or two-page statement certainly can be included at this point, but a three- or four-page statement should not. If you include portions of the statement, make a note that the entire statement is available for inspection upon demand. When you have several witnesses, all of whom say essentially the same thing, the best manner of handling this is to include an excerpt from your best witness, and then put a notation that these facts are supported by statements from witnesses Jones, Smith, and Brown. Again include the comment that all the statements will be mailed to the reader upon request. In this manner you get all the pertinent information to the Defendant without burdening him or her with an extraordinarily bulky tome.

You should also go through the other discovery materials looking for language that constitutes an admission or that provides essential facts that may be necessary for other materials you are enclosing. For example, if you are going to enclose an expert's report (and you must), you ought to set forth the pertinent facts upon which the expert relies in preparing the reports. Many of these facts may be included in answers to Interrogatories, Requests for Production, Requests for Admissions, or the matter set forth in an Answer. Your rule of thumb has to be that, if they are helpful use them, but at the same time try to restrict them to ''one-liners'' as much as possible.

A very necessary portion of your liability discussion will be reports from your experts. You must include them in order to be persuasive in this brochure.

Mary Jones was a 26-year-old woman with diabetes when she initially came to John E. Smith, MD for care during the pregnancy of her second child. Dr. Smith's obstetrical group had cared for her during her first pregnancy; thus, Dr. Smith was aware of the nature of the care and that Mrs. Jones was a diabetic. (See Smith depos. Pg. 6 and 9.) At the first visit he performed tests which indicated a high urine sugar count. He did not perform the additional tests necessary to determine exactly the extent of her diabetic control. (See Smith depos. Pp. 12 and 13.) The additional tests were not performed until several weeks later. (See Smith depos. p. 16.) That delay constituted negligent conduct. (See report of Dr. Joseph White.) Additionally, Dr. Smith did not commence any alteration in her insulin dosage for many weeks thereafter. (Smith depos. P. 22) That delay was also conduct below accepted standards of medical care. (See report of Dr. Joseph White and also report of Dr. Black.)

Mrs. Jones was followed in the office only by Dr. Smith through the early stages of her pregnancy. None of the numerous diagnostic tests available to Dr. Smith were performed. (See report of Dr. Black.) Eventually, he felt the need for ultrasound tests to resolve the discrepancy between fetal size as noted by physical examination and expected size as estimated by Mrs. Jones' last menstrual period. (See Smith depos. Pp. 31-33.) It was in July of 1989 that she had her first ultrasound, and it was in August of 1989 that she had her second ultrasound, both at the Main City Hospital. (See records attached.) Of interest is the fact that the second ultrasound showed an increase in amniotic fluid which caused the doctor who read the ultrasound to suggest correlation for possible hydramnios. Dr. Smith never followed up on this obvious signal of eventual danger. (See Smith depos. P. 33.)

Figure 13.1. Case Summary

Hopefully none of these reports will be more than three pages; if they are longer than that, it is suggested that you recontact your expert and try to get that person to condense the report into something you can use. As previously mentioned, you can always state in one sentence that this report is a condensation of a longer one and that the longer one is available upon request. Among the types of reports to which I make reference at this stage would be the expert's report in a medical malpractice case, a report of an accident reconstruction specialist in an auto case, the report of an engineer or chemist in a product liability case, the opinion of a railroad engineer in an FELA case, and the opinion of an air traffic controller or FAA specialist in an airplane crash. All these reports should be attached at this point in your brochure and should have been discussed in your narrative statement.

Finally, your defense attorney or claims person may either be unknowledgable in matters of law as they pertain to your case, or perhaps a little too weary to look up the law. Nonetheless, it is in your best interest that they thoroughly understand the legal principles that apply in this instance. So you might want to include a short, pertinent legal discussion concerning the liability of the Defendant. If you have the law on your side, why not say so? If there are legal problems in the case, you might as well bring them out in the open and discuss them just as you would in argument before the Court. Equally important is the issue of evidentiary issues on which a good defense attorney may be relying as a means of causing you all kinds of problems. If such exists, you might as well confront them now. Explain to defense council and to the claims personnel that:

You have a good legal position;

It enables you to introduce your expert or to prove some other vital element of the case which they may erroneously believe cannot be done.

If in fact there is such a genuine problem, you might as well address it now rather than waiting to do so before a trial judge.

This memo should not exceed three pages, and you should include a minimal number of citations—only those that are truly in point. And a further comment is appropriate: do not include quotations from the opinions. There simply isn't enough space available to do everything. Naturally you will make reference to any relevant statutes; again, merely refer to the statute instead of quoting from it, unless the quotation can be done very simply and conveniently. The key to your approach has to be a recognition that you are trying to write a persuasive memo and not a detailed, exhaustive brief. The memo is essential, but it doesn't have to be long.

4. Medical Information. This writer was once criticized by a senior partner for spending too much time working on the liability side of a case and not enough time working on the medical and damages side of a case. It was a valid criticism, and you should spend a great deal of your time working on the medical aspects of your brochure. You will have to include some portions of a hospital record; since these records are frequently very lengthy, you must be judicious in excerpting those portions of the record that illustrate the point that you are trying to make. Do not include, for example, the entire cover sheet of a record, or the entire history or physical, or the complete operative record. Each of these has a lot of unnecessary miscellany that will just simply clutter up your brochure and distract the reader.

By way of illustration, every operative record begins with the words "after the patient was appropriately prepped and draped'' and then describes all the preliminary cutting and tying off before getting to the part of the anatomy or procedure with which you are concerned. All of that preliminary material should be ruthlessly excluded. If your case is about a neurosurgeon who is doing a laminectomy, and who manages to cut a nerve while doing it, get to that portion of the operative record that describes what the surgeon did in two or three sentences. Those are the sentences that you will want to excerpt and include in your medical discussion. Likewise, if a baby was damaged during delivery, numerous descriptive phrases will set forth the damage to the newborn (putting in the APGAR scores), and you can pull out those sentences and phrases rather than including the entire description of the child upon delivery to the neonatal ward.

Medical reports are usually not lengthy. Perhaps you share with me the annoyance that most medical reports are too brief and fail to adequately discuss the nature of the treatment rendered by the physician and the prognosis. Whatever medical reports you attach to the brochure—and they should be attached at this point—should include the physician's diagnosis, the nature of the treatment in some detail, the prognosis, and a statement as to causation. An ideal medical report consists of two full pages, preferably three, although it is unlikely that most doctors are going to routinely dictate a three-page report, although they may do so if specifically requested. Try to be certain that you have included reports from each of the significant physicians, since, as we all know, modern medical treatment in a serious case will frequently call into play the services of several medical disciplines—orthopedic, neurology, surgery, internal medicine, and various subspecialties.

In the case of a serious injury with long-term ramifications, it is essential that you get detailed discussion of future medical care from the doctors involved, Frankly the subject is important enough that you should do everything in your power to convince the principal treating physician or physicians to submit a separate report on this subject. Two or three pages are ideal. If you cannot get that much, or if they will not do it, then try to get them to devote one page of their report to this important subject.

The necessity and seriousness of this subject are illustrated by the case of a child who has been badly burned. A plastic surgeon will tell you that he simply cannot do some necessary surgery while the child is still growing and that it is going to have to wait until the child is approximately 16 or 18 years old, which may be ten years in the future. Somebody has to tell the defense attorney and the insurance company in detail the medical treatment this child is going to need at that time. A conscientious doctor will understand your need for such a report and be able to give it to you in sufficient detail to enable the defense team to understand all the treatment that is going to be necessary;

When this treatment is likely to be given;

The duration of the treatment and extensiveness of it; and

Some comment concerning the cost either based on present day values or an estimated future value. (Perhaps the latter is best left to an expert on the cost of medical care.)

This section of the brochure is an appropriate place at which to put photographs of your client, of the various medical implements that he or she is required to live with, and of prostheses and scars.

5. Itemized Breakdown of Medical Expenses. Your client generally incurs medical expenses up to the time of the preparation of this brochure, may be incurring some medical expenses at the present time, and could possibly be subject to numerous such expenses in the future. These have to be spelled out for the claims personnel in great detail, since they have to do with finances. Medical expenses generally comprise the following:

1. Hospital bills;
2. Doctor's charges;
3. The cost of drugs and medications;
4. The cost of prostheses;
5. The expense of physical therapy or rehabilitation; and
6. Counseling; and
7. Home care services including such things as the cost of visiting nurses, live-in assistance, and supplies such as oxygen, hospital beds for use at home, and exercise equipment, and wheelchairs.

An example of the kind of estimate you may have to prepare is seen in Figure 13.2.

All the bills for these things must be accumulated, with the totals in each category itemized and listed on a separate sheet of paper. Do not attach the bills to the brochure. At this point all you have to do is to list the totals, making note of the fact that the actual bills are available to the reader upon request. You should break the bills down into the three categories of:

1. Past expenses;
2. Current expenses; and
3. Future expenses.

The primary admonition with regard to this material is that it be as complete as possible. Before you begin to sort out your bills and itemize them,

Figure 13.2. A typical medical expense estimate

Medical Equipment/Supplies	Frequency of Need Frequency of Repairs	Cost
Electric Hospital Bed	Every five (5) years.	$1740/bed
	Repairs on head and foot spring may be needed every two years.	Repair cost can not be predicted but minimum charge would be $50.
Patient Lift	Every five (5) years	$915/patient lift
	Repairs may be needed annually for sling, straps and pump.	$150 for repairs
Britax Car Seat	Three or four a lifetime	$435/car seat
Pogon Stroller	Two or three before he needs a high strength lightweight wheelchair with special adaptations.	$399+ depending on adaptations.
	Upholstery and wheels may need repair every year.	
TLC Bath Transfer Aid	Every two or three years throughout life.	$315/TLC
High Strength Lightweight Wheelchair with custom modifications and custom quick release insert designed for positioning.	Every three (3) years	$3,000/wheelchair
	Adaptations may need repair annually.	$60 for tire replacement. $200/insert modifications.
Tumble Form Insert	Four or more a lifetime	$545 to $695/basic insert dependent on size.
Side Lying Positioner	Four or more a lifetime	$225/positioner

prepare a checklist of the types of bills, set up folders according to the types, and put the respective bills into the appropriate folders. You'll be surprised to find that your client may well have utilized one surgical supply company for a period of many months, and then switched to another one and that you don't have the bills for the second company. Very commonly, clients go to several pharmacies for the purchase of their drugs and medications. While you may have the bills from two of the pharmacies, you don't have them from the most recent one. The billings for home nursing care are always a major headache unless your client went to only one company providing that service and stayed with them. Then you will be able to get the names of the personnel who worked for your client, the hours, and the charges. Not every client is that organized, and sometimes a client retains "casual" or "itinerant" persons to provide home health care, and you will have an awful time trying to get these persons to identify for you their hours, duties, and charges. In these kinds of situations, just say a prayer that they were paid by check.

In any event, the bills have to be carefully and completely accumulated, itemized, and totaled for the purposes of this brochure.

6. Opinion Letter from Medical Cost Expert Re: Future Expenses. The cost of future medical expenses can create a headache. You may have to expend a considerable amount of time and effort trying to locate the persons whose job it is to project such costs and to identify one who would be willing to submit a report and, if need be, to testify. Medical doctors are of absolutely no help; they know medicine, not economics. The truth of the matter is the average doctor has no more idea of the cost of one day's hospital stay ten years from now or the cost of an operation in the near future than you do. The best place to turn for an expert in this field is either to the health insurance industry or to a university whose economics department or medical school contains specialists who make it their business to estimate these future costs. University personnel are ideal for this purpose since they are easy to contact and talk with, and their work takes them into the medical financial field concerned with future costs. Another source of information is your local Blue Cross/Blue Shield organization, and a third is major corporations who operate health maintenance organizations (HMOs). As a matter of personal preference, and because of the convenience of nearby universities, this writer prefers to contact economics professors or some of the senior administrative officials of the local Blue Cross organization.

Obviously, any person who submits a report or who testifies on the subject of the future cost of medical treatment must qualify as an expert. Since one is dealing with future events, the entire matter is one of speculation, although it may be classified as necessary and legitimate speculation. And, like the weather forecaster, there is no assurance that these persons are going to be correct! Nonetheless, they represent the only proof that we have and all concerned have to rely on their good judgment. Before that judgment can be verified as ''good'' or ''sound,'' these experts have to have a reasonable degree of education, training, and expertise in this field. In short they have to be experts with all the qualifications necessary for any other type of expert. Don't even both trying to get an ordinary economist or businessperson to do this work for you. The field is significantly specialized that you have to go to somebody who is involved primarily in medical economics.

There is not yet any particular type of training for economists who become a part of the medical industry, but there are economists who spend years working for this industry and develop their expertise by virtue of their employment. These are the persons to look for to submit an opinion letter on the subjects in which you are interested. The curriculum vitae of one such person is Figure 13.3.

Figure 13.3

John M. Jones
100 White St.
Pittsburgh, PA 15219

Phone: (412) 123-4567 (Home)
       (412) 890-1234 (Office)

EDUCATION: Bachelor of Science in Mathematics
Westminster College, New Wilmington, PA, June, 1970

Associate of the Society of Actuaries, July, 1979

Member American Academy of Actuaries, January, 1981

EXPERIENCE: I have been a member of the Actuarial Department of Blue
Cross of Western Pennsylvania for almost thirteen years since
my graduation from college in June, 1970. In my present
position as Associate Actuary, the following are some of my
duties:

1. Prepare and file all necessary documents with the Pennsylvania State Insurance Department requesting adjustments to subscription rates and projection factors for all
benefit plans offered by Blue Cross of Western Pennsylvania. The preparation of these documents require the
analysis of current cost levels, and based on this analysis
a projection of future costs for each benefit plan. I have
also appeared before the Pennsylvania State Insurance Department at rate hearings to support information contained
in the rate filing documents.

2. Monitor cost and usage trends for the different benefit
programs offered by Blue Cross of Western Pennsylvania
for use in the rate filings and for financial forecasts.

3. Rerating of large experience rated accounts such as United
States Steel, J & L Steel, Westinghouse Electric Corporation, etc.

4. Benefit design and product development.

5. Analyze outstanding claims liability for all types of cover-
ages offered by Blue Cross of Western Pennsylvania.

Quite naturally your interests are going to be directed to the fields of medical treatment that physicians have pointed out to you, including hospitalizations, operations, possible utilization of rehabilitation centers or physical therapy groups, cost of medications, and costs of prostheses and medical equipment. Ideally, the economist and the doctor could sit down together and discuss the future medical needs, but that is generally unlikely. You are probably going to have to rely on your physician to present a detailed report concerning future medical needs, then submit that report to your economist who can then make the necessary projections concerning the cost. If consultation between them is needed, then try a telephone consultation. In any event, your economist will have to prepare a detailed report, which must be a part of this brochure and the total cost of the future medical expenses will be included on the page relating to medical costs.

7. School Records and College Transcripts. If you make a point about the success of your client in school, get the appropriate records from the school attended. Quite naturally everything depends on the age of your client and whether he or she performed extraordinarily well in school. If your client is or was a student who did A-B work in school before the accident, suffered a serious injury and is now receiving C-D grades, it is appropriate that you dig out the old records and attach them to the brochure. These grades can be easily secured with an authorization signed by the parent and mailed to the administrative office of the grade school, high school, or college. A certification or seal is not really necessary at this point, although as a matter of convenience (if the case is not settled and you need these records at trial) it might be worth while to have this done.

If the transcripts do not amply demonstrate that your client was an excellent student before the accident, then do not use them. Don't try to make the grades something they're not. If it turns out that your client has two As, one B, one C, and two Ds, the transcript is really not good enough to use. It doesn't prove anything more than the fact that your client was an average student. You simply hurt yourself by trying to submit the A grades while hiding the D grades, and the deception can be easily uncovered and will destroy the trusting relationship you are trying to create.

School records are also good proof of your client's athletic ability. Your client may well have won an award or letter, or participated on the swimming or football team. These things are all matters of record with the school, and those records may be used by you as proof of that particular ability.

The same type of thing exists with regard to scholastic achievement in addition to grade records. A student may be awarded a letter for performance on a debate team, appointed to the National Honor Society, or the editor of the school newspaper. Each of these items can be verified from the records of the school, should be ordered, and should become a part of the brochure. If you are dealing with an outstanding student who has received numerous honors, it is better to list them on a single sheet of paper and not include the actual records from the school.

Finally, a letter from a teacher or principal can be very important. The letter should summarize the area of expertise of the student, the contact between the teacher and the student in this field of endeavor, and should express in strong and definite terms the student's unique ability while working under the supervision of the teacher. It should be a great deal more than a vague letter of recommendation and should be set forth in one page. A prime source for a letter of this nature would be a teacher, coach, counselor, or administrator.

All of this material is very helpful in impressing the person who reads your brochure about the outstanding accomplishments of your student-client before the accident.

8. Wage Records. To prove a loss of earnings, a reduction in earnings, or a reduction in earning capacity, wages records are essential in every case involving a person who either is or was working.

When you decide about the kind and number of records needed, you must consider the age of your client, the work history including the variety of jobs the individual may have had, the earnings at those jobs, and the earnings potential in the future including the likelihood of promotions and progression. If it is pertinent, you can devote one full page in a brochure to a "work history," which itemizes the jobs held by your client and presumably would indicate a steady progression to better jobs and higher pay, but you should not even try to document this history in the brochure. If documentation is appropriate, you should limit yourself to employment matters within a reasonable period of time, usually over the past five years.

The employment and payroll records are relatively easy to secure by means of an authorization directed to the personnel or payroll department of the employer. As with a student, however, you should search around for other documents that may be helpful in proving your client's extraordinary skill as a worker and his or her participation in company activities. It could well be that your client has:

Served on a labor-management committee that was instrumental in solving some problem at the workplace;

Was commended for saving a life of a fellow employee by the prompt application of CPR;

Came up with a new idea that improved the nature of his or her work for the benefit of coemployees and the company and received either a commendation or a monetary award.

You are looking for any kind of documentation that establishes that your client was an active, interested, and extraordinary employee. If you can find one or two commendations, be sure to include them in the brochure.

Letters from supervisors and administrators praising the skill of your client, indicating the likelihood of promotion, and discussing the promotions that he or she might have attained within the company are also very valuable. It is true that they are frequently difficult to secure since the persons involved are not used to writing such letters and are somewhat reluctant to do so both because of shyness and the belief that the company could be exposed to a theoretical liability. Nonetheless, an attempt should be made to secure these letters if your client believes that a supervisor or senior executive would be willing to say kind and good things about him or her. If you can get such a letter—especially one that indicates that your client could well have become president of the company—then by all means make every effort to do so. In the brochure you are going to be talking about your client's future. If you can document the fact that in employment, he or she had a very bright future, you are certainly going to be ahead of the game.

9. The Economists Report. The economist, working with the medical doctor, is the most important person you will work with, and his or her report is essential in your brochure. The economist makes the projections of future economic loss—the fabled "bottom line," the total of the financial losses. You must make certain that you get a good one.

Since the economist is going to be establishing losses in large amounts of money—occasionally several million dollars and usually many hundreds of thousands of dollars—it is essential that:

1. The projections be accurate and reasonable; and
2. They be conservative in nature.

You cannot frighten anyone by shouting about a multimillion dollar loss that cannot stand up to sharpeyed scrutiny. You can worry a lot of people by coming up with a rock solid loss of, say, $1,200,000 that will draw the reluctant approval of your opponent's accountants. That is what you are after: substantial, conservative estimates that withstand challenge.

You must always meet with your economist to discuss the details of the information you have collected including the past work history, payroll records, likelihood of promotion, types of work your client can presently perform and its pay scale, work expectancy, inflation, increase or decrease in benefits, and other related matters that must be considered before a report is written. The economist must have a firm grasp of all the details before a sensible report can be prepared.

The economist's report should:

Spell out the facts upon which he or she is relying;
List any statistics, surveys, reports, or treatises that have been utilized; and
Set forth firmly the anticipated total loss of your client.

This report, dealing as it must with large sums of money, will be subject to intense scrutiny and review. It should be direct, to the point, and as accurate as circumstances will allow. Note in Figure 13.4, which is a preliminary report, the additional information the economist will need.

10. Report of the Employment Specialist. An expert in the field of employment opportunities, another specialist whose report you must have, can tell you many things about your client's job opportunities, and this data is important to your economist. The types of information you are interested in are:

1. What kind of work can my client do today?
2. What job opportunities exist in this type of work today?
3. What is the pay scale of this work?
4. What is the likelihood of my client securing such a job in the area in which he or she lives?
5. What effects do age and sex have in relation to this job market?
6. Can my client be retrained? If so, what are the recommended occupations for which he or she might qualify?
7. As to these new occupations, what are the job opportunities, the pay scale, the chances of my client getting such a job given the problems of age, sex, and geography?

It gets complicated. In essence what you want the employment specialist to tell you are the facts in regard to:

1. Your client's current (or former) occupation;
2. The kind of jobs your client, as a disabled person, can secure and the kind of future opportunities (if any) existing in that job;
3. If retraining is possible, what kind of work your client should aim for and what the future holds in that job.

Remember and plan around one fact: disability is not the totally catastrophic event that it was even a few years ago. While all disabilities have tragic

---

SMITH COLLEGE
Pittsburgh, Pennsylvania 15219

January 12, 1992

Mr. David T. Donnelly
4800 Library Road
Bethel Park, PA 15102

Dear Mr. Donnelly:

At your request and with the information provided me by your office, I have prepared the following economic projection of the net economic loss for John Jones.

This report on the net economic loss is based upon the following:

1. That based upon the educational levels attained by his parents and that his mother is a fulltime teacher, it is reasonable to assume that he would graduate from college.

2. That among the variety of occupational opportunities that he might have chosen, the projected choice is that of a high school teacher at a beginning salary at the time he would be entering the labor market of $25,298. This was arrived at in the following way. The projection is based upon a beginning salary at the present, 1988, of $21,000. The average earnings for teachers in high school in 1984-85 were $24,276. Assuming that he would have entered the labor force in 2007, a beginning salary of $21,000 in 1988 adjusted by a productivity factor each year of 1.88% would be $25,298 by 2007. Then that same productivity factor is applied each year during his worklife expectancy. It is reasonable to assume that a person's productivity increases over time as he becomes more experienced on the job and as promotions are earned. Sources: *Occupational Outlook Handbook*, 1986-87 Edition, bureau of Labor Statistics, U.S. Department of Labor, Washington, D. C., and *Multifactor Productivity Measures, 1985: Private business, Private Nonfarm Business and Manufacturing*, USDL 86-402, October 2, 1986, Bureau of Labor Statistics, U. S. Department of Labor, Washington, D. C.

3. That his worklife expectancy as of the time of graduating from college would be 36.6 years. Source: *Worklife Estimates: Effects of Race*

Figure 13.4 (continued)

and Education, Bulletin 2254, Bureau of Labor Statistics, U. S. Department of Labor, Washington, D. C., February 1986.

4. That his loss of fringe benefits would be 18.3% of his salary. This was the government's figure of fringe benefits as a percent of wages in 1977. This figure had grown from 11.2% in 1966. The current figure is not available, but it is reasonable to assume that it would be equal to or probably higher than 18.3%, but 18.3% is the figure used in making this economic projection. Source: *Handbook of Labor Statistics,* Bulletin 2070, 1980, Bureau of Labor Statistics, U. S. Department of Labor, Washington, D. C.

5. That institutional care would begin at the age of six and continue through his lifetime. The projection is based upon a current cost of $168 per day or $61,320 per year. Source: The Verland Foundation Inc., Sewickley, PA, January 27, 1988.

6. That his life expectancy at the present time is not known due to his condition. Therefore projections have been developed based upon his living to age 31, 36, 41, 46 and 51.

With the above taken into consideration, the projections of his net economic loss would be as follows:

Net earnings loss:			$1,334,942			
Net loss of fringe benefits:			244,294			
Total of these losses:			$1,579,236			
Institutional care costs:						Net Economic Loss
To age 31-25 years: $1,533,000	+	$1,579,236	=	$3,112,236
To age 36-30 years: 1,839,600	+	1,579,236	=	3,418,836
To age 41-35 years: 2,146,200	+	1,579,236	=	3,725,436
To age 46-40 years: 2,452,800	+	1,579,236	=	4,032,036
To age 51-45 years: 2,759,400	+	1,579,236	=	4,338,636

It is important to note that additional income has not been factored in for such things as coaching, working with students in extra-curricular activities, teaching summer sessions, or earning additional income in doing other work in summer. And the cost of physical, occupational and speech therapy has not been factored in. As of January 21, 1988 Blue Cross had paid for this. Costs for the variety of equipment and medical supplies that will be necessary for his care throughout his lifetime have not been determined.

Sincerely,

consequences, many employers today are willing to hire the disabled for certain types of work. There is also the new Americans with Disabilities Act—and there will be other laws at the state level—which gives badly injured persons employment rights or opportunities they never had before. You and your employment specialist have to discuss this matter in some detail with regard to your client's future job opportunities.

From this expert you need a good, detailed report, setting forth an opinion with regard to the manner in which injuries have affected the client's employability and financial future. Like the other reports, this one should be succinct, to the point, and not more than two pages long. Do not include supporting data, although it may be referred to. Just be sure that the report is strong and accurate so as to set forth your position clearly and be able to withstand attacks by the defendant.

11. Specialty Matters. In every serious injury case there are unique circumstances that require special attention on the part of the attorney as he or she computes losses to the client. Some of these novel situations would include the following:

Education or Job Retraining. When you are representing a school-age client, there are some cases in which the cost of a higher education represents a probable loss. In other cases, when a client is already employed but cannot return to the previous job, the cost of retraining comes into play. In either event, the attorney has to gather data concerning a school providing the needed education, the types or kind of courses the client must study, the tuition costs, the length of time needed to complete the education, and the cost of room and board, books, and the usual miscellaneous fees. These charges can be set forth on one page of the brochure with the documentation not attached but available if requested.

The Cost of a House. When representing a seriously injured young person who will be disabled in adulthood and will have no parent with whom to live, you must think about the special care the client will need in the future. Among the special items is so basic a matter as shelter—somewhere to live. The attorney must consider such things as:

> What size shall the house be?
>
> What special facilities must be provided—ramps, extra wide doors, elevator, modified plumbing or toilet needs, special railings, lowered shelves, etc.?
>
> Where shall it be located? In a familiar neighborhood or a new one?
>
> Can an existing house be renovated or should a new one be built?

After you have pondered these matters, you will have to meet with an architect and/or contractor to price out this house. Then you will need a letter from such person outlining the specifications of the house and the cost. See Figure 13.5.

Figure 13.5

Dear

Please find enclosed sketches and a list of modifications for a home for John Jones.

In sorting through possible options, it became apparent that the most practical and economical route would be to purchase and erect a house from Ryan Homes and then modify it to the specifications required.

I have selected the model "The Adams" for several reasons.

1. It provides bedroom and daily living space on one level for _____
2. It can be easily modified to accommodate _____, his parents, and his sisters with the least amount of disruption.
3. It provides one of the most resalable designs should the _____ decide to move in the future.
4. It is one of the most economical homes in its class, available in todays market.

This particular home is available in the Cranberry West plan of homes in Butler, PA, which at this time, has level lots available.

The estimates for modification and construction are based on current rates and can be used as a reliable guideline, however, detail pricing will depend upon site locations, time, and alternative modification suggestions.

In this estimate I am assuming that _____ condition will not permit him to care for himself and will always require assistance in mobility, food consumption, and hygiene. Should his prospects for independence change, further modifications to electrical outlets, switches, and cooking areas will have to be made.

Base price for Ryan home "The Adams" erected on a lot in Cranberry West, including site preparation	$56,095.00
Additions to base home provided by Ryan (including appliances)	8,545.00
Modifications required for _____	21,200.00
TOTAL PRICE FOR HOME	$86,650.00

Cost of a Car or Van. An adult client needs transportation. Vehicles can be purchased or modified to suit the needs of disabled persons, and your client should be entitled to this necessary expense. Inquiry to new car dealers can give you an idea of what is available and the cost of these vehicles. That cost should be included in your brochure. Don't forget that cars wear out. Therefore, you must include this cost as one recurring about every five years.

Companions, Tutors, Nurse's Aides. Some disabled clients will need the services of another human being after the spouse or parents have died or are otherwise rendered incapable of providing care. Think about this. It is rare that 24-hour care is needed, but common that part-time help is required. Minimally, one may need a person to clean the house, wash clothes, and cook meals. Numerous home health care and house cleaning services exist today to provide their services. You will need a letter from such an organization with respect to the needs of your client.

Tutors and companions may also be needed, and these can be provided for a cost. Once again, you must assess the needs of your client and include these costs in your brochure.

12. Summary Page. On one page you should set down a summary of all past, present, and future losses that must be incurred by your client. These should be broken down into the categories of:

1. Medical expenses;
2. Wage losses;
3. Special expenses; and
4. Compensation for pain, suffering, and inconvenience.

This page should also include bare-bones details about your client: age, birth date, marital status, children, occupation, life expectancy, and work expectancy. It should be designed so that, at a glance, a reader can have all pertinent economic data. An example of such a document is shown in Figure 13.6.

13. Demand Page. One of the primary reasons you are preparing this brochure is to justify your demand. That demand is important enough to require a page of its own.

Briefly, and simply you should discuss the injuries to your client, the totals of expenses and losses incurred or to be incurred, the changes in life style, and the description of the pain your client has endured in the past and may be required to suffer in the future.

Make your demand high but sensible, bearing in mind that you are setting down an initial negotiation position. But don't be absurd (a common failure of Plaintiff's attorneys at this point). If you would be happy to settle for $300,000, then make a demand of $375,000 and not $2,500,000. Allow yourself a little room for negotiation, but don't make a fool of yourself. One thing you must remember is that an outrageous demand simply shuts off the defense and

Figure 13.6

I.	*Home Equipment & Supplies*	
	1. Liken -	$763,022.80
II.	*Home Care*	
	1. Murphy Quality Care	
	Private duty nursing 25.00 per visit	
	1 visit/wk. × 52wks/yr. × 16.5 yrs. =	$21,450.00
	Physical therapy 45.00 per visit	
	1 visit/wk. × 52wks/yr. × 16.5 yrs. =	$38,610.00
	Speech therapy 45.00 per visit	
	1 visit/wk. × 52 wks/yr. × 16.5 yrs. =	$38,610.00
	Home health aid 6.85 per visit (Cost uncertain)	$0.00
III.	*Home*	
	Home suited and adapted for the handicapped.	
	Land site	$25,000.00
	Ryan home—The Brentwood	$77,500.00
	Modifications for handicapped	$8,250.00
IV.	*Institutional Care*	
	1. Northern Panhandle Behavioral Ctr. - $138/day	
	53.2 yrs. × 365 days/yr. × $138/day =	$2,679,684.00
V.	*Lost Wages*	
	1. Life expectancy—71.6 yrs.	
	2. Work expectancy—57.5 yrs.	
	3. High school education of parents	
	4. Estimated lost earnings—	$1,121,083.00
	5. Estimated lost fringe benefits—	$98,767.00
	GRAND TOTALS	$4,871,976.80

destroys everything you have striven for in preparing this brochure. Most sensible and realistic defense attorneys and claims persons won't even respond to a preposterous demand. By so conducting yourself, you will have accomplished nothing.

Finally, if you can make reference to a verdict or to settlements of other, similar cases in the range of your demand, mention them and be explicit. The argument has to be that your demand represents the ''going value'' of this type of case. If you don't know of any such cases, then refer to Modern Jury Verdicts or some other manual that will lend credence to your claim.

THERE—YOU'RE DONE!

When you are finished with your brochure, take the time to look it over and see what you have accomplished. It will certainly be something you can be proud of if you've stuck to the guidelines in this chapter. It may not be a work of art, but it was never meant to be. It only needs to be an interesting, illustrated, well-documented handbook about your case that will convince your opponent of two cardinal facts:

1. That he or she cannot win this case; and
2. That your demand is reasonable and ought to be paid.

SUMMARY OF CONTENTS OF BROCHURE

1. Photographs;
2. History of the case;
3. Discussion of liability;
4. Medical information;
5. Medical expenses;
6. Report of medical cost expert;
7. School records;
8. Wage records;
9. Economist report;
10. Report of employment specialist;
11. Specialty matters;
12. Summary page;
13. Demand page.

14

Structured Settlements: Protecting Your Client's Future

INTRODUCTION

Clearly a phenomenon of the last few years, the structured settlement is the product of the substantial verdicts and settlements that have come into being in that time. A structured settlement is a boon to an insurance company or a Defendant corporation in that it does not require them to pay out a very large sum of money at one time, or they can pay it to a subsidiary which earns money on the principal invested. It is equally a boon to many Plaintiffs—in fact, you might say to all Plaintiffs—except the extremely rare individual who is either educated in financial matters or by nature of his or her standing in life is used to handling large sums of money.

The fact remains that 95 percent of all injured Plaintiffs do not fall into either of these catorgories. If you take a moment to consider your client's financial education and experience it becomes pretty clear that rarely have these persons had so much as $10,000 in hand at one moment. He or she never dreamed of having $100,000 at one time. The average person, when given the opportunity of getting his or her hands on a large sum of money, immediately thinks of luxuries such as a fancy car, a dream vacation, or expensive jewels and furs. This leads to catastrophe if one is concerned about that individual's long-term financial well being. Thus the structured settlement is one of the best innovations to have come down the road in a long time as far as the average plaintiff is concerned.

Additionally, payments received under the terms of a structured settlement are *tax free*. There is no income tax on these payments. This fact can be terribly important to a client when you consider that monthly income can be $2,000 or $5,000 and that lump sum payments often amount to $10,000 and more.

This method of payment had been enthusiastically endorsed by the insurance industry, as well as by thoughtful Plaintiffs and their attorneys, as an innovative way to meet the demands and needs of both groups who are usually at odds with one another.

Listen to a concrete illustration of a situation in which you might find yourself one day. The client was a 17-year-old boy whose family was poor. As the case was to be settled in the near future, the parents came to the attorney and advised him that they did not want their son to get his hands on a large sum of money for fear that he would squander it. It was expected that the anticipated settlement would clear the young man about $30,000. A complicating factor was the fact that the settlement simply could not be negotiated before he attained the age of 18, and after that age the entire sum of money would have to be given to him and he would be free to do with it as he would. The client was a sensible achiever and the family thought that the attorney could reason with him in terms of plans regarding the money received from the settlement.

The answer to the problem was clearly a structured settlement. Shortly thereafter the case was settled for the sum of $45,000. Of this sum, $15,000 was paid in cash at the time of settlement to be used for the payment of attorney's fees and also to give the young man some money with which to buy a second-hand car, since that was (typically) his foremost desire. The balance of the money was structured so as to be paid out as follows:

$2,500 on December 15, 1990
$2,500 on December 15, 1992
$2,500 on December 15, 1994
$2,500 on December 15, 1996
$2,500 on December 15, 1998
$7,500 on November 25, 1991
$10,000 on November 25, 1995
$15,000 on November 25, 2000
$25,000 on November 25, 2005

These dates and amounts were selected after conferences with the client, his parents, and a representative of the insurance company. The total payments to him will amount to $70,000 plus the money to buy a car at the time of settlement.

As you can imagine, there is absolutely no way in which an 18-year-old boy would have the ability or interest to invest his share of the settlement to produce that kind of money, and the odds are 99 out of 100 that he would have spent this money in a matter of months.

The net result was that the client was happy, the parents were delighted, and the attorney was pleased because this young man, coming from a poverty-stricken background, was given a start in life that is very rare. It is important to remember that without current concepts of structured settlements this would never have been accomplished. Counsel may have tried to direct him to a financial advisor, the parents may have exhorted him not to spend the money, but he most certainly would have disregarded everyone and the money would be gone.

It is worthy of mention that the insurance company proposed three other payout plans, which were considered and rejected. One variation, for example, called for a cash payout at settlement and then monthly payments to age 30. This is merely mentioned to illustrate the flexibility of these plans.

And flexibility is certainly the outstanding attribute of structured settlements. The only limits are those on the imagination of the Plaintiff's attorney and of any financial advisor that may get involved in this matter. You can vary the initial cash payout, provide for monthly payments, provide for lump sum payments for a period of years, skip them for awhile, and then provide for larger lump sum payments at a later time. The amounts of the lump sum payments can vary. You can begin with monthly payments, stop them, institute periodic lump sum payments, change over again to monthly payments for a given period of time, and then end up with a large lump sum payment. You can change the time periods involved—for example, providing lump sum payments yearly for the first 5 years followed by a hiatus for a period of years, and then lump sum payments thereafter for every 5 or 10 years. There are so many opportunities to take care of all of the future needs of your client that working with these structured settlements becomes fun.

Nonetheless, structured settlements have their own serious problems. Among these are the following:

1. What are the client's needs?
2. What kind of payouts best satisfies those needs?
3. What kind of guarantees does one have that the payor will still be a viable organization 30 or 50 years from now?
4. What happens if the client dies?
5. How much consideration should you give to the inflation factor?

These are just some of a host of considerations that the attorney is going to have to think about when negotiating such a settlement and dealing with the client.

Figure 14.1. An Overview of Structured Settlements

1. *Why structure a settlement?*

    a. *Tax benefit:* Future payments are free of federal income tax.

    b. *Common sense:* It keeps the money out of the hands of the injured Plaintiff and family; very few Plaintiffs or their families can resist the urge to spend when they make a significant recovery.

    c. *Managed investment:* It is a safe, reasonably lucrative, long-term investment.

    d. *Planning:* It is a flexible investment vehicle so that large sums of money can be available at times of need in the future.

2. *Determine the needs of the client.*

    a. *Age 18:* College fund, special training.

    b. *Age 25:* First job, first nice apartment, first nice car—a lot of needs at this age for clothing, furniture, transportation, wedding, etc.

    c. *Ages 30–35:* Downpayment on a house or beginning a business.

    d. *Ages 60–65:* Retirement fund.

    e. *Special medical expenses:* Operation, replacement of medical equipment or prosthesis, replacement vehicles for physically handicapped.

    f. *Special needs:* Person who cannot return to work might need monthly income, occupational retraining, or a combination of both.

    g. *Catastrophic injury:* Prepare a Lifetime Care Plan.

3. *Negotiating the structured settlement.*

    a. Negotiate a dollar amount for the settlement with the understanding that a portion of the settlement will be structured. You must know the present value of the total package.

    b. Annuities must be purchased from a Best A+ rated (or Standard & Poors or Moody's) *Life* insurance company.

    c. Coordinate the dollars available to spend with the needs of the client. Be flexible and obtain various plans. Mix and match the elements of the various plans.

    d. Consider an inflation factor if the settlement will require payments many years down the road.

    e. *Rating the client:* With a seriously injured client, the annuity company will assign a reduced life expectancy. They will *rate* the injured party as a 30-year-old or a 35-year-old even though he or she may be 10 years old. Argue for a higher rating, perhaps 40 or 45 years old, which will produce a lower life expectancy and higher payouts.

Figure 14.1. (continued)

    4. Who should structure?

        a. Any minor receiving more than $10,000 or $15,000.

        b. Any catastrophically injured client regardless of age.

        c. Any individual having a specific future financial need.

            (1) College expenses;

            (2) Purchase of home;

            (3) Funding retirement.

        d. Any individual not comfortable with, or capable of, managing a significant sum of money.

    5. Do you have to structure every penny?

        No. With large settlements it is often smart to establish a guardianship account in the trust department of a local bank. Deposit $100,000 or $200,000. (Most banks will insist on at least $100,000.) Have the monthly checks or lump sum payments from the structured settlement made payable to the bank as guardian. The bank can then provide for the financial needs of the client and deposit any excess funds into the guardianship account. That guardianship account is invested by the bank, thereby giving the client a diversified portfolio and a managed, liquid investment.

WHEN SHOULD YOU USE STRUCTURED SETTLEMENTS?

Structured settlements are of value in the following types of cases:

The Minors Case

In view of the fact the minor cannot spend the money, and considering the long life expectancy of a minor, these cases are prime for the utilization of a structured settlement. (Remember that the longer you delay payouts, the higher the eventual payments are going to be by virtue of the fact that the insurance company is going to have this money for a longer peiod of time in which to invest it.) Many judges who have to approve a minor's settlement will themselves make inquiry about a structured settlement. There really is no excuse not to use a structure unless you are dealing with a very small sum of money, or the minor is close to attaining majority and the sum involved is of such a nature that it really should be paid directly to him or her. Outside of these reasons, every minor's settlement should be structured.

A Decedent's Case

When one is dealing with a decedent, survived by a spouse and perhaps children, every effort should be made to structure the settlement. Many spouses are not up to the necessity of dealing with a large sum of money (even after one or two years from the date of death), and when there are minor children the necessity becomes more imperative. One has to bear in mind that some spouses do not remarry and do get old, and some arrangements for the later years must be made. As far as children are concerned, you must consider such things as a college education for the children and the advantages of having a sizable sum of money available when the child reaches age 25 or 30. It is very nice to receive a large sum of money in your adulthood when one is newly married, starting a family, or looking to buy a new house. All of this can be arranged by means of a structured settlement.

The Financially Unsophisticated Client

Probably 95 percent of your clients fall into this category. They simply have not had a large sum of money at one time, do not know how to invest it, and are inclined to feel that they have struck the pot of gold at the end of the rainbow—and that it's party time! These people need help, and every attorney has the duty to use every ounce of persuasiveness to convince such clients to accept a structured settlement.

Where Long-Term Medical Treatment Is Required

For a seriously injured and disabled client, the attorney has to look down the road and contemplate the type of additional treatment that is going to be required and the cost of that treatment. Many children have the type of injury that cannot be operated on until physical maturity (approximately age 16 or 17), and even adults may suffer from a condition that is going to require extended medical treatment at various times in the future. At the present time, a hip replacement is a procedure that usually has to be redone every 10 to 15 years. If one is dealing with a 40-year-old man, he ought to plan for at least two or three such operations in the future. If you are dealing with a very serious injury such as paraplegia, you have to plan extensively for significant medical treatment in the future since these people are known to have serious psychiatric problems, urinary tract diseases, infections, and dermatological problems, in addition to the problem causing the paralysis.

The Spendthrift Client

Every attorney is well aware that some of his clients live by the philosophy, "Have a dollar, spend a dollar." These people are often very difficult to reason with. Yet if you can convince them to invest the money by way of a structured settlement, they are going to be far, far ahead of the game, rather than receiving all of the money in one lump sum and having to overcome the temptation to spend it. If a structured settlement is not entered into, the chances are very strong that within six months or a year of the settlement the client is going to be broke.

The "Financial Planner" Client

This person—just the opposite of the spendthrift client—is forward-looking and is desirous of handling these funds very carefully, but simply doesn't know how. Sometimes it's a matter of education; sometimes it's a matter of not having the time or inclination to properly invest the money. And there may be some disinclination to entrust the money to the services of financial managers. This type of careful client will probably be very interested with working with his or her attorney to arrange a structured settlement, and such an arrangement will certainly be to the benefit of this client.

IMPORTANT MATTERS TO CONSIDER

As you think about the purposes of the structured settlement, consider some or all of the following matters:

The Immediate Needs of the Client

These can include:

> The true need to purchase an automobile (some clients have never had the money to buy one);
> The immediate payment of some medical bills;
> Repayment of persons from whom the client has borrowed money;
> The need to purchase a house or to move from an undesirable rental neighborhood;
> The cost of experimental or unique medical treatment which can only be secured at some distance from the client's home, and at an expense that the client must bear individually.

All of these things have to be considered as you contemplate the amount of cash payment up front.

Monthly or Yearly Income Requirement

Almost all seriously injured or disabled persons are desperately in need of money. Many of them have been living on public assistance, the loans of relatives, or the sharply reduced income from a disability plan. After you have arranged for payment of past debts, the next order of business is to try to decide what amount of money, on a monthly basis, will enable the client to live comfortably and how these monthly payments are going to fit into the overall structure. Questions will pop up concerning the amount, how long the monthly payments will last, how they should be interspersed with lump sum payments, and whether there is any time period in which the monthly payments should be stopped or increased. You and your client will have a merry time debating this subject.

Attorney's Fee

Quite naturally the attorney is entitled to be paid for services rendered in handling the case and negotiating the settlement, and this fee is going to have to be paid from the proceeds of the settlement. Shall it be paid in full as part of the initial cash payout? That is usually done, but if other ways of payment are to be arranged, it must be decided at this point. Incidentally, as of 1992, the Internal Revenue Service no longer allows for structuring fees.

SPECIALTY NEEDS OF THE CLIENT

High on your list of things to do is an evaluation of the special needs of your disabled client, how much they will cost, and when in the future they are likely to occur. While obviously these needs vary from client to client, they tend to fall into certain similar categories:

Education and Tuition

When representing a young client, you clearly have to anticipate the costs of a college education. It is possible that the child may not be smart enough to get into a college or may lack the desire to do so, but if that decision is ten or more years into the future, the attorney has no alternative but to plan for the possibility that the child will go to college.

Advanced education or retraining of an older client is also a matter that may have to be considered. In this instance, however, you know whether the client is interested in training, when the schooling will begin, and the length of the training desired.

In both instances, the attorney must consider tuition costs, room and board, and the cost of books, supplies, and miscellaneous expenses. This may require a meeting with a knowledgeable person at a university or trade school.

The Cost of a House or Car

If your client is a 10-year-old child, severely injured, you cannot assume that the parents will be around forever to provide housing and transporation. In due course the child becomes an adult and parents die. At some point the client will want a house and a car, and considerable thought has to be given to these matters. What amount of money will have to be set aside? When shall the expense be incurred? Shall payment be made in a lump sum, or shall it be the more usual "down payment and mortgage" arrangement? As to a car, you must plan for replacement every several years.

Future Medical Care

Many cases will require planning in this area. There may be one or more operations needed in the future, followed by extensive rehabilitation or physical therapy. If medical insurance is likely not to pay the entire bill, then these costs have to be worked into the structure. Many prostheses are like cars; after several years of wear and tear they have to be replaced. How often will this occur in the case of your client, when, and at what cost? Figure 14.2 shows the kinds of devices and the related costs.

Housekeeper, Aides, Nursing, Tutors

A bedridden child may need a nurse's aide, a therapist, and a tutor. A brain-damaged adult may need a full-time companion. A crippled and irascible senior citizen may require a person to house clean and cook meals—and that is all he or she may want you to arrange. In each case it is something different and something special. But you must ask, "How long shall I plan for this to last? Where do I get such persons and what do they charge? What level of skill is needed?" These are difficult questions to answer, but the attorney must have these answers and then work the figures into the framework of the structured settlement.

Travel and Entertainment

Sick and disabled persons do not manage money well. Ordinarily, people save money from their monthly income for vacations, entertainment, and travel. When dealing with a disabled client, it is far better not to work this figure into the

Figure 14.2

Medical Equipment/Supplies	Frequency of Need Frequency of Repairs	Cost
Electric Hospital Bed	Every five (5) years.	$1740/bed
	Repairs on head and foot spring may be needed every two years.	Repair cost can not be predicted but minimum charge would be $50.
Patient Lift	Every five (5) years	$915/patient lift
	Repairs may be needed annually for sling, straps and pump.	$150 for repairs
Britax Car Seat	Three or four a lifetime	$435/car seat
Pogon Stroller	Two or three before he needs a high strength lightweight wheelchair with special adaptations.	$399+ depending on adaptations.
	Upholstery and wheels may need repair every year.	
TLC Bath Transfer Aid	Every two or three years throughout life.	$315/TLC
High Strength Lightweight Wheelchair with custom modifications and custom quick release insert designed for positioning.	Adaptations may need repair annually.	$60 for tire replacement. $200/insert modifications.
Tumble Form Insert	Four or more a lifetime	$545 to $695/basic insert dependent on size.
Side Lying Positioner	Four or more a lifetime	$225/positioner

monthly allowance but to make it a lump sum amount payable annually (June of each year, beginning at age 18, for example). In that manner, the money is segregated and identified as intended for a specific purpose. If you try to work it into the monthly allowance, the odds are high that it will be spent for other purposes and will not be available when needed.

These items cover the bulk of the "special needs" of your client. If you pay attention to them and plan carefully, you can insure that your client can achieve a good quality of life in the future.

PREPARING THE STRUCTURE

After analyzing the various requirements of your client, you begin the hard work of preparing a structured settlement to fulfill these needs. You have to begin with what is commonly called the "up-front money"—the sum to be paid immediately at the time of settlement. Generally it is going to consist of three items:

1. Money to pay the client's past-due bills and expenses.
2. Money to fulfill a client's immediate needs. This can be anything from "fun money" for that (controlled) spending spree that many clients yearn for and expect, to the necessity of getting the client out of a miserable, rented apartment into a home of his or her own.
3. The attorney's fee.

Once this item is decided, there comes the second crucial item of monthly income. The client must have a steady source of income. Naturally this will have been discussed at length and all sources of miscellaneous income will have been considered: pension, SSI, insurance, part-time work, and any other source of money to be received on a routine basis.

Incidentally, never forget that the costs of everything are increasing steadily, that this will continue to occur, and that it is essential to build into this monthly income some kind of inflation factor. This can be an agreed-upon figure, or it can be keyed to an objective, governmental statistic. In any event, it must be considered or else the satisfactory figure of, let us say, $2,000 per month today may diminish in buying power to a very unsatisfactory $1,500 a month several years from now.

The easy part of the structure is now done and the whole thing is beginning to take shape.

Now fit in those specialty needs in both amount and time.

When will those future operations occur, how many, and what will they cost?

When will the client need a car, what kind, and at what cost?

When will the car have to be replaced?

If a client needs a tutor today what will that cost and how long need it last?

When will the child need money for college and what will that cost?

Just take these one at a time and fill in an outline listing years, event, and cost. Slowly but definitely the structure begins to take shape.

There will be compromises. After all, you are dealing with definite but limited amounts of money. To get a tutor you may have to drop the nurse's aide; to work in a college education you may have to forget the car; and if a large sum is to be used at age 30 to buy a house, you may have to reduce monthly income at ages 60 to 80.

At this stage, you will be conferring with the client, an actuary or accountant, and the insurance representative. You will have a telephone in one hand, and the fingers of the other hand will be rapidly plying a computer until your head spins with figures. Nervous prostration marks the end of every bargaining session. Figure 14.3 shows the type of computation you will get involved with

Figure 14.3.

Settlement: $1,750,000.00
Attorneys fee and costs: 583,000.00
Cash needed by client: 55,000.00
For Structure: 1,112,000.00
Possibility No. 1:

	Input	*Solution*
Interest rate	8.00%	8.00% (Interest rate guaranteed by the annuity company. Usually very close to the current rate on certificates of deposit.)
Cost of Living Increase	5.00%	(the inflation factor)
Term (in years) 21 (payments are for the life	21	of the child with 21 years of payments guaranteed.)
Mode (Payments per year) Actual Pay $6,168.00	12 Annual $74,016.00	payments per year $6,168.00—amount of monthly payment
Dollar Increase	0	0
Present Value		$1,112,013.26
Simple Additional P.V.		0
Total P.V.		$1,112,013.24 cost of Annuity

Possibility No. 2:

Interest rate	8.00%	8.00% Interest rate
Cost of living increase	3.00%	(lower inflation factor)
Term in Years	20	20 (payments for life with 20 years guaranteed)
Mode (payments per year) Actual Payment $5,125.00	12 Annual $61,500.00	payments per year $5,125.00 monthly payment
Dollar Increase	0	
Present Value	$762,560.80	$762,560.80 cost of annuity
Simple Additional P.V.	0	
Total P.V.		$762,560.80

(This allows for $349,453.00 extra. Shall it be used for lump sum payments at various time intervals? Increase monthly payments and some used for lump sums? Take some as cash and put in bank for a liquid investment? What is best for the client?)

during negotiations. This illustration of an attorney "playing with the computer" shows variations in cost of living increase (5 percent and 3 percent), term (20 years and 21 years), and monthly payment ($6,168 and $5,125) that were being discussed at one point during settlement discussions. It also shows that one structure (I) uses up all the money in monthly payments, while (II) will have money left over for lump sum payments—or for whatever. Which is best? What do you want?

It's wild but it's fun. Somewhere, somehow, the figures will come together and the actuary says "OK," the insurance representative agrees it can be done, your client assents, and you have a settlement. At that point you will be ready for a day off and a round of golf.

ILLUSTRATIONS OF STRUCTURED SETTLEMENTS

Let's take a look at three different settlements and something of the ideas that went into the method of structure:

A Small Minor's Settlement

12-year-old girl; $25,000 settlement.

Settlement year: 1990

Attorney's fee: $8,000

Balance to structure: $17,000

1992 lump sum: $3000.00

This money is designated to pay for a dermabrasion procedure to correct superficial facial scarring.

1996 (age 18): $4,250

1997 (age 19): $4,750

1998 (age 20): $5,250

1999 (age 21): $5,750

These payments are designed to assist the child when she is either in college, in a technical school or beginning her working career (down payment on a car, money for apartment, etc.).

2008 (age 30): $15,000

At this age the young woman may be beginning a family and looking for a house. This money is available as a lump sum to provide a down payment for a house or some other significant purchase or use.

Thus the total payout from this $17,000 investment is $35,000.

The parents of this child could never have done this. They are financially unsophisticated. They never owned a share of stock or one certificate of deposit, and they wouldn't know how to invest this money or where to go to accomplish this purpose.

A Substantial Minor's Settlement

12-year-old boy; $190,000 settlement

Settlement year: 1990

Attorney's fee, costs, medical liens, etc.: $77,450.83

Balance to structure: $112,549.17

This young man received a serious injury but made an excellent recovery. He will have no future medical bills. He is bright and studious and comes from a relatively poor family. His parents had no idea what to do with this money or how to plan for his future. They could provide for this child and wanted no money during his minority. The structure was as follows:

1996 (age 18): $12,000

1997 (age 19): $12,000

1998 (age 20): $12,000

1999 (age 21): $12,000

These payments are designed to assist the child for educational purposes and, if he did not go to school, to enable him to buy a car or possibly have his own apartment.

Note: The parents did not want any substantial amounts payable to this child during what they termed "his foolish years." We wholeheartedly agreed with that assessment.

2003 (age 25): $80,000

2008 (age 30): $100,000

2013 (age 35): $250,000

We rejected *monthly payments* over his lifetime as being too low (even with an inflation factor) to make a significant impact on his life.

The $80,000 lump sum payment was deliberately kept low because it was felt that at age 25 this young man would still be prone to wild extravagances, given his neighborhood and likely friends. The large payment ($250,000) was set at age 35 because it was felt that by then the man might be interested in business opportunities or investments and would have the money to accomplish these purposes.

In this case the total payout from this investment of $112,549.17 will be $478,000.

IS THE STRUCTURED SETTLEMENT AN ARROGANT EXERCISE IN DIRECTING ANOTHER PERSON'S LIFE?

Arrogant? No. Necessary? Yes. Directing another person's life? Yes.

It can't be helped. The alternative is putting the settlement proceeds into an investment that matures when the minor reaches age 18 and then giving that young person a large sum of money.

In American culture, 18-year-olds are not known for their financial savvy, self-discipline, or long-range vision. With a little help from their friends, they will find a way to blow a large sum of money very quickly. This is an axiom of life that will brook no argument.

Equally important is the fact that common sense—and an accountant's good advice—demand that these settlements be structured. If you are going to negotiate a structured settlement, it has to be done *now*! There is no chance to wait until the young person matures and can be consulted in this matter.

So the truth is that we are dictating the financial aspects of a minor's life. Let it be done wisely and in good faith, and there need be no apologies for it.

A High Settlement for a Minor Child

8-year-old boy: $615,000 settlement

Settlement year: 1991

Attorney's fee, costs, medical liens: $225,000

Balance to structure: $390,000

This child, mentally and physically handicapped, will be dependent for his entire life. His parents have adequate medical insurance and are both employed at good jobs. They do not need money at this time.

1991: $25,000 to be placed in a trust fund. This is emergency, "what-if" money to be available should something untoward occur.

1991-1996 (to age 13): $300 per month plus an inflation factor of 3 percent. This monthly income is primarily designed to assist the parents by hiring babysitters, buying needed clothes or equipment, and dealing with miscellaneous needs.

1997-2001 (ages 13-18): $1,500 per month with 3 percent inflation factor. Now the child is getting big. He will need clothes, furniture, more expensive equipment, perhaps some training or aides not covered by insurance.

1997 (age 18): $25,000—At age 18, or shortly thereafter, he may have to move into his own home or a group home, have to buy a van, or may need training in some skill or occupation. This money is available for that purpose.

2002 (age 19 to death): 20 years is certain. $3,500 per month plus 3 percent inflation factor. This is designed to give the adult a reasonable lifestyle for all of his days. Hopefully it will provide for him.

Three Unusual Factors in This Structure

1. Rating the Beneficiary. This child was 8 years old at the time of settlement. His normal life expectancy was 64.5 years. The annuity company must assume it would make payments throughout the normal life expectancy of 64.5 years and that the payments would normally be computed on this basis. However, given this child's injuries, it is unlikely he will live that long. So arguments began.

The annuity company on its own rated the child as a 32-year-old man. Accordingly, the life expectancy was reduced to 41.9 years. This allowed for higher monthly payments based on the dollar investment.

We believed that was still incorrect.

We argued that the child should be rated older yet. We provided the annuity company with detailed medical documentation on all the child's medical problems. We also provided supplemental reports from our experts and treating physicians. Eventually, the child was rated as a 45-year-old. Life expectancy was now 30 years and permitted much higher monthly payments with the same dollar investment.

2. Lifetime Care Plan. In determining the amount of money necessary for this child over a period of 25 to 40 years, it was necessary to develop a Lifetime Care Plan. Much of the work was previously done in building the damages phase of the case. What medical needs will the child have at ages 15, 25, or 35? Where will the child live? What level of independence will the child attain? Based on the answers provided, how much money will the child need?

The expert was a woman who began as a pediatrician but who had gone on to specialize in pediatric rehabilitation. She prepared for us a detailed Life Plan that provided answers to all the questions.

A good three- or four-hour meeting with an expert who is experienced in providing long-term care to the physically and mentally handicapped is a "must" to secure the answers to the various questions. You have probably already retained such an expert in the preparation of your case. Use him or her now to plan your settlement.

3. Inflation Factor. When dealing with payments over a period of 25 to 40 years, an inflation factor is imperative. A lot of money in 1960 is not so much today.

Three percent is a reasonable figure, though medical costs in recent years have been significantly higher than that. I prefer a factor of 5 or 7 percent, but the cost of such an inflation factor is very high. It will produce much lower monthly payments in the early years. In negotiating the structure, you must balance the negative impact of inflation against the cost of the inflation factor.

SOME ADDITIONAL CONSIDERATIONS

1. *Agree on a settlement figure and then negotiate the structure.* If you focus on the future payments without knowing the present cost of the annuities, you can wildly miscalculate the value of the settlement. Look at the payouts for the examples cited. Could you accurately project the value of the settlement knowing only the future payments and estimating the interest rate?

Insurance companies love to say that the IRS prohibits their disclosure of the present cost. Ask for a copy of the revenue ruling supporting the prohibition. There is none.

You must agree on a settlement figure with the concurrent understanding that the balance due the client will be structured. Only then can you begin to negotiate an appropriate structure.

2. *Tax benefit.* All future payments are free of tax just as in the routine bodily injury settlement *if the* structure is negotiated as part of the settlement. Do not expect to control with specificity the placement of the various investments that fund the future payments You can insist only that the insurance company purchase the annuity from a Best A + -rated life insurance company. If you actually attempt to *direct specific investments*, the IRS may insist that you are exercising control and thus that interest earned is taxable just as it would be if you settled for a lump sum and purchased a certificate of deposit.

3. *Structures are not often desirable for reasonably well-off middle-aged or older couples.* They generally prefer to manage their investments themselves and do not have the financial demands of the young. A structure can be advisable, however, for individuals within 10 or 15 years of retirement or for

someone who desires to fund a child's education. In that event, a deferral of some or all of a settlement to a point 10 years later will produce a significant tax-free lump sum of money.

4. Structured settlements are a must for any catastrophic injury, regardless of age.

WHO ADMINISTERS THIS SETTLEMENT?

Really there are two parts to this question: (1) who runs the show insofar as making payment is concerned, and (2) who administers the fund after payment is made?

As far as payment is concerned, nearly every major insurance company today either has its own independent subsidiary that will undertake payment of the settlement, or will refer you to an independent financial institution that will perform this task. Since this settlement may continue for as long as 60 or 70 years, the financial solvency of such an institution is of prime consideration. You can take several protective measures:

1. The best that you can do is to demand that the company have the highest possible rating with such firms as Standard & Poor's, Moody's, and A.M. Best.

2. You can try to compel the casualty company to guarantee the payment of the proceeds in the event of default by the obligor insurance company.

3. You can purchase insurance to guarantee the payout, but this can be expensive.

Beyond these things there is no realistic way to absolutely guarantee that a payor will be around 30 or 40 years into the future.

The administrator of the funds, upon receipt, has to be a bank. This is the only type of organization geared to receiving money, investing it for some period of time, making routine payments according to a schedule, and being accountable to the recipient and/or the courts. A judge will nearly always insist upon a bank in the case of a minor, incompetent, decedent, or a client who simply cannot handle his or her financial affairs. A bank has the right personnel, facilities, experience, and accountability in matters of this kind. The attorney would be making a grave error by accepting an appointment as administrator because of the voluminous details involved. And good old "Uncle Joe," whom everyone thinks is a great guy and good with figures, frequently turns out to be a crook when substantial sums of money begin to flow through his hands. On balance, *it has to be a bank.*

AFTER THE SETTLEMENT—CLOSING THE CASE

It goes without saying that court approval of your settlement will be required in the case of minors, decedents, and incompetents. If, by chance, in your state such approval is not required, get it done anyway with any Petition, Motion, or other pleading that you can dream up that will get this matter before a judge. There is a possibility in these settlements for misunderstanding, regrets, change of mind and heart, recrimination, and complaint. Remember that you are dealing with years and years of a client's life—and lifestyle. Things that are agreeable today become subjects of controversy tomorrow. Protect yourself. A brief hearing in court together with an Order approving the settlement is the best protection. If that cannot be, then:

1. Give the client a copy of all papers;
2. Take the time to go over every sentence of the settlement papers;
3. Have the accountant, actuary, or any other person who participated in the settlement planning, present at this discussion;
4. If possible, videotape the meeting or tape record it;
5. At the very least, have the client sign a document acknowledging that this entire settlement has been explained in detail and that it is completely satisfactory.

After all the paperwork has been completed, an administrator is appointed, and the checks begin to come in routinely, there are still going to be numerous, practical problems about which the client will contact the attorney. In the beginning these will be problems with the bank which is, after all, a new element to be dealt with. Perhaps the client does not get along with the bank officer to whom this matter is assigned, and the attorney will have to intervene to get someone else involved. A check may be delayed or a payment by the bank is not sent out. There is a normal adjustment period during which the client and bank personnel get to know each other and fully understand what is to be done and when. The attorney is the buffer, coordinator, and compromisor in these minor and exasperating conflicts. This should last about two or three months, and then the attorney must get out of this matter and stay out. The alternative is a nervous breakdown! Remember that the client and the administrator have a long-term commitment to each other and the nit-picking sources of disagreement are endless. No attorney in his or her right mind can stay in the middle of this relationship without being severely burnt. As with marital disputes, the best advice is to stay out!

So the settlement is concluded and the case is closed. The attorney who has done the job well can have the satisfaction of knowing not only that the amount of the settlement was a good one, but that the client is well cared for during the remainder of his or her life or a substantial part of it. It is a good feeling to know that due to your efforts the client is financially secure. It makes the effort worthwhile.

Index